# The Leadership Class in Scottish Education

# The Leadership Class in Scottish Education

WALTER M. HUMES

Department of Education
University of Glasgow

JOHN DONALD PUBLISHERS LTD
EDINBURGH

ISBN 0 85976 137 1

Exclusive distribution in the United States of America and Canada by Humanities Press Inc., Atlantic Highlands, NJ 07716, USA.

Phototypeset by Quorn Selective Repro, Loughborough.
Printed in Great Britain by Bell & Bain Ltd., Glasgow.

# *Acknowledgements*

A great many people have helped to make the completion of this book possible by giving generously of their time to answer my questions, by supplying me with documents to which access is normally restricted, and by commenting on and criticising my arguments.

I wish to express a particular debt of gratitude to David Strachan, Coordinator of the Parental Choice Project at Glasgow University. He has been extremely assiduous in drawing my attention to references and passing on numerous items of information relevant to my research: but for his efforts, I would have missed a significant amount of useful material.

Maria Gibbons, David Hamilton, Leslie Hunter, Alastair Macbeth, Malcolm MacKenzie and David Strachan have all read sections of the book in draft form and I have benefited greatly from their observations. Hamish Paterson has read the whole text and I am extremely grateful to him for his detailed comments and for his encouragement. In fairness to all of these people, however, I must stress that I have not always followed their advice, and responsibility for the final version is mine alone.

In so far as I have managed to acquire an understanding of the way the Scottish educational system operates, it has to a large extent depended on the insights of people working in a variety of posts — as head teachers, advisers, lecturers, researchers, administrators, etc. Also important has been the contribution of successive groups of M.Ed. students at Glasgow University — and, in particular, the members of my seminars on contemporary issues in education — who have helped to keep me in touch with the points of view of classroom teachers. It would be impossible for me to give an exhaustive list of all those who have been of assistance, but the following are deserving of special mention: David Betteridge; Andrew Bruce; Dugald Cantlay; Margaret Crombie; John Darling; William Dunn; David Eastwood; Ian Flett; the late Charles Forbes; Nigel Grant; William Hannah; David Hartley; Dan Hood; Jean Hunter; John Hunter; Bill Inglis; Gordon Jeyes; Frank McEnroe; Gilbert Mackay; Andrew McPherson; Pat Murray; Percy Quinn; Ian Stronach; Geoffrey Tharme; Rosemary Wake; John Watt; Douglas Weir; Eric Wilkinson.

Finally, I wish to thank John Tuckwell of John Donald Publishers for his readiness to take on the project, for his patience while it was being completed, and for the keenness of his editorial eye.

Walter M. Humes

# *Contents*

# *Key to Acronyms and Abbreviations*

| | |
|---|---|
| ADES | Association of Directors of Education in Scotland |
| ALCES | Association of Lecturers in Colleges of Education in Scotland |
| ALSCI | Association of Lecturers in Scottish Central Institutions |
| ASTMS | Association of Scientific, Technical and Managerial Staffs |
| AUT | Association of University Teachers |
| CBI | Confederation of British Industry |
| CCC | Consultative Committee on the Curriculum |
| CES | Centre for Educational Sociology |
| CI | Central Institution |
| CNAA | Council for National Academic Awards |
| COPE | Committee on Primary Education |
| COSE | Committee on Secondary Education |
| COSLA | Convention of Scottish Local Authorities |
| CSYS | Certificate of Sixth Year Studies |
| DES | Department of Education and Science |
| EIS | Educational Institute of Scotland |
| ESRC | Economic and Social Research Council |
| FACLS | Federation of Associations of College Lecturers in Scotland |
| FE | Further Education |
| *GH* | *Glasgow Herald* |
| GTC | General Teaching Council |
| HE | Higher Education |
| HMCI | Her Majesty's Chief Inspector |
| HMDSCI | Her Majesty's Deputy Senior Chief Inspector |
| HMI | Her Majesty's Inspector |
| HMSCI | Her Majesty's Senior Chief Inspector |
| MSC | Manpower Services Commission |
| NAB | National Advisory Body |
| NAS/UWT | National Association of Schoolmasters/ Union of Women Teachers |
| NCITT | National Committee for the In-Service Training of Teachers |
| NICCER | National Inter-College Committee for Educational Research |
| OU | Open University |
| PAT | Professional Association of Teachers |
| QUANGO | Quasi-autonomous non-governmental organisation |
| RIU | Research and Intelligence Unit |
| SCDS | Scottish Curriculum Development Service |
| SCE | Scottish Certificate of Education |
| SCEEB | Scottish Certificate of Education Examination Board |
| SCET | Scottish Council for Educational Technology |
| SCOTBEC | Scottish Business Education Council |
| SCOTEC | Scottish Technical Education Council |
| SCOTVEC | Scottish Vocational Education Council |
| SCOVACT | Scottish Council for the Validation of Courses for Teachers |
| SCOVO | Scottish Vocational Preparation Unit |

| | |
|---|---|
| SCRE | Scottish Council for Research in Education |
| SEB | Scottish Examination Board |
| SED | Scottish Education Department |
| SFHEA | Scottish Further and Higher Education Association |
| SIO | Scottish Information Office |
| SMDP | Scottish Microelectronics Development Programme |
| SSRC | Social Science Research Council |
| SSTA | Scottish Secondary Teachers' Association |
| STEAC | Scottish Tertiary Education Advisory Council |
| STUC | Scottish Trades Union Congress |
| SUCE | Scottish Universities Council on Entrance |
| SUCSE | Scottish Universities Council for Studies in Education |
| *TESS* | *Times Educational Supplement Scotland* |
| *THES* | *Times Higher Education Supplement* |
| UGC | University Grants Committee |
| YOP | Youth Opportunities Programme |
| YTS | Youth Training Scheme |

# 1
# *From Description to Interpretation*

## Aims and Methodology

This book has two principal aims. First, it attempts to offer a description of the main structural features of the Scottish educational system at both national and local level: thus the various functions of the Scottish Education Department (SED), regional education authorities, the Scottish Examination Board (SEB), the Consultative Committee on the Curriculum (CCC), the General Teaching Council (GTC) and other important bodies are outlined and their interconnections traced. That there is a need for such an account is evident in the fact that the best existing description, the second edition of S. Leslie Hunter's *The Scottish Educational System*, was published in 1972 and, inevitably, is now out of date in many respects, especially following the reorganisation of local government in 1975. Hunter's book remains, however, a very valuable source, and the present writer's indebtedness to it will be apparent at several points.

The second aim involves going beyond description in a deliberate and conscious way, and, in this respect, marks a major departure from earlier studies of the structure and organisation of Scottish education. What will be attempted is the development of a critical interpretation of the way power is exercised by many of the people who occupy influential positions within those institutions that constitute the Scottish educational system. Their styles of leadership, the political roles they assume, the coherence of the public statements they make, and the quality of the contribution they make to the formulation of educational policy, will all be subject to detailed examination. The conclusions that are reached, it should be admitted at the outset, are not particularly favourable and represent a direct challenge to some of Scottish education's most cherished orthodoxies. It will be argued that the need for such a revisionist account is not only long overdue but also a necessary precursor to meaningful reconstruction.

These two aims — the descriptive and the interpretative — will be pursued concurrently. Even if it were possible to separate them, it would not be desirable, for it would lead to discontinuities of presentation and necessitate a measure of repetition. In any case, however ostensibly neutral a 'straightforward' account of the workings of Scottish education might claim to be, it would inevitably imply an interpretation, simply by virtue of its selection and ordering of material. There are, moreover, certain advantages in being explicit about the interpretative stance that is being adopted. The interest of readers, even where they disagree profoundly with what is being said, is likely to be more strongly engaged. Too many books on education seem dull because the writer is over-cautious about declaring his or her position and conforms too readily to the approved — and highly suspect — models of 'objective' social science. It is hoped that the argument advanced in this volume will at least stimulate the reader to further reflection on the subject, even if some of the critical ideas are rejected.

To the student seeking to understand the way Scottish education works, several methods of investigation present themselves. The most obvious approach is *via* the legislative framework: here the focus is on the requirements of acts of parliament, the circulars and memoranda issued by the Secretary of State for Scotland, the statutory responsibilities of local government, and so on. This line of enquiry might be extended by looking at the policy-making process as a whole, to which government ministers, other politicians, officials, trade unionists and pressure groups of various kinds all contribute. In this way, the political-administrative dimension of Scottish education would receive fairly comprehensive coverage.

An alternative approach would be to concentrate on socio-cultural processes: that is, the complex fabric of norms, values, beliefs and traditions which combine to produce particular responses to specific educational issues at a given period in history. In many respects this is a more difficult undertaking than that which takes the legislative framework as its starting point. It calls for a level of analysis that goes deeper than the formal institutional structures which embody the educational system, and requires the investigator to try to assess, among other things, the importance of the Scottish educational tradition, its relation to other influences within Scottish culture, and their combined effects on those involved both in policy formulation and in the routine business of teaching and learning. This seems an altogether more amorphous kind of exercise, one which cannot rely on the clear signposting provided by acts of parliament. It may, nevertheless, be important, for too exclusive a concern with the framework of law is likely to produce a limited understanding of the cultural and ideological pressures which have caused it to emerge in the particular form it has. The socio-cultural approach, then, is less tidy than the political-administrative, but it may lead to a deeper awareness of the underlying character of Scottish education.

Another strategy would be to start 'from the inside' of the educational system by eliciting the subjective experiences of men and women closely involved in its day-to-day workings. The views of teachers, administrators, inspectors, researchers, etc. could be sought and the accumulation of their perceptions could be used to construct a picture of channels of communication, networks of influence, and the machinery of decision-making. Gradually a composite view of the structure as a whole would begin to emerge. This procedure might be described as phenomenological in the sense that it would accord more value to the lived experience of the primary agents of the educational process than to some external management model of how it is assumed to operate. There are, however, limitations and dangers. It is not possible to guarantee the representativeness of informants, and too exclusive a reliance on subjective accounts might make it difficult to raise the level of analysis above that of journalistic reportage.

All methodologies have their characteristic strengths and weaknesses, and claims that one particular form of enquiry affords the most penetrating insights should be treated with scepticism. For this reason the present study will be eclectic in character and will draw on a range of investigative styles. As can be seen from the acknowledgements, part of the research involved talking to many people working at different levels in Scottish education. Their comments assisted in at least three ways: they provided factual information of a kind that was often not available from written sources; they contributed specific examples of the way Scottish education operates, some of which have been used to illustrate particular ideas; and they helped to shape, and in certain cases modify, the interpretative line of the argument. But personal impressions, however carefully considered and however soundly based in experience, are not enough. They need to be supplemented by a detailed study of the institutional and bureaucratic contexts in which decisions are made, the value systems which those contexts generate, and the public presentation of approved policies emanating from them. Direct access to the inner workings of central and local government is not easy, but there is a large body of material in the form of reports, minutes, newsletters, etc. which can be consulted and from which much can be learned. Usually documents of this kind are not widely read, but they have provided a major source for this study and they are quoted extensively in several of the chapters. They have proved particularly useful in respect of the interpretative part of the exercise: many official statements emerge as deeply ironic when compared with what actually happens at the level of practice.

The reasons for this disparity are partly explicable in terms of the nature of bureaucracy itself, but it will be argued that ideological and cultural explanations are also important. Thus, for example, the significance of the widespread invocation of professionalism among Scottish teachers and of highly selective appeals to certain forms of nationalism will have to be examined. These issues, in turn, introduce a series of directly political questions about the climate of ideas which serves to sustain the structure as a whole, the distribution of power in Scottish society, the place of the SED within the Scottish Office, and of the Scottish Office within the British system of government. Here again some of the discontinuities between standard accounts of what is said to take place and what actually takes place will be apparent.

Methodological purists will no doubt object to the proposed eclecticism. It has been preferred to other approaches because of a firm conviction that it is only when political-administrative, socio-cultural and phenomenological strategies are combined that an adequate appreciation of the forces at work in Scottish education can be gained. Any one on its own is insufficient, and while their deployment together will certainly pose many problems, it is hoped that the results will justify the effort.

## The Received Wisdom

Since the view of Scottish education to be presented in succeeding chapters will be strongly critical in a number of respects, it will be useful to start by offering a brief description of what might be called the received wisdom; that is, the conventional version of the relative powers of the various educational bodies which carry responsibility for the running of the system, and of the principles and values underlying the existing arrangements. This will serve as a reference point for later discussion.

The official account of the administrative arrangements is set out in a series of 'Factsheets' produced by the Scottish Information Office (SIO). These suggest that 'Public sector education in Scotland is a partnership between central and local government'.[1] Although the SED supervises the system as a whole, it 'acts in co-operation with the regional and islands area authorities'.[2] It is claimed that a great deal of power is devolved: 'The central government does not run any schools or colleges; nor does it engage any teachers; nor does it prescribe any textbooks or curricula'.[3] Particular stress is laid on the absence of interference in curricular matters. 'The primary curriculum is not centrally prescribed; within the overall policy of the education authority, headteachers are free to devise the type of education best suited to the circumstances of their pupils.'[4] Similarly, 'the secondary school curriculum is not prescribed by law and education authorities and headteachers have considerable freedom to decide what courses should be available in any individual schools'.[5]

The general picture, then, is one of democratic involvement in which absolute authority is not located in any single institution but is distributed throughout the many agencies which comprise the educational service as a whole. 'Partnership', 'cooperation' and 'consensus' are the terms most often invoked. The development and implementation of policy is invariably presented as a collaborative exercise. Thus, for example, in the programme of research following the Munn and Dunning reports — which led to the introduction of Standard Grade courses at the start of session 1984–85 — many different individuals and groups, not just SED officials, 'played a key part in the process'[6]; members of Joint Working Parties of the CCC and SEB, staff in colleges of education, advisers, administrators, and teachers in schools used for piloting materials and courses.

This official explanation has been supported — albeit with qualifications of varying force — by a number of commentators. An interesting historical slant on the background to current circumstances has been offered by James Scotland,[7] who identifies the 1960s as a period when a deliberate policy of devolving power from the Secretary of State to local authorities and other agencies was pursued. According to his analysis, this pattern can be seen in the areas of examinations, curriculum and teacher entry. The inspectorate ceased to administer the Scottish Certificate of Education (SCE) examinations, and a separate statutory body (the Scottish Certificate of Education Examination Board — SCEEB — which later became the SEB) was set up in 1963 to take over this responsibility. Again, with the establishment of the CCC in 1965 'the Secretary of State had set up [another] influential body of which he was not in command'.[8] And similarly, by creating the GTC he 'gave away his power not only to control admission to the profession, normal and exceptional, but also his right to expel or discipline unsatisfactory teachers'.[9] This last move also served to increase the freedom of the colleges of education: they were, says Scotland, 'permitted to acquire increasing independence in their work',[10] a process already promoted by the terms of the Teachers (Training Authorities) Regulations of 1958, which provided for the administration of the colleges by independent boards of governors.

Within this overall account, the position of teachers has often been selected for particularly favourable mention. One writer states that 'Scottish teachers exercise much greater control over the affairs of their own profession than teachers in England — or indeed anywhere else in the world'.[11] And another makes the point that 'Teachers in Scottish schools do not teach with the feeling that 'Big Brother' in the form of the Scottish Education Department or its inspectorate is watching them. There remain large areas of freedom for teachers in the classroom situation'.[12]

These comments, like those of James Scotland, were written some time ago, but the political-administrative dimension of the received wisdom continues to receive support. Alastair Macbeth, in an article which appeared in 1984, states that 'decision making ... is diffused through the system' and 'there is a multiplicity of ... bodies and groups involved in the educational partnership'.[13] It will be seen shortly that Dr Macbeth has reservations about another dimension of the received wisdom but he nonetheless concludes that in his personal view 'the current structure of government in Scottish education has much to commend it'.[14]

The way in which Scottish education is organised is also frequently cited as evidence of the distinctiveness of Scottish society and culture. Along with the church and the law, education is regarded as an important means of preventing complete assimilation to English norms and practices. One of the standard textbooks on the Scottish political system puts the point forcefully: 'Education is one of the best-defined 'arenas' of Scottish life, and one which most strongly maintains the boundary of the Scottish political system'.[15] Its author, James Kellas, explains this in terms of 'the autonomy of the policy-process in Scottish education',[16] which he relates to the role of the Scottish Office in framing legislation:

> All of the so-called 'educational' decisions about Scottish education are made within the Scottish political system. The legislation governing education in Scotland is Scottish legislation which has been drafted in the SED, with the help of Scottish educational organisations, and debated largely by Scottish M.P.s. Its administration is in the hands of the Scottish Office.[17]

This insistence on the distinctiveness of the Scottish educational system has a cultural and historical aspect as well as a political one. Despite a few voices of dissent, there persists in the popular mind a general belief that Scottish education has been, and continues to be, both different from and, in many respects, superior to that offered in state schools in England, and that these differences and superiorities are based on the evolution of certain social and intellectual principles that have no real equivalent south of the border. The proposals of John Knox and his fellow-reformers in the *First Book of Discipline* of 1560 are usually identified as the first comprehensive embodiment of these principles: they advocated a national system of education, open to all, and catering for all stages, from elementary school to university. Offering a succinct account of the essential features of the updated Scottish educational tradition is not easy, but the following characteristics are picked out by both James Scotland and, more recently, Henry Cowper and Willis Pickard: the value attached to education as a general social good; equality of opportunity for all pupils; democracy in terms of the social mix of schools and the absence of a significant private sector (except in Edinburgh); a bias in favour of academic learning; a preference for curricular breadth rather than specialisation; resistance to experimentation in teaching methods; an emphasis on practicality in the training of teachers; a concern for economy and efficiency of provision; general acceptance of the authority of the teacher.[18]

These characteristics should not, of course, be regarded as static. They are inevitably subject to cultural forces tending to produce change, and it would not be inconsistent for someone to believe, in general terms, in the merits and distinctiveness of the Scottish tradition in education, while defending recent policies in terms that involve some modification of that tradition. For instance, the provisions of the Standard Grade examination have been described as an attempt to correct the academic bias of the Ordinary Grade which it replaces. Similarly, it might be argued that, notwithstanding the general tendency to pedagogical conservatism, teaching methods have changed significantly in recent years — mixed-ability grouping and team-teaching might be cited as examples. Commitment to the tradition need not involve inflexibility and a resistance to change *per se*. What it does require, however, is a belief in the value of cultural continuity and a conviction that *some* principles are absolutely fundamental. It is probably fair to say that, of the principles identified above as constituting the Scottish educational tradition, equality and democracy are appealed to most frequently.

It thus emerges that the received wisdom contains both political-administrative and socio-cultural elements. The legislative framework is said to allow for a series of checks and balances, which ensure that the SED does not become too dominant: moreover, the opportunity for other groups to influence the policy process — through bodies such as the CCC, the SEB and the GTC — is considerable. This structural provision — the argument continues — is protected by the independence enjoyed by Scotland in determining its own educational legislation and by the continuing potency of an educational tradition that embodies democratic and egalitarian principles.

## Criticisms of the Received Wisdom

The basis tenets of the received wisdom have, until now, not been subject to a full frontal attack. A number of limited criticisms have, however, been expressed, and when these are put together, doubt is cast on the comfortable view favoured by official spokesmen and their apologists.

Probably the fullest set of critical comments is to be found in an Open University (OU) course unit, prepared by a team of writers chaired by Sir Toby Weaver, formerly Deputy Secretary at the DES in London: the role of the SED was examined as part of a wider study of the control of education in the whole of Britain.[19] Their review of the evidence about the way power is distributed leads them to the conclusion that 'the SED exercises a considerable degree of control over the provision of education in Scotland. By comparison with the DES, the SED is more overtly involved in curricular matters, and the Scottish education authorities do not provide an effective counterbalance to central direction'.[20] The reference to involvement in curricular matters, it should be noted, runs directly counter to that part of the received wisdom which places emphasis on the freedom of local government and, indeed, individual headteachers. The OU team are also less than fully convinced by the claim — exemplified in the writings of James Scotland — that 'the department [i.e., the SED] is much less autocratic than it was in the past, [and] that its inspectors no longer function as departmental policemen . . . '[21] They show more sympathy for the view that the department 'has skilfully succeeded in making gestures towards local authority autonomy by giving away unimportant functions while retaining overall direction and control of the system'.[22]

The significance of the setting up of the SCEEB, the CCC and the GTC is also questioned. With regard to the first, it is acknowledged that 'this has been seen by some as an attempt to lessen central influence', but an alternative possibility is advanced — 'it may well have been a purely administrative device to relieve the inspectorate of the crushing burden of work which administering the examination system entailed'.[23] Likewise, the CCC, despite disclaimers to the contrary, is not really intended to 'encourage curricular innovation 'from the grass roots' '; its real function is to issue reports which 'are interpreted as 'handbooks of best practice' carrying departmental authority'.[24] And, as for the GTC, 'Not even [its] most fervent admirer . . . would claim that the council has given teachers equal 'partnership' status in the control of education'.[25] Far from being a 'watchdog' for the teaching profession, it often seems to act as 'a lapdog of the Secretary of State'.[26]

A proper evaluation of these remarks will clearly require a detailed examination of the relative powers exercised by the various agencies but, for the moment, two general points are worth making, which may go some way towards explaining the disparities between the received wisdom and the alternative interpretation favoured by the OU course team. The first concerns the difference between formal and informal power. An individual or an organisation may possess limited formal authority but may nevertheless exert considerable influence over a wide range of matters. There can be many reasons for this: a desire for clear leadership by those affected by the decisions taken; a recognition of expertise; a sharing of ideological assumptions between the agents and recipients of authority (so that the exercise of informal power is not perceived as an illegitimate abuse of formal office). Less benign explanations are also possible. Informal power may be viewed as a form of manipulation because those who exercise it are often successful at persuading others that decisions have been arrived at through a process of democratic consultation when, in fact, the real decision-making may have taken place behind the scenes. Members of the inspectorate might be cited as an example of a group of people in Scottish education who have been remarkably successful in acquiring a substantial amount of informal power over and above that which comes from their formal position.

The second point concerns the fact that social institutions develop over time and what may have seemed, and been intended as, liberating at one period may come to be perceived as, and may actually turn out to be, restricting at a later period. It is easy to fall into the assumption that educational reforms act progressively in the direction of greater freedom. This need not be the case. James Scotland's analysis was published in 1969, that of the OU team ten years later. In 1969 the SCEEB, the CCC and the GTC were all relatively young bodies and their innovative potential may have seemed promising. By 1979, however, their spheres of operation had become more clearly defined and doubts about their effectiveness in acting as counterweights to central control had already been expressed. Iain Thorburn, in an article severely critical of all three bodies, made the important point in 1977 that 'The existence of a structure brings [the] temptation to believe the problem it has been set up to deal with has been solved'.[27] In other words, the simple fact that the SCEEB, the CCC and the GTC were in existence did not guarantee that they would develop as independent bodies. Moreover, the form of their evolution depended not only on their own efforts but also on the policies of successive governments. It is at least arguable that their effectiveness has been further weakened with the election, in 1979, of a party firmly committed to the principle that the function of central government is to govern. Where a tendency to capitulate has already been established, the task of translating that principle into reality is made very much easier.

Reservations have also been expressed about the claimed distinctiveness of the Scottish educational system and the alleged autonomy which it enjoys in relation to the DES. A much more recent study of the Scottish political system than Kellas's locates the activities of the Scottish Office very firmly within the British system of government and expresses scepticism about the extent of its independence. Its authors state: '... the Scottish Office is an integral part of central government'[28] and 'the structural differences in Scottish Office administrative arrangements have not resulted in substantive policy autonomy'.[29] Unfortunately, they have relatively little to say about education as such, but an unpublished study by Alastair Macbeth, based partly on interviews with SED and DES personnel, lends support to their general argument. Dr Macbeth suggests

> that the Scottish educational system, while technically separate from that of England, is more similar to it than many suppose; that the DES has influence on the nature of Scottish education; that the shift of power towards the centre over the past century has occurred in both the English and the Scottish systems, though more so in Scotland ...[30]

It should be added that Dr Macbeth values the British dimension and believes that the trends he describes should not necessarily be regarded as pernicious. The essential point, however, is that his conclusions represent a further challenge to the received wisdom. Elsewhere, he states, *contra* Kellas, that regular administrative and inspectorial contact between staff in Edinburgh and London means that 'DES thinking may pre-condition SED thinking'[31] to a greater degree than the formal, structural arrangements might suggest, though he is careful to add that 'It is difficult to pin down the extent of DES influence on Scottish education and it doubtless varies with personalities and issues'.[32]

An important question to arise from this difference of interpretation is what function the continuing belief in an autonomous Scottish educational system serves. Dr Macbeth notes that, notwithstanding his own reading of the situation, 'Scotland prides itself in having a separate and institutionalised education'.[33] And he adds, 'Its separateness is something to which politicians can point when they want to appeal to sentiments of nationalism'.[34] This again highlights the importance of looking at political-administrative and socio-cultural factors together. The formal structures, viewed at a superficial level, give credence to the notion that the Scottish system is separate and distinct; in addition, that idea is culturally reassuring and forestalls potentially strident reactions which might result from any suggestion that the SED merely follows the DES. Periodic appeals to sentiments of nationalism also serve the function of placing would-be critics at a disadvantage. Almost any criticism, however legitimate, can be made to seem an attack on a fundamental Scottish institution, a betrayal of national pride. It is only a small step from accusations of being anti-Scottish to accusations of being pro-English, a prospect that most Scots would not contemplate lightly. The irony of this situation should not be missed. If the superficial level of analysis is rejected in favour of one which reveals the extent of central control and the misleading character of claims that the Scottish system is autonomous, then it is the proponents of the received wisdom, not their critics, who emerge as guilty of cultural betrayal. That they have managed to avoid being exposed to this charge is a testimony both to the skill with which they operate and to the susceptibility of many Scots to a form of nationalistic flattery that is designed to ensure docility through reassurance.

The argument about distinctiveness is closely related to the significance attached to the Scottish educational tradition. Here too recent research has raised some question marks. R.D. Anderson,[35] in a scholarly study of the period 1820–1914, which, among other things, casts doubt on G.E. Davie's reliance on anglicisation as the major explanation for the changes in the Scottish university system in the nineteenth century,[36] notes the extremely malleable character of historical invocations:

> It is a striking fact that in Scotland educational debates invariably included an appeal to the past and to the national tradition, which was used both to defend the status quo and to make genuine innovations more acceptable. When rival models of educational change were put forward, both sides tended to appeal to the Knoxian ideal, often with some plausibility, and to accuse their opponents of abandoning it and of yielding to English examples.[37]

He also notes the danger that 'constant evocation of past glories might become a substitute for hard thinking about contemporary problems, and that constant and complacent assertion that Scottish education was democratic might cover its actual evolution on class lines'.[38] This is a point that the OU team, dealing with the more recent past, allude to as well. They refer to the Scottish educational tradition being 'over-idealized and romanticized' and go on:

> Perhaps its most damaging manifestation is in a certain complacency about the superiority of the Scottish system which has allowed the moderately academically able to flourish but has, to date, rather neglected the others.[39]

Taken together, these observations begin to raise the possibility that Scottish education may be much less 'democratic' and 'egalitarian' than is often supposed. Hamish Paterson has commented that 'if Scottish schools were ever democratic, they were democratic in a particular way which emphasised social division, competitive liberalism and individual achievement at the expense of others'.[40] Historically, the conflict was between the value attached to *individual* academic achievement and the 'democratic' assumption that achievement was open to all. In fact, the defining characteristics of academic success required that there should be large numbers of academic failures, and this was formally enshrined in the bipartite system of secondary education that prevailed until the 1960s. Institutional division was legitimised by the 'findings' of the mental testing movement, which made the allocation of different 'types' of children to different schools a relatively easy matter (and in which, incidentally, Scotland played a leading part[41]). Maintenance of a belief in the 'democratic' character of the system was possible for two related reasons: the seemingly objective, scientific character of the tests employed to separate children; and the uncritical acceptance of the view that success was dependent purely on ability, not on factors such as wealth or class. Thus even those who failed were inclined to accept the 'justice' of the outcome.

Secondary schooling is no longer selective, of course, but some of the old divisions certainly remain. It will be surprising if the differentiation of courses within the Standard Grade programme does not become, in practice, a differentiation of 'types' of pupil. The fact that this will take place within a single institution called a comprehensive school may soften the impact, but it is unlikely to provide an adequate justification for the exaggerated 'democratic' claims that are often made on behalf of Scottish education.

Similar caution is required in relation to equality. A major recent study, drawing on extensive data collected over a number of years, expresses scepticism about 'the folk image of the lad o' pairts, and the accompanying notion of equality', and concludes, 'Scottish education since the war has been neither meritocratic nor equal; the levels of inequality are similar to those observed in England and other Western societies'.[42] This gap between the received wisdom and the actual situation as revealed by a careful longitudinal analysis of the relation between social class and educational achievement should come as no great surprise. A re-examination of the various components of the Scottish educational tradition highlights the fact that the features that were identified —equality, authority, democracy, practicality, scholarship, etc. — need not be mutually reinforcing.

The stress on academic learning, for example, coexists uneasily both with the claims about equality and with some interpretations of practicality in education. Again, the acceptance of the authority of the teacher indicates that there are definite limits to the kind of democracy that is deemed appropriate. It thus emerges that the internal coherence of the Scottish educational tradition is less than fully convincing.[43]

It would, however, be too extreme to say that it should be regarded as an elaborate illusion, a collection of misleading myths that bear no relation at all to reality. A myth has been defined as 'a story that people tell about themselves ... for two purposes ... first, to explain the world and, second, to celebrate identity and to express values'.[44] The 'mythology' of Scottish education as expressed in the 'traditional' part of the received wisdom is an important part of Scottish consciousness, a celebration of the past and an explanation, albeit a highly confusing one, of the present. The question that arose in relation to the 'distinctiveness' argument reappears in a new guise: what purpose do appeals to the Scottish educational tradition serve?

Their main purpose would seem to be to encourage a high degree of cultural solidarity among Scots by submerging critical problems — which, when examined closely, begin to look rather disturbing — under an idealised conception of tradition. In a sense, it is the *idea* of the Scottish educational tradition, rather than the substance, that matters. As has been shown, it would be difficult for anyone to believe rationally and consistently in all the features that comprise it. Thus the tradition is usually invoked vaguely or selectively rather than as part of a carefully articulated, logical argument. It also serves as a focus for misplaced sentiment — perhaps, it has been suggested, a necessary focus given the absence of 'a deliberative and legislative body through which the aspirations of [Scottish] people might be expressed and the public actions of [Scotland's] representatives or their agents called to account'.[45]

The maintenance of solidarity and continuity within the educational system can be related to Scottish culture as a whole. Just as there is an idealised and sentimentalised version of Scottish education, so there is an idealised and sentimentalised version of Scottish culture which seeks to disguise potential sources of division. The tendency to subsume the whole of Scottish life under an improbable model which combines elements of Knox, Burns, Hampden, Red Clydeside and a kailyard perception of community life (in which the dominie features as a folk hero) continues, despite the fact that there is, and always has been, considerable cultural variation within Scotland — between, for example, Highlands and Lowlands, Catholics and Protestants, Edinburgh and Glasgow. Another indicator of significant cultural diversity is the existence of three native languages — English, Scots and Gaelic. From the point of view of political control, however, cultural diversity always poses problems; thus the attraction of idealised models, whether of education or of Scottish society as a whole. This helps to explain, for example, the record of neglect and hostility on the part of the SED to Scots and Gaelic.[46] The more powerful the forces tending towards uniform conceptions of education and society become, the easier it is to dismiss variations as aberrant or deviant. In such circumstances, the significance of differences in such areas as language, class and religion can be discounted. The warm embrace of the idealised model — which has a psychologically consoling as well as a socially reassuring aspect — serves to defuse potential conflicts.

The absence of conflicts may seem a welcome state of affairs, but if it is achieved at the cost of failing to address substantive issues, the result may well be unhealthy as far as the longer-term functioning of a society and its institutions is concerned. It has been suggested that the principal features of the received wisdom — its projection of an image of democratic partnership and devolved authority, its insistence on the distinctiveness of Scottish education, and its commitment to an idealised version of the Scottish educational tradition — are all, on closer inspection, in need of extensive qualification, if not outright rejection. Their unqualified perpetuation has, however, certain advantages for those concerned with the administration of Scottish education, in the sense that the features invoked all serve to disarm criticism. An important consequence is that credibility is given to a misleading conception of cultural solidarity and the reality of social divisions is ignored. The role of the educational system in this process is central. As one recent observer has remarked: 'education is one of the principal ... underpinnings of Scottish civil society and culture', and 'as a national system it presents relatively few varieties of styles of authority and social organisation'.[47] In these respects, Scottish education may be regarded both as a symptom and a cause: a symptom of the uncritical and unhealthy acceptance of academic and other forms of authority, and a cause of the social and cultural evasion which characterises much of Scottish life.

## The Immediate Context

It may be objected that the events of the last few years have overtaken many of the criticisms considered in the preceding section. Henry Cowper and Willis Pickard, for example, assert that 'The disconcerting tendency to surround Scottish educational achievements with a smug complacency no longer persists to any great extent'.[48] The publication of a number of polemical pieces of a critical kind, written from very different political standpoints, might be cited in support of this view.[49] Attention could also be drawn to the recent curricular and examination reforms introduced for 14–18 year olds and to a number of initiatives in other areas — for example, primary education, special education, parental choice of school, in-service training of teachers. Taken together, these developments might be regarded as evidence of a healthy, responsive educational system, alert to the needs of a changing society. In January 1984 the present Minister responsible for Scottish education wrote:

> This year is one which will mark a watershed in almost every area of Scottish education. The foundations for change have been laid and many of the bricks are already in place.[50]

He also claimed that the system as a whole was 'facing up successfully to the current challenges of radical change'.[51]

How valid are these as objections to the line of attack that has been initiated? With regard to the statement of ministerial confidence, it should be said that some of the developments that are now taking place — e.g., those in special education — are certainly to be welcomed, though it remains to be seen whether the actual outcome is as good as the advance publicity. Much more fundamentally, however, neither the belated recognition in some quarters of the deficiencies of Scotland's educational self-image, nor the promises held out by the current series of reforms, begins to tackle the underlying ideological issues. There has, for example, been almost no critical consideration of the institutional framework within which 'solutions' are sought, far less of the relation between the political context within Scotland and the educational system as a whole. It has been blandly assumed that the agencies which have been active in the 'reform' process — the SED, the CCC, the SEB, etc. — are well qualified to promote genuine improvements and fully committed to a vision of Scottish education which is in the interests of the whole community. The possibility that these bodies may themselves constitute a major part of the difficulty has not been seriously entertained. In other words, both the identification of and the response to educational problems have taken place within very circumscribed parameters.

On reflection, however, this myopia is perhaps not so astonishing. After all, many of the same people who presided over the creation of the problems are now charged with resolving them and, indeed, are already claiming credit for some kind of breakthrough. What is lacking in all this is any real understanding of the forces at work in the institutional and bureaucratic agencies which have generated these 'reforms'. 'Deficit' theories of educational failure, whereby blame is attached to pupils, their parents or the community at large, are rarely extended to those who actually run the system, that invisible hierarchy of educational officials who lie behind the front-line ranks of classroom teachers. The sophisticated understanding which sociologists have developed in relation to the 'hidden curriculum' — that is, the value system that underlies the formal processes of schooling and that may undermine their stated aims — has, by another interesting feat of partial vision, not been applied to the upper layers of educational officialdom. One of the principal goals of the present volume is to remedy that deficiency. But, before it can proceed further, it is necessary to add to the conceptual apparatus to be employed: the penetration of complex institutions requires the use of tools appropriate to the task. These will be introduced in the next chapter.

*Notes and References*

1. SIO Factsheet 15, 'Scottish Education', n.d., p. 2.
2. SIO Factsheet 20, 'The Scottish Office', n.d., p. 7.
3. SIO, 'The Educational System of Scotland', HMSO, 1977, p. 21. SIO Factsheet 15 (see Note 1 above) is a revised and updated version of this booklet.
4. SIO Factsheet 15, p. 3.

5. SIO Factsheet 29, 'Scottish Secondary Education: 'Standard' Grade', n.d., p. 4.
6. *Ibid.*, p. 13.
7. James Scotland, *The History of Scottish Education*, Vol. 2, University of London Press, 1969, pp. 185–187.
8. *Ibid.*, p. 187.
9. *Ibid.*, p. 186.
10. *Ibid.*, p. 185.
11. G.S. Osborne, *Change in Scottish Education*, Longmans, London, 1968, p. 79.
12. S. Leslie Hunter, *The Scottish Educational System*, 2nd ed., Pergamon Press, Oxford, 1972, p. 39. Hunter also contends, however, that 'control from the centre is a reality' (*ibid*, p. 38) and, as will be shown in later chapters, is fully alert to the extent of the SED's influence.
13. Alastair Macbeth, 'The Government of Scottish Education: Partnership or Compromise?', in D. McCrone (ed.), *The Scottish Government Yearbook 1984*, Unit for the Study of Government in Scotland, Edinburgh, 1983, p. 167.
14. *Ibid.*, p. 184.
15. James G. Kellas, *The Scottish Political System*, 2nd ed., Cambridge University Press, 1975, p. 199.
16. *Ibid.*, p. 197.
17. *Ibid.*, p. 199.
18. See Scotland, *op. cit.*, Vol. 2, Chapter 17 and H. Cowper and W. Pickard, 'Education', in D. Daiches (ed.), *A Companion to Scottish Culture*, Edward Arnold, London, 1981, pp. 109–113.
19. Mary Gethins, Colin Morgan, Jennifer Ozga and Ray Woolfe, *The Welsh Office, the Scottish Education Department and the Northern Ireland Office: Central or Devolved Control of Education?*, Unit 3, Course E222, Open University, Milton Keynes, 1979.
20. *Ibid.*, p. 26.
21. *Ibid.*, p. 22.
22. *Ibid.*, p. 22.
23. *Ibid.*, p. 25.
24. *Ibid.*, p. 25.
25. *Ibid.*, p. 24.
26. *Ibid.*, p. 24.
27. Iain Thornburn, 'The new consultation', *TESS*, January 28, 1977, p. 2.
28. Michael Keating and Arthur Midwinter, *The Government of Scotland*, Mainstream, Edinburgh, 1983, p. 13.
29. *Ibid.*, p. 25.
30. Alastair Macbeth, 'The DES and Scottish Education', unpublished paper presented at a seminar on the DES held at Cambridge University, September 19-21, 1983. I am grateful to Dr Macbeth for permission to quote from this paper.
31. Macbeth, 'The Government of Scottish Education: Partnership or Compromise', in McCrone, *op. cit.*, p. 171.
32. *Ibid.*, p. 172.
33. *Ibid.*, p. 168.
34. *Ibid.*, p. 168.
35. R.D. Anderson, *Education and Opportunity in Victorian Scotland*, Clarendon Press, Oxford, 1983.
36. G.E. Davie, *The Democratic Intellect: Scotland and her Universities in the Nineteenth Century*, 2nd ed., Edinburgh University Press, 1964.

37. Anderson, *op. cit.*, p. 23.

38. *Ibid.*, p. 26.

39. Gethins *et al, op. cit.*, p. 28. The statement goes on, reinforcing part of the earlier argument, 'Allied to this complacency is a certain acceptance of authoritarianism in education, a lack of innovation from the local or individual school level, indeed a certain lack of tolerance by the centre to departures from normal practice'.

40. H.M. Paterson, 'Incubus and Ideology: The Development of Secondary Schooling in Scotland', in W.M. Humes and H.M. Paterson (eds.), *Scottish Culture and Scottish Education, 1800–1980*, John Donald, Edinburgh, 1983, p. 205.

41. See J.V. Smith and D. Hamilton (eds.), *The Meritocratic Intellect: Studies in the History of Educational Research*, Aberdeen University Press, 1980.

42. J. Gray, A.F. McPherson and D. Raffe, *Reconstructions of Secondary Education: Theory, Myth and Practice since the War*, Routledge and Kegan Paul, London, 1983, p. 226.

43. For a fuller discussion of this issue, see W.M. Humes, 'The Cultural Significance of Scotland's Educational System', in McCrone, *op. cit.*, pp. 149–166.

44. Gray, McPherson and Raffe, *op. cit.*, p. 39.

45. *Ibid.*, p. 44.

46. See Keith Williamson, 'Lowland Scots in Education: An Historical Survey', Parts I and II, *Scottish Language*, No.1, Autumn 1982, pp. 54–77 and No.2, Autumn 1983, pp. 52–87. Also Victor E. Durkacz, *The Decline of the Celtic Languages*, John Donald, Edinburgh, 1983.

47. Bob Tait, 'Doubts and Fears about Socialism', *Radical Scotland*, June/July 1983, p. 15.

48. Cowper and Pickard, 'Education', in Daiches, *op. cit.*, p. 109.

49. See, e.g., Alex Fletcher and John Mackay, *Scottish Education — Regaining a Lost Reputation*, 1978, cited in 'Where the parties stand', *TESS*, June 3, 1983; D. Jenkins, K. Reid and D. Skinner (eds.), *Scotland a Half-Educated Nation*. Callendar Park College of Education, 1980; and N. Grant, *The Crisis of Scottish Education*, Saltire Society, Edinburgh, 1982.

50. Allan Stewart, '1984: a watershed year' *TESS*, January 6, 1984, p. 4.

51. *Ibid.*, p. 4.

# 2
# *Analytic Concepts*

## Introduction

The aim of this chapter is to explain some of the central concepts that will be used in analysing the Scottish educational system. Three of the concepts — bureaucracy, professionalism and ideology — are very widely employed in a variety of contexts, and the literature dealing with them is vast and often conflicting. All that can be attempted here is an indication of the senses in which these terms will be used in the present volume. No claims are made that these senses are definitive, simply that they represent reasonable interpretations which can serve to illuminate the functioning of Scottish education. The fourth concept — leadership class — is more problematical, partly because it does not enjoy the wide currency of the others, and partly because it implies a degree of cohesion among those so designated, an interpretation which cannot be properly assessed until the evidence of succeeding chapters is considered. Nevertheless, even if a final judgement about the *connotative* force of the term must be postponed until later, it is important to try to indicate its *denotative* significance at this stage.

## Bureaucracy

Most modern studies of bureaucracy still take as their starting point the work of the German sociologist, Max Weber (1864–1920).[1] Weber abstracted the most typical features of bureaucratic organisations and offered an 'ideal type' which has served as a theoretical model for many subsequent empirical investigations.[2] The principal characteristics of this 'ideal type' are: the fixed designation of official duties to be carried out on the principle of the division of labour; the use of hierarchical forms of organisation to establish clear lines of authority and accountability; the application of a consistent system of abstract rules in the interests of maintaining uniform standards of performance; the exclusion of personal considerations by officials in the discharge of their duties so that impartiality is maintained; the appointment of staff on the basis of formal qualifications and under conditions of employment which give relative security of tenure; a concern for maximising organisational efficiency.

This account is in line with Weber's emphasis on legal-rational authority in modern society and, taken as a whole, it presents bureaucratic structures in a reasonably favourable light. They are seen to be a logical means of coping with the immensely complex nature of social, industrial and political life in advanced cultures. Weber was certainly aware of potential dangers within bureaucracies, but it was left to later writers to elaborate on these. The extent to which the aim of efficiency, which the formal structure is intended to facilitate, can be modified and, in some cases, undermined by the actual processes of bureaucratic operation, now receives a great deal of critical attention.[3] This increasing focus on *process* rather than *structure* has led to the term bureaucracy and its derivatives frequently being used to express an adverse judgement, signifying obstruction, delay and incompetence. Bureaucracy has, in fact, come to be regarded as a major social problem, and relatively few commentators are now prepared to defend it with vigour as an organisational form.[4] It should be noted, however, that it is hard to see how many of the expectations of citizens in modern society could be met without an extensive network of large, and often complex, institutions dealing with a wide range of activities (legal, medical, educational, etc.). The critical question is how far they actually fulfil the functions they are supposed to and how far they generate functions which serve the interests of officials instead of those of the public.

Definitional problems come to the surface at this point. Many alternative ways of defining bureaucracy have been suggested,[5] but a principal weakness of purely formal, structural accounts is their neglect of the human dimension, the fact that organisational goals have to be translated into action by people rather than machines. This is perhaps particularly true in the field of education. For this reason, the working definition of bureaucracy that relates most closely to the concerns of the present study is 'rule by officials'. It should be noted, however, that it will not be argued that everything can be reduced to a matter of personal motivation: the word 'rule' indicates a context of authority and a framework of order in which the private purposes of individuals have to be worked out. Some of the most interesting aspects of bureaucratic organisations can, indeed, only be understood if attention is focused on the *interaction* between administrative and personal aspirations. Viewed in this way, it becomes meaningful to speak of the 'bureaucratic personality' as well as the 'bureaucratic institution'.[6] It will be instructive to refer to some of the forms in which the conjunction of organisational and human purposes manifests itself.

The emphasis on applying abstract rules impartially, which was a feature identified by Weber, leads to the development of a neutral, impersonal style by officials. This can be employed to serve another, more self-interested goal — the masking of personal and political rivalries, both inside and outside the organisation, and the emotions associated with them. There are facial as well as verbal elements in this. The bureaucratic face displays formal cordiality, but there need be no corresponding emotional engagement. Similarly, the language employed is polite and objective, with a marked preference for the passive voice in the written mode. Used with subtlety, this style can be deployed to convey messages other than those apparent on the surface. Skilled bureaucrats 'become masters of the presentation of self and learn to communicate, when necessary, through indirection'.[7]

Also worthy of comment is the effect of the hierarchical structure favoured by most bureaucracies on the personalities and values of officials. The relationships between junior and senior staff develop in identifiable ways. For example,

'Subordinates in a hierarchy will say and do certain things to make their immediate superior feel important'.[8] Quality of performance is obviously an aspect of this, but so too are friendliness, real or feigned, flattery and imitation. Even where the focus is on performance, it is important that success should reflect on the leader. If failure should occur, however, there is no corresponding displacement of blame onto the senior member. Related to this, it is assumed that gradations within the hierarchy reflect not just levels of authority but also levels of competence. 'Expertness and hierarchical authority are not distinguished but are presumed identical.'[9]

Acceptance of this belief is regarded as an important indicator of commitment to the organisation and thus acts as a crucial test of loyalty, perhaps the most esteemed bureaucratic quality of all. A high rating on loyalty — to one's superiors and to the whole structure of bureaucratic norms and practices — can sometimes compensate for certain deficiencies in job performance. Several studies have pointed to this as an explanation for the promotion of persons with inferior performance ratings over colleagues with stronger credentials.[10] Where this occurs, however, a side-effect which is likely to have dysfunctional consequences is that able people who are passed over will begin to doubt and perhaps even challenge the expertise of their superiors. Nevertheless, in large bureaucracies it is actually very difficult for individuals to do very much about incompetent superiors because criticism will be perceived as threatening to the hierarchy as a whole, not just to those whose abilities are being called into question. Occasionally. disenchantment leads some employees to leak information to outside bodies, such as the media, in the hope that mistakes will be exposed publicly. This is relatively rare, however, for the retribution against 'disloyal' and 'untrustworthy' individuals is usually strong. Retribution is meted out even if the motives are less displeasure at being passed over than commitment to some extra-organisational principle — for example, of a moral sort. The pressures to conform to internal norms of behaviour, even if they violate standards that are highly valued in other contexts, can be very powerful indeed.

In these circumstances, it is hardly surprising that bureaucratic settings sometimes generate a kind of social paranoia. This can be illustrated with reference to another important characteristic, the concern with confidentiality. Ascending the hierarchy of a bureaucracy involves a progressive initiation into the inner workings of the structure. To those who are deemed worthy of advancement, the process acts as confirmation of their worth: they have passed the loyalty test, and access to restricted information is one of the rewards. It is a mark of both power and status. But it is also a source of fear. The status symbol is only potent in so far as others are denied it. This means that care must be taken to ensure that subordinates and outsiders do not share the inner knowledge given to senior officials, and so energies are directed towards various strategies of containment. Concern about the disclosure of information thus becomes a major preoccupation of bureaucratic élites. The effects of this process at a political level are described in the early work of Karl Marx in a way that again indicates the importance of the interaction between structural and personal values:

> The general spirit of bureaucracy is the official secret, the mystery ... Conducting the affairs of state in public, even political consciousness, thus appear [*sic*] to the bureaucracy as high treason against its mystery. Authority is thus the principle of its knowledge and the deification of authoritarianism is its credo. But within itself this spiritualism turns into a coarse materialism, the materialism of dumb obedience ... As far as the individual bureaucrat is concerned, the goals of the state become his private goals: a hunting for higher jobs and the making of a career ... Bureaucracy has, therefore, to make life as materialistic as possible ... Hence the bureaucrat must always behave towards the real state in a Jesuitical fashion, be it consciously or unconsciously ... The bureaucrat sees the world as a mere object to be managed by him ... The bureaucracy is the illusory state alongside the real state, it is the spiritualism of the state. Everything has, therefore, a double meaning: the real and the bureaucratic one.

This statement is interesting for several reasons, not least its irony in the light of the development of oppressive bureaucracies in Communist bloc countries. It links the concern with confidentiality and secrecy both to authoritarianism and to the conflation of public and private goals. It also draws attention to the transformation of the real world into what Marx calls 'spiritualism', an arcane belief system which serves to justify the actions of the bureaucrat. And again, the statement raises the question of the degree of consciousness involved in the 'Jesuitical' manoeuvres adopted to disguise the various forms of self-interest which arise. In this respect, two opposing explanations can be constructed. Accounts of bureaucratic behaviour which attribute a high level of consciousness to officials tend in the direction of conspiracy theories and are often inclined to assume that institutions are subject to simple and direct control by efficient élites. Conversely, accounts which suggest that officials are often unaware of the forces that move them to act in particular ways tend in the direction of false-consciousness theories and are often inclined to assume that institutions possess a potent life of their own which is almost impossible to control.

The truth, in the majority of cases, probably lies somewhere between the two. In most complex institutions, senior officials will require a measure of reflectiveness about the work they are engaged in, but it seems likely that for much of the time it will be directed at the achievement of agreed organisational goals: the reflectiveness will, in other words, take place within a framework of largely unquestioned assumptions. The underlying features of the bureaucratic structure itself will not be questioned and certainly not in so far as these serve the interests of the leadership group. At lower levels of the system, the importance attached to loyalty and conformity ensures that the scope for critical reflection is minimal. This helps to explain the relative stability and inertia of bureaucratic hierarchies. On the face of it, the potential for disaffection within the structure is considerable. As fewer people move up each rung on the ladder of power, so the number who 'fail' increases. Their acceptance of that 'failure' is promoted partly by the formal and contractual restrictions on their defined roles (as described by Weber), and partly by their progressive initiation into an organisational ethos which encourages the uncritical acceptance of internal institutional norms and their dissociation from external value systems of a potentially contaminating sort. Thus, although alienation may occur, it will not find expression as open rebellion: instead it will simply be part of the private world of individual officials, who may use it as a perverse kind of consolation for their failure to reach the top or as reassurance that they have not been totally 'corrupted'.

These, then, are some of the main aspects of the concept of bureaucracy that will feature in succeeding chapters. Reference will be made both to structures and processes, but there will be a greater concern than in conventional sociological accounts to explore the inter-connectedness of, on the one hand, organisational forms and practices, and, on the other, the perceptions and goals of the senior officials responsible for the functioning of the institutions in which they are employed. After all, education is — or should be — an enterprise concerned with human values and it would seem unsuitable to apply an entirely impersonal, managerial mode of analysis. It is hoped that, in adopting this approach, the risks of *argumenta ad homines* will be avoided, but it will be necessary to refer to particular people and their involvement in specific episodes in the administration of Scottish education in order to substantiate the general argument that will be advanced.

## Professionalism

The traditional professions are those of medicine, the law and the church. Nowadays a great many other occupations lay claims to professional status (e.g., engineering, journalism, social work, advertising) — so much so, in fact, that the indicators of professionalism have become extremely blurred. However, in the case of teachers and others employed in education, the concern has always been to emulate the traditional professions, especially the law and medicine, in terms of standing and remuneration. They have, it must be said, not fully succeeded in this aspiration, for a variety of reasons that will emerge in the course of discussion. First, however, some attention must be directed to the question of what it is that distinguishes high status, 'professional' occupations from less highly regarded forms of employment. A large number of criteria have been proposed by different writers on the subject, and attempts have been made to draw distinctions between semi-professionals and full professionals, and between restricted professionals and extended professionals.[12] None of the proposed criteria of professionalism are conceptually water-tight, but the following, inter-related features emerge as especially important in most accounts.

First, professionals require extensive knowledge and skill in their chosen field: this means that to qualify they must undergo a lengthy period of education and training, in the course of which they are subject to a 'process of socialization into professional values'.[13] Secondly, the expertise which professionals possess is highly valued by society: they provide a vital service, the loss of which would be regarded as extremely damaging to the life of the community. Thirdly, the element of service and the initiation into professional values lead to the development of an ethical code, which makes explicit the obligations of professionals to their clients. Fourthly, both the expert knowledge which the professionals possess and their sense of obligation to their clients make it desirable that they should be organised on a self-regulating basis and be responsible for their own registration and disciplinary procedures. Fifthly, this degree of relative autonomy extends to the exercise of everyday responsibilities: professionals bring their knowledge and skill to bear on complex and varied situations, and their expertise entitles them to exercise their independent judgement in offering advice.

It should be noted that some of these criteria stress the duties which professionals owe to their clients, while others indicate the benefits which accompany professional status. The balance between these two elements is critical, and a recurring issue in the recent literature on the subject is the extent to which professional groups have become more concerned about looking after their own interests than those of the public whom they supposedly serve. A number of studies have traced the historical development of different occupational groups and have suggested that establishing the distinctiveness of members' expertise, gaining collective control of the organisation of the profession, and securing advantageous career opportunities for members, have become more significant motives than any associated with the idea of disinterested public service.[14] One example might be the growth of the academic community in the twentieth century, a process marked by increasing specialisation, the pursuit of more advanced qualifications, and the deployment of forceful arguments in favour of a high measure of freedom of action notwithstanding demands for a greater proportion of the nation's financial resources. It would seem, moreover, that the academic community, because of its power to define what counts as worthwhile knowledge and its capacity to determine the way in which that knowledge is classified, has been a particularly potent influence in establishing the legitimacy of the claims of different groups to professional status.

When it comes to other levels of the educational system, the picture is more complicated, and some of the reasons for the uncertain position of primary and secondary teaching begin to emerge. The knowledge and skill which school teachers possess is generally regarded as less esoteric and easier to acquire than that of doctors and lawyers: this may be partly a matter of familiarity, since most people have direct and extended experience of the educational system, whereas they lack similar experience of the medical and legal worlds. Again, the precise nature of the training required for teaching is difficult to specify and open to dispute: sometimes, in fact, it is asserted — not least by trainee teachers themselves — that formal training is of limited value and that personality factors are as important as skill factors in determining success. This scepticism can extend to qualified and experienced teachers, but the power of the professional model is such that they are generally careful not to give public expression to it. Instead, they compete with each other in respect of assumed levels of professionalism: thus graduates feel themselves better placed — and so more 'professional' — than non-graduates; and teachers of academic subjects tend to feel superior to teachers of practical subjects. In recent years the situation has altered somewhat with the appearance of the BEd degree and the gradual move towards an all-graduate teaching force, but the essential point remains — namely, that the existence of different entry routes, of varying periods of training, and of courses related to different age ranges, has cast doubt on the precise character of the professionalism that is invoked. As an element in the propaganda of teachers' organisations, the concept of professionalism continues to feature prominently, but its exact designation is vitiated by internal prejudices and divisions.

There is another respect in which the professionalism of teachers is compromised. Increasingly, classroom teaching has come to be regarded by educators themselves as a modest rung on the ladder of career advancement, and there are grounds for thinking that status differentials *within* education have developed to a greater extent than those within medicine or the law. In the case of the latter occupations there are certainly differences between junior and senior partners, between registrars and consultants, and between solicitors and advocates, but the professional standing of those occupying even the least exalted position is not normally in doubt. There is a fair measure of uniformity of status, for example, between all general practitioners within the National Health Service and all solicitors in private practice. Within teaching, however, there are very considerable variations, reinforced by an elaborate and highly differentiated promotion system. Thus, in Scotland, there are, at secondary school level, assistant teachers, assistant principal teachers, principal teachers (subject), principal teachers (guidance), assistant head teachers, deputy head teachers and head teachers. In addition, there are many career opportunities in education for which a period of classroom teaching is regarded as a necessary preliminary but which are rewarded more generously — these include the advisory service, the inspectorate, college lecturing, educational administration, and some posts in examining and research. The occupants of these positions are sometimes regarded as refugees from the classroom but, should they be troubled by that jibe, they can console themselves with the financial and other advantages which they enjoy. However, if the net result is that 'success' in the educational world is partly defined in relation to the ability to secure a non-teaching job, the worth of what classroom teachers do is inevitably devalued and this, in turn, casts further doubt on the nature of their professionalism. The issue is not usually confronted in this way, partly because classroom teachers themselves, not surprisingly, are unwilling to acknowledge the extent to which a hierarchical career structure which, through their representatives, they have endorsed, creates what might be called 'professional slippage': that is, a situation in which the more specialist opportunities that arise, the less prestige the unpromoted teacher enjoys.

There is yet another, and perhaps more fundamental, reason why the ambiguous nature of professionalism in education is not addressed directly. Those who do manage to 'escape from the classroom' are usually careful to continue to pay tribute to the professionalism of their former colleagues. Some of these tributes are no doubt genuine and reflect an awareness of the demands and the difficulties of work in schools. Other motives are, however, also in evidence. Non-teaching jobs are usually, in some sense, parasitic on the work of schools. College lecturers and advisers seek to influence the form and content of lessons: inspectors monitor standards and act as agents of reform; administrators control resources and exercise power over appointments. In each case, the authority of the non-teaching 'experts' depends on the existence of a large body of 'ordinary' staff whose actions they seek to control in some way. This creates a problem of legitimacy in the sense that the longer the non-teaching 'experts' have been away from classroom situations, the weaker their credibility becomes. The problem can, to some extent, be overcome by the simple existence of an elaborate hierarchy and the promise of advancement to those who accept its approved norms. But reliance on the hierarchy alone would tend to become too authoritarian and might prove counter-productive. This is where the importance of appeals to professionalism comes in. They serve the useful function of disguising the power element inherent in the complex stratification of education by appealing to an occupational ideal which seems to offer the prospect of a desired status and respect, and, at the same time, characterising critical conduct as *un*professional. Professionalism thus becomes a mechanism of control which operates as effectively against members themselves as against would-be members who lack the necessary qualifications and training. Furthermore, the effectiveness of the control is increased by the fact that the principal agents are not wholly external officials but are themselves former teachers who have a stake in the promotion of professional values. Viewed in this light, the highly ambiguous character of the concept of professionalism becomes apparent. It is something which classroom teachers aspire to but feel they have not fully secured; it is something which conflates the interests of clients and those of members; it is something which can be exploited by those who exercise authority over classroom teachers.

The existence of a sizeable number of relatively high-status non-teaching jobs within the educational system (inspectors, administrators, etc.) raises a further issue that bears on professionalism. Men and women occupying these positions are, to a much greater extent than classroom teachers, part of the bureaucratic machinery of central and local government. While teachers are undoubtedly affected by that machinery, their contact with it is peripheral rather than central. At the simplest level, teachers are not located in the institutions where important policy decisions are reached. They are, it is true, usually consulted — on a representative basis — about matters that affect them, but the nature of the consultative process itself is part of a wider network of bureaucratic conventions. By contrast, the occupants of senior posts in education are closely tied to national and/or regional administration, and part of their work involves learning to cope with bureaucracy. This raises a critical question: to what extent do the values of professionalism and bureaucracy coincide and to what extent do they conflict?

Some aspects of professionalism seem, on initial inspection, to contain the potential for resistance to bureaucratic pressures. The emphasis on service to the client, for example, seems to belong to a different value system from the concern with loyalty and conformity to the organisation which was noted as a significant feature of bureaucracies. However, writers who have examined the rise of professionalism suggest that, once established, and particularly where successful establishment depends on evolving a working (and often financially dependent) relationship with state agencies, altruistic qualities — such as service to the client — become secondary to qualities which are quite compatible with bureaucratic values. As Marten Shipman has observed:

> The spread of professions has accompanied the rise of bureaucracies . . . Bureaucracy and professionalization have been developed in harness despite their apparently conflicting values; advanced industrial societies seem to be fertile ground for both.[15]

He goes on to explain the process in these terms:

> The commons factor linking the bureaucrat and professional is that the steps in their careers are clearly laid out. The procedures that mark the bureaucracy also mark out orderly career patterns. The signs are the negotiated scales, the posts of responsibility, the increments, the sequence of promotions, the security of employment . . . Professionals press for bureaucratization because it guarantees a secure future.[16]

This, it should be noted, is a long way from the notion of dedicated, disinterested service to others. The balance between the duties and the rewards of professional status has been tipped very firmly in favour of the latter. For senior officials, however, it remains important to continue to invoke those parts of the traditional rhetoric of professionalism which stress altruism; a twin purpose is served by so doing — the maintenance of self-esteem and the projection of a socially worthy public image.

But the argument can be pushed too far. Despite a fair measure of congruence between bureaucratic and professional value systems, tensions and conflicts continue to surface. In the case of the teaching profession in Scotland, this is particularly apparent when the role of those organisations, such as the Educational Institute of Scotland (EIS), which exist to represent the interests of teachers, is examined. Here a desire to act in a manner that conforms to the approved norms of professionalism coexists uneasily with an awareness that the strategies associated with trade unionism sometimes seem to offer a better chance of success in achieving objectives relating to pay and conditions of service. Even so, it is worth pointing out that trade unions have evolved their own forms of organisation which, in many respects, are quite compatible with bureaucratic systems. Some of these continuities and discontinuities will be considered in more detail in a later chapter.

It has been suggested that professionalism is something that teachers have long aspired to but, despite a great deal of lip service being paid to the importance of what they do, they have not been fully successful in their efforts. Their continuing obsession with professionalism can, indeed, be adduced as evidence of their failure to achieve it. This failure is partly explicable by external factors, most notably the unwillingness of successive governments to make the considerable financial commitment which would be necessary to enhance the status of teachers significantly. In addition, however, there have been a number of internal factors which have served to undermine the pursuit of full professional standing. The division of labour within education and the gradual expansion of non-teaching posts which, rightly or wrongly, have come to be more highly regarded and more highly rewarded than the work of classroom teachers, are major elements in this. It can be argued that this 'élite' group functions partly by using the attractions of professionalism as a mechanism of control in its dealings with teachers. However, neither teachers nor those who have moved on to become part of the educational bureaucracy have been prepared to confront the deep ambiguities of the concept, and they have certainly not shown any disposition to reject it as a false ideal.

## Ideology

Bureaucracies and professional groups need to be understood not merely in terms of the structures and processes that constitute their surface configurations: it is also necessary to dig beneath the surface and attempt to trace those subterranean movements, at the level of ideas, attitudes and values, that shape their public and private actions. This level of analysis can be described as ideological in that it is concerned with the belief system that underlies the forms of expression that bureaucrats and professionals characteristically adopt. Raymond Williams has identified one important meaning of ideology as 'the set of ideas which arise from a given set of material interests or, more broadly, from a definite class or group',[17] and it is in this sense that it becomes meaningful to speak of a 'bureaucratic ideology' and a 'professional ideology' to refer to those fundamental tenets shared by members of these overlapping groups.

However, in attempting to extend the analysis from structures and processes to ideas and values, a number of problems are encountered. Although a great deal has been written on the subjects of bureaucracy, professionalism and ideology in general, the specifically Scottish literature is thin and, in relation to education in particular, almost non-existent. David McCrone has observed: 'The power of bureaucratic authority in Scotland is very significant, and yet our understanding of it is poor'.[18] And John Wilson has commented that 'We know next to nothing about Scottish teachers as a professional group'.[19] These observations identify real difficulties for the investigator seeking to develop a deeper level of analysis but they do not undermine the importance of the enterprise. Indeed, they prompt a question which may suggest a way forward. Why is it that the bureaucratic and professional dimensions of Scottish education — and, by extension, their ideological underpinning — have received so little attention? Several explanations are possible. First, it might be argued that there is general satisfaction in Scotland with the performance of professionals and bureaucrats within education, and that the issue is not seen as problematical or worthy of investigation. This would doubtless be an appealing explanation for members of the groups concerned but it must, at best, be judged improbable and unconvincing in the light of the material presented in Chapter 1. That part of Chapter 1 which deals with the Scottish educational tradition — in particular, the tensions between democracy, authority, equality and competition —suggests a second possible explanation for the failure to look at bureaucratic, professional and ideological issues in a critical way. Just as the inherent conflicts in the Scottish tradition are painful to contemplate, especially when juxtaposed with the favoured self-image of educational excellence, so the attempt to uncover ideological assumptions may carry the danger of revealing features that are disturbing rather than reassuring. There may, in other words, be a measure of unconscious psychological resistance to undertaking the enquiry for fear of what it might uncover. The fact that the most likely enquirers are to be found within the educational system itself, and are therefore also the people who would be most affected by any critical conclusions, serves to intensify the attractions of evasion.

A third possible explanation, which is not incompatible with the second, takes the argument further by attempting to establish links between the ideologies subscribed to by particular groups in education and the economic and political basis of power within Scottish society as a whole. One general (i.e., not specifically Scottish) interpretation that has enjoyed a fair amount of currency in recent years is that 'educational ideology has the dual function of legitimating a specific power grouping while at the same time acting as an agent of social control'.[20] This kind of explanation, it should be said, has usually been applied to the power relationships between teachers and pupils, but it can be extended and, in certain respects, is perhaps more appropriate to the relationships that exist between educationists themselves and between educationists and other social groups. The process of legitimising specific power groupings involves setting limits to the kinds of enquiries that are regarded as worthwhile:

> By defining what ideas and arguments should be regarded as legitimate and a normal part of political discourse, a dominant ideology controls the kinds of issues which are allowed to enter the political arena.[21]

If the logic of this argument is accepted, then it may be that investigations into the ideological basis of Scottish education and, in particular, into the unstated value and belief systems of bureaucrats and professionals, and their relation to wider social and economic structures, have been discouraged because they have been perceived as potentially threatening. Furthermore, in so far as members of these groups actually determine what is to be investigated, their chances of controlling the terms of the debate are that much greater. This process need not be undertaken, or even regarded, as an exercise in deliberate suppression: it can exist at the level of instinctive response and be received at the level of unreflective acceptance.

The philosopher, Patrick Corbett, has described the ideological relationship between dominant and subordinate groups in a somewhat simplified, but nonetheless powerful and impressive, way:

> It will escape no one but the simplest devotee that ideologies serve the interests of certain institutions, and therefore of those who hold office in those institutions. Men enjoy power, and the fruits of power. They like to make other men act as they decide;

> the spectacle is pleasant in itself and brings material gains. But how can other men be made obedient? It is impractical to be always telling them and forcing them to act as you desire. That takes too much time; it is also too rigid, and is liable to produce resistance. More effective is to persuade them that obedience is in their own real interest; more effective still is to persuade them that what looks like obedience is really nothing of the kind, but rather the fulfilment of some plan or necessity which transcends the lives and needs of any individuals. (That the plan or necessity in question ministers much more to the lives and needs of some people than it does to those of others is merely incidental, and to be accepted as part of the nature of things.) These lines of thought thus lead to the conclusion that the social function of ideologies is to condition men intellectually to obedience.[22]

Corbett's account allows for a range of strategies of control. The preferred mode is non-repressive and, indeed, inexplicit: the validity of authority is simply taken for granted, both by those who exercise it and those who are subject to it. Should persuasion be necessary, the initial appeal is to the identifiable interests of those whose 'cooperation' is sought. Direction is a last resort, but it nonetheless remains a possibility.

Some of the aspects of bureaucracy and professionalism described in the preceding sections fit this explanation quite well. The emphasis on organisational loyalty, on operating within a framework of rules or conventions, and on establishing the distinctiveness of those who qualify for entry to the ranks, all tend to promote conformity and therefore acceptance of the basic ideological assumptions. That is not to say that tensions do not exist. On the contrary, an effective ideology must be able to accommodate some tensions while ensuring that they do not pose a real challenge to the structural foundations on which the exercise of power depends. An interesting example of the way this works — an example which perhaps has particular relevance to Scotland —arises in relation to social class. Traditionally, questions of class have provided a major source of social conflict. It can be argued, however, that the growth of professional and bureaucratic ideologies has served to neutralise the conflict to some extent. Ozga and Lawn,[23] drawing on the work of Larson,[24] have commented on the ideological functions of professionals and bureaucrats in advanced capitalist societies: they note the mutually reinforcing character of many of these functions and, in particular, they observe that 'the ideology of professionalism . . . acts to deny the importance of class conflict by opening up the possibility of 'professional' status to all classes, and by stressing the accessibility of educational opportunity'.[25]

Now Scotland has often been held up as an example of a relatively classless society, especially in comparison with England. Despite a substantial body of evidence to the contrary,[26] this belief has persisted, not least among Scots themselves. It is, in fact, another aspect of the Scottish educational tradition and the kailyard version of community life which emphasise opportunity and solidarity, social advancement and fatalistic acceptance. If, however, it is true that the uncritical acceptance of professional and bureaucratic ideologies results in the disguising or denial of class conflict, then education, as a major instrument for the induction of such acceptance and as a major arena for the activities of professionals and bureaucrats, must play a significant part in this process. To the extent that they reinforce the myth that class is not a major issue in Scottish society, educationists thus perform an important ideological function that extends beyond their own immediate area of operation: they help to sustain the belief that differences in power and economic status depend on an entirely rational exercise in social selection in which rewards are distributed fairly.

The contradictions in this position are not hard to see. By seeking to secure parity with other professions, teachers show themselves to be part of a wider movement of competing interests, class interests, the validity of which is denied by the orthodoxies of the Scottish educational tradition, to which they happily subscribe. The pursuit of class advantage for themselves can thus coexist with an unreflective acceptance of the myth of classlessness. This fundamental inconsistency is not addressed simply because the ideological sub-structure on which it is based exists at the level of unconscious assumption and is never subjected to critical scrutiny. If it were, it might provoke an acute existential dilemma for teachers.

Clearly the political ramifications of this line of enquiry are considerable and extend beyond the scope of the present volume. For example, one important area that needs to be addressed is how dominant ideologies within Scottish education relate to dominant ideologies within Scottish society as a whole. Here again the absence of a developed body of literature on the subject is apparent. There have been a number of useful, but inevitably limited, articles by journalists about the power exercised by influential groups in Scotland. Chris Baur, for example, has suggested that the people who 'fix the nation's agenda' are a relatively small group who 'all know each other' and share the same basic beliefs — 'a tight circle of politicians, businessmen, civil servants, lawyers, trade unionists, churchmen, academics and a nostalgic sprinkling of titled gentry'.[27] Beneath this upper echelon there is a sizeable group, including many in the field of education, who are beneficiaries of Scottish Office patronage — that is, appointees to one or more of the 4,000–5,000 jobs on committees, panels, boards, working parties, etc. which are controlled by the Secretary of State and his advisers.[28] In the course of Chapters 3 and 4 further consideration will be given to the view that those who control and those who receive Scottish Office patronage share broadly similar, if unstated, assumptions about the nature, distribution and exercise of power in society. Education constitutes only one arena for this network of influence, but it can be argued that it is a particularly important one, given its power to define what counts as worthwhile knowledge and therefore set limits to 'valid' forms of intellectual enquiry. A possible criticism of leading Scottish educationists is that they have failed, because of their close association with ideologically dominant groups, to promote an adequate cultural understanding of the very society whose interests and traditions they claim to represent.

These are wide-ranging issues on which a final judgement must, for the moment, be postponed. One immediate task presents itself — the identification of the people who constitute the dominant group in Scottish education and the justification of their designation as a 'leadership class'.

## Leadership Class

The term 'leadership class' serves here as a general label for those who occupy senior positions in the world of Scottish education, and it will be useful to give some examples before going on to explain the use of the concept. In simple descriptive terms, the members of the leadership class can be identified quite precisely: career civil servants of Assistant Secretary level and above within the Scottish Education Department (SED); members of Her Majesty's Inspectorate (HMIs); at local level, Directors of Education and their staffs; Principals of Colleges of Education; and, not least, the leading office-bearers in a range of important educational bodies, including the Consultative Committee on the Curriculum (CCC), the Scottish Examination Board (SEB) and the General Teaching Council (GTC). This last category covers people from a wide variety of educational backgrounds — head teachers, principals of colleges of further education, lecturers, advisers, etc. The essential point is that their membership of the leadership class does not depend so much on the post from which they earn their living as on their involvement, at a senior level, with national bodies such as the CCC or SEB. Thus, for example, only a small minority of head teachers can legitimately be regarded as belonging to the leadership class.

These are the people who, collectively, set a large part of the agenda of Scottish education and contribute significantly to the formulation and implementation of policy. They are professionals and bureaucrats — often both — and in some cases there would be scope for a nice semantic argument about whether 'bureaucratic professional' or 'professional bureaucrat' would be the better designation. It would, however, be wrong to suggest that the world of the leadership class is entirely enclosed and immune from outside pressures. Many people in Scottish education have a peripheral connection with it. For example, classroom teachers are well represented on the subject panels of the SEB, and representatives of teachers' organisations have regular contact with directorate staff at local level and with SED staff at national level on matters pertaining to salaries, conditions of service, etc. A full and fair account of the processes by which decisions are reached must include an analysis of these links and their significance in terms of the distribution of power and the principles of democracy and partnership. In other words, it would be wrong to present, *ab initio*, a picture of the leadership class as monolithic and all-powerful.

The need for caution is reinforced by the rather problematic nature of the term 'leadership class' itself. Raymond Williams has observed that 'Class is an obviously difficult word, both in its range of meanings and in its complexity in that particular meaning where it describes a social division'.[29] Tracing its historical development, he notes that it can be used 'as a general word for a group or division', 'as a would-be specific description of a social formation' (e.g., middle class, working class), as an explanatory term in accounts of the economic and political relations of different social groups (e.g., productive class, privileged class), and as an indication of 'self-description and self-assignation' (e.g., class consciousness, class struggle).[30] Often these senses overlap and inter-relate in ways that conflate birth, status, wealth and power. Quite obviously it is impossible to be narrowly prescriptive about usage, and attempts to draw tight conceptual distinctions, while they often highlight important shades of meaning, are usually less than fully convincing. A.H. Halsey, for example, relies on the concepts of class, status and party in explaining the differential distribution of power in society and the stratification system which embodies it — 'classes belong to the economic, status groups to the social, and parties to the political structure of society'.[31] He goes on to state that classes derive from the division of labour and 'make up more or less cohesive and socially conscious groups' based on occupation and income: status is formed out of the tendency 'to attach positive and negative values to human attributes, and to distribute respect or honour and contempt or derogation accordingly': parties 'form out of the organized pursuit of social objectives; they are political parties, pressure groups, associations, and unions of those who consciously share a planned movement for the acquisition of power'.[32]

This classification is useful, but it is difficult to apply it in a consistent fashion to the real world in which economic, social and political structures penetrate each other at many points. In the field of education, for example, senior civil servants and local government officials are very much part of the political arena and, even although they may not seek direct power, of the kind acquired through the ballot box, they undoubtedly possess executive power and, indeed, there are often suspicions that their influence extends beyond that: collectively, they function as an internal pressure group on the policy-making process, a role made more effective by the fact that it is played, for the most part, with the subtle indirectness characteristic of complex bureaucracies. They can also be regarded as part of the historical development of the division of labour and the growth of a particular economic category, the professional service class. Furthermore, their employment in bureaucratic organisations, in which levels of responsibility and reward are formally designated in a hierarchical career structure, makes them part of a system in which success is partly defined by the acquisition of status and prestige. Thus all three of Halsey's categories are involved, and it would be misleading to limit the use of class to the economic system, strictly defined. They are all relevant to the present study, though it remains to be seen whether some elements turn out to be more critical than others from an interpretative point of view.

'Leadership' poses fewer problems of a semantic kind. Two main senses can be distinguished: first, it can refer descriptively to those who hold the dignity, office or position of leaders ('the leadership'); and, secondly, it can refer evaluatively to the possession of qualities indicative of fitness to lead. The second sense, it should be noted, is capable of ironic deployment, especially where those who hold senior office think that they do possess leadership qualities while others beg to dissent from that opinion.

The phrase 'leadership class' is preferred to other possible terms — for example, élite —because it gives a prominent place to questions of power. As T.S. Eliot has shown, élites need not be connected very closely to the political process — artistic and literary élites provide examples of this.[33] A leadership class, on the other hand, especially where its authority depends on its place within the bureaucratic machinery of central and local government, is very much part of the political process. To make this point is not to prejudge the nature or the amount of political power that is involved: it is simply to insist that a proper understanding of the way any state educational system functions depends, in part, on locating its principal agents within the decision-making machinery of government.

In the case of Scottish education, the various groups which were mentioned at the start of this section as constituting the leadership class — whether professionals or bureaucrats or both — operate in the context of local and national government, to which they are formally accountable, and this raises the difficult question of where power really resides. Within the Scottish Office, for example, there is a Parliamentary Under-Secretary of State for education, and civil servants within the SED are answerable to him and, through him, to the House of Commons. At local level, there are elected councillors who serve on education committees under the chairmanship of a fellow member: non-elected officials, such as Directors of Education, are assumed to serve the democratic process and are expected to implement the agreed policies of the region. This framework of representative government may seem to cast doubt on the viability of the notion of a leadership class of bureaucrats and professionals. Are they not merely the functionaries of national and local politicians and, in that sense, do they not possess a very limited kind of power? There are several important issues involved here: the extent to which national and local politicians do have carefully considered educational policies; the degree of congruence between the thinking of politicians and officials; the amount of delegated authority which officials are allowed or contrive to exercise; the ability of senior bureaucrats and professionals to use their expert knowledge to advance or block particular policies. These are complex matters which cannot be pronounced upon at this stage. What can be said, however, is that in recent years there has undoubtedly been a growing concern about the ability of the legislature to keep the executive in check, a problem acknowledged by some senior civil servants themselves. Part of the explanation is historical. With the expansion of the welfare state in the post-war period the number of people employed as public service professionals increased markedly, and the capacity of elected representatives to maintain effective oversight of all their activities was severely stretched. Even the present Conservative government, which is firmly committed to a reduction in the public sector and to greater accountability of officials, finds it hard to make significant inroads into the bureaucratic structures which, ostensibly, they control.

These points suggest that the relationship between politicians and officials is a critical area and, in subsequent chapters, it will be necessary to consider specific examples illustrating the way that relationship manifests itself in Scottish education. It is unlikely that an entirely uniform pattern will emerge, and the peculiar political situation in Scotland, whereby the majority party at Westminster is in a minority in terms of parliamentary and local government seats held in Scotland, complicates the matter further. Nevertheless, this issue must be addressed if the functioning of the leadership class is to be properly understood.

The peculiarity of Scotland's political position also arises in relation to the role of two institutions which exert powerful pressures on the educational system but which, technically, are not part of its formal structure. First, there are the universities, which, through the Scottish Universities Council on Entrance (SUCE), set up in 1969, and their strong representation on the SEB, have exercised a considerable influence on the school curriculum, especially at the upper levels of secondary education. The universities are not, however, responsible to the SED, though many contacts between university staff and SED officials take place on a variety of bodies: they are financed through the University Grants Committee (UGC), established in 1919, which has United Kingdom responsibilities, and are ultimately subject to controls deriving from the Department of Education and Science in London.

The Scottishness of the Scottish universities has, in fact, been a vexed question for a long time, and there is an increasingly vocal lobby arguing for a measure of devolution (and, in some cases, even complete independence) from the existing U.K. structures. This issue will be considered in some detail in Chapter 9 when the whole question of the structure and management of tertiary education in Scotland will be explored. The role of the universities in the in-service training of teachers will also be subject to critical examination in Chapter 9. Yet another area in which the universities will feature is the field of educational research, which has implications for all types of institutions. One of the justifications for the existence of an academic community is its supposed commitment to the disinterested pursuit of knowledge, and it will be instructive to examine the extent to which staff in university departments of education in Scotland have lived up to that ideal.

Secondly, the role of the Manpower Services Commission (MSC), established in January 1974, should be noted. In many ways, the MSC has represented a challenge to the traditional leadership class in Scottish education, not least because it had its origins outside Scotland. As David Raffe explains:

> The MSC has always been a British body. (Northern Ireland has its own manpower ministry.) It was initially responsible solely to the Employment Secretary, but since July 1979 the MSC has reported 'to the Secretary of State for Scotland in respect of its activities in Scotland to the extent that it is possible to distinguish a specific territorial dimension to them. Any functions of the MSC relating to matters which cannot be identifiably split between the countries continue to be matters for the Secretary of State for Employment, acting in conjunction with the Secretary of State for Scotland.'[34]

This ambivalent position makes it difficult to classify the MSC in relation to conventional educational agencies in Scotland, but it does serve to highlight, once again, the wider political context within which educational policy develops. In this respect, public presentation has been perceived by government as a critical issue, as can be seen from the development of the Youth Opportunities Programme and the Youth Training Scheme. Both of these programmes, for which the MSC has been responsible, have had considerable repercussions on the educational provision for 14 to 18 year olds. Partly as a reaction to the many criticisms of YOP schemes, including major objections from the education lobby, the YTS, started in 1983, is being presented in a different light. 'Both the government and the MSC have made it clear that the new Youth Training Scheme ... is not a youth unemployment measure. It is 'first and last a training scheme'; it is 'not about youth unemployment'.'[35] This change of public projection, when viewed in a Scottish context, can be regarded as evidence of a growing accommodation between industrial and educational interests, a process advanced in 1984 when the person appointed as Chairman of the MSC in Scotland was none other than the Chairman of the CCC. The potential for compromise and mutual assimilation in this move is considerable and suggests a desire on the part of the Scottish Office to defuse incipient hostilities. This concern to arrive at an acceptable *modus vivendi*, and to ensure that the various territorial sensitivities are not too outraged, will later be shown to be characteristic of the leadership class in other areas of Scottish education.

The universities and the MSC, then, do not fit conveniently within the network of formal structures which constitute the Scottish educational system. A proper exploration of the way the MSC functions in the Scottish context would require a separate enquiry. The universities, however, cannot be left out of the picture and, as has been explained, they will be looked at critically in common with other important bodies in Scottish education. But the first task is to study those groups which make up the central core of the leadership class — SED officials, key figures in educational quangos, members of the directorate. The existing literature dealing with these groups is very thin indeed. Apart from a largely historical text written by the present Principal of Jordanhill College of Education, the work of the inspectorate has not been subject to external investigation.[36] Again, there is no study of the SED as a whole comparable to Sir William Pile's book on the DES,[37] and there is no work on Directors of Education in Scotland which compares with that of Bush and Kogan on their English equivalents.[38] In other words, the formally constituted leadership class in Scottish education has, until now, received very little in the way of critical scrutiny. The present work is designed to make a modest start to the important task of remedying that deficiency.

*Notes and References*

1. See Max Weber, *Economy and Society: An Outline of Interpretive Sociology*, 3 vols., ed. G. Roth and C. Wittich, Bedminster Press, New York, 1968.

2. A concise account of Weber's analysis of bureaucracy is to be found in P.M. Blau and M.W. Meyer, *Bureaucracy in Modern Society*, 2nd ed., Random House, New York, 1971, pp. 18–23.

3. See, e.g., R.K. Merton, *Social Theory and Social Structure*, 3rd ed., Free Press, New York, 1968, pp. 73–138.

4. One notable exception is C. Perrow, *Complex Organizations: A Critical Essay*, 2nd ed., Scott, Foresman, Glenview, Illinois, 1979.

5. See M. Albrow, *Bureaucracy*, Macmillan, London, 1970, pp. 84–105. Albrow suggests that there are seven modern concepts of bureaucracy: bureaucracy as rational organisation;

bureaucracy as organisation inefficiency; bureaucracy as rule by officials; bureaucracy as public administration; bureaucracy as administration by officials; bureaucracy as the organisation; bureaucracy as modern society. These alternatives give varying emphasis to the elements of structure and process but, as Albrow himself admits, they overlap to such a degree that it is extremely difficult to maintain conceptual clarity. For a useful discussion of Albrow's classification, see D. Warwick, *Bureaucracy*, Longman, London, 1974, Chapter 1.

6. The account that follows is indebted to Part III ('Bureaucracy and Personality') of *Bureaucracy as a Social Problem*, ed. W.B. Littrell *et al*, Jai Press, Greenwich, Connecticut and London, 1983.

7. N. Williams, G. Sjoberg and A.F. Sjoberg, 'The Bureaucratic Personality: A Second Look', in W.B. Littrell *et al, op. cit.*, p. 178.

8. *Ibid.*, pp. 179–180.

9.Blau and Meyer, *op. cit.*, p. 71.

10. Williams, Sjoberg and Sjoberg, *op. cit.*, p. 181.

11. Quoted in Warwick, *op. cit.*, p. 30.

12. See, e.g., G. Langford, *Teaching as a Profession*, Manchester University Press, 1978; E. Hoyle, 'Professionality, professionalism and control in teaching', *London Educational Review*, Vol.3, No.2, 1974, pp. 13–19; A. Etzioni (ed.), *The Semi-Professions and their Organization*, Free Press, New York, 1969.

13. Eric Hoyle, 'The Professionalization of Teachers: A Paradox', in P. Gordon (ed.), *Is Teaching a Profession?*, Bedford Way Papers 15, Institute of Education, University of London, 1983, p. 45.

14. See Harold Silver, *Education as History*, Methuen, London, 1983, p. 138ff.

15. Marten Shipman, *Education as a Public Service*, Harper and Row, London, 1984, pp. 129–130.

16. *Ibid.*, p. 130.

17. Raymond Williams, *Keywords*, revised edition, Fontana, London, 1983, p. 156.

18. David McCrone, 'The Social Structure of Modern Scotland', in H.M. Drucker and N.L. Drucker (eds.), *The Scottish Government Yearbook 1981*, Paul Harris, Edinburgh, 1980, p. 55.

19. John D. Wilson, 'Selecting Teachers for Development', in W.B. Dockrell (ed.), *An Attitude of Mind: Twenty-Five Years of Educational Research in Scotland*, SCRE, Edinburgh, 1984, p. 171.

20. Brian Salter and Ted Tapper, *Education, Politics and the State*, Grant McIntyre, London, 1981, p. 50.

21. *Ibid.*, p. 54.

22. Patrick Corbett, *Ideologies*, Hutchinson, London, 1965, p. 57.

23. J.T. Ozga and M.A. Lawn, *Teachers, Professionalism and Class: A Study of Organized Teachers*, Falmer Press, London, 1981.

24. Megali Larson, *The Rise of Professionalism: A Sociological Analysis*, University of California Press, 1977.

25. Ozga and Lawn, *op. cit.*, p. 19.

26. See, e.g., Gordon Brown and Robin Cook (eds.), *Scotland: the Real Divide*, Mainstream, Edinburgh, 1983.

27. Quoted in McCrone, *op. cit.*, p. 59.

28. See Douglas Reid, 'Who Runs Scotland?', *Sunday Standard*, October 3, 1982, p. 13.

29. Williams, *op. cit.*, p. 60.

30. *Ibid.*, pp. 60–69.

31. A.H. Halsey, *Change in British Society*, 2nd ed., Oxford University Press, Oxford, 1981, p. 22.

32. *Ibid.*, pp. 21–22.

33. T.S. Eliot, *Notes Towards the Definition of Culture*, Faber, London, 1948, Chapter II.

34. David Raffe, 'Youth Unemployment and the MSC: 1977–1983', in D. McCrone (ed.), *The Scottish Government Yearbook 1984*, Unit for the Study of Government in Scotland, Edinburgh, 1983, pp. 193–194.

35. *Ibid.*, p. 188.

36. T.R. Bone, *School Inspection in Scotland, 1840–1966*, SCRE, Edinburgh, 1968.

37. Sir William Pile, *The Department of Education and Science*, Allen and Unwin, London, 1979.

38. Tony Bush and Maurice Kogan, *Directors of Education*, Allen and Unwin, London, 1982.

# 3

# *The Scottish Education Department*

## Introduction

It will be instructive to begin by quoting a short official statement, published in April 1984, about the work of the Scottish Education Department:

> The public education system is supervised by the Scottish Education Department. It acts in co-operation with the regional and islands area authorities which are direcly responsible for the service within their areas, and for educating around 910,000 pupils in about 3,900 schools.
>
> The Department maintains much of its contact with education authorities and bodies through more than a hundred Inspectors of schools, almost all of whom have had teaching experience. The staff, including the Inspectorate, totals about 550.
>
> In general, the Department seeks to ensure that the education service is adequate to meet changing needs and priorities in schools and also in further education. It determines the amount of money to be spent on educational buildings, prescribes standards and advises on designs for these buildings, gives guidance on the content of education and, with the co-operation of the General Teaching Council, seeks to match the supply of teachers to the demand. The Department directly finances the central institutions and colleges of education, each of which has its own board of governors, and it directly administers students' allowances.
>
> The Department also exercises a general supervision of the provision for community education including youth and community and adult education and it gives grants to a number of voluntary organisations. It looks after the Secretary of State's responsibilities for the arts and for sport and physical recreation, including his relations with the Scottish Sports Council. It is directly responsible for the Royal Scottish Museum and it is closely associated with the National Museum of Antiquities of Scotland, the National Galleries of Scotland and the National Library of Scotland.
>
> In the financial year 1982–83 the Department spent nearly £200m on education, most of it on student allowances and grants to colleges of education and central institutions. Local authority expenditure in the same year amounted to nearly £1,350m including loan charges, this expenditure being assisted by rate support grant. SED also pays grants to residential special schools and to many bodies operating in informal education, recreational and other fields of education.
>
> The Department exercises certain responsibilities for Scottish universities, although these, like other universities in Britain, are primarily the concern of the Department of Education and Science.[1]

It would be unfair to subject this statement to detailed critical scrutiny, for it is intended simply as a basic description of the main functions of the SED. Nevertheless, it raises, directly or indirectly, several very important issues. First, it occurs in the context of an account of the Scottish Office as a whole, thereby drawing attention to the significance of the wider political arena within which the SED operates. Secondly, the references to co-operation with the regional and islands authorities and with the General Teaching Council are in line with that aspect of the received wisdom about Scottish education, discussed in Chapter 1, which stresses partnership and democracy. It will be recalled that some commentators have argued that there is a much greater degree of central control than the received wisdom suggests. Thirdly, the statement refers to the staff of the SED totalling about 550, of whom more than 100 are inspectors with a background in teaching. Another official publication explains that 'HM Inspectorate exists as a distinct unit within the framework of the Scottish Education Department',[2] an explanation that prompts questions about the precise relation between HMIs and other civil servants within the Department, and about the qualifications and background of SED staff who have not had teaching experience. Finally, and perhaps more interestingly of all, the statement, by referring to the Department's concern to ensure that the education service is adequate to meet changing needs and priorities, touches on a whole range of matters concerning the way in which educational policy is initiated, developed and implemented. Who is involved in this exercise? What are the processes that have to be gone through? How successful is the SED in carrying out its responsibilities?

These are interpretative and evaluative questions of a kind that the statement, given its limited purpose, could not be expected to answer. But they refer to matters that must be investigated if the workings of Scottish education are to be properly understood. As was stated at the start of Chapter 1, interpretation cannot be avoided: even ostensibly neutral, 'factual' accounts imply an interpretative stance, however submerged it may be. The programme for this chapter is, therefore, not simply to offer information about what the SED does but to consider the significance of its mode of operation. This will involve looking at the political background against which the work of the Department is carried out, the personnel within it, and the organisational structures through which policy is implemented. In addition, a detailed examination of a particular episode in SED administration will be undertaken with a view to forming an assessment of the quality of performance of senior officials. It should be noted that, while reference will be made at several points in the present chapter to members of the inspectorate, a detailed consideration of their work will not take place until Chapter 4.

## The Political Context

The activities of the SED must first be understood within the framework of the Scottish (and British) political system and the cultural functions that system serves.[3] In previous studies of Scottish education there has often been a tendency to regard the SED as some sort of autonomous agency, cut off from the vulgar world of political dealing. This is a naive view, though it is worth pointing out that it is one that senior members of the educational leadership class do not discourage. It helps to sustain the myth that they are disinterested preservers of a great tradition and are not subject to compromising influences. One of the principal arguments of this chapter will be that, although Scottish education may rank low on the political agenda of the major parties, its operation can be adequately explained only if its location in the world of politics is understood.

The SED is one of five major departments within the Scottish Office: the others are the Department of Agriculture and Fisheries for Scotland, the Industry Department for Scotland, the Scottish Development Department and the Scottish Home and Health Department. 'Each department is under the charge of a Secretary who is responsible to the Secretary of State for the work of his department.'[4] In addition, there is a Central Services Unit, headed by a Deputy Secretary, which provides a range of important services (financial, statistical, legal, personnel, information, etc.) for the five departments. The cost of running the Scottish Office was 77.9m in 1982–83.[5] This figure included the salaries of Ministers and the staffs of Central Services and the five functional departments.

The Secretaries of the SED and the other departments, together with the Deputy Secretary (Central Services), meet regularly under the chairmanship of the most senior civil servant in Scotland, the Permanent Under Secretary of State (at present Sir William Kerr Fraser), as a Management Group 'to ensure co-ordination of work, to consider common problems across the whole field of Scottish Office responsibilities, and to advise the Secretary of State and his ministerial team'.[6] This arrangement is designed to facilitate the flow of information between departments and to encourage a 'corporate' view of policy and administration. Whether it is entirely successful in this respect is open to debate. Keating and Midwinter argue that the Management Group's emphasis is 'on administration rather than policy co-ordination, and it concentrates on internal management and inter-departmental issues. Agendas do not include current policy issues, which are pursued independently by departments in direct contact with Ministers'.[7]

This raises the question of the relation that exists between senior civil servants and politicians within the Scottish Office. Formal responsibility for the work of the various departments rests with the Secretary of State who is, in theory at least, directly answerable to parliament. Clearly, however, it is not possible for one person to maintain detailed control of all the work carried on in the Scottish Office, and the ministerial burden is shared with four colleagues — a Minister of State and three Parliamentary Under-Secretaries of State. The position is complicated by the fact that the portfolios of the junior ministers do not correspond exactly to the remits of the five administrative departments. Thus Michael Ancram acts as Minister for Home Affairs and the Environment, John Mackay for Health and Social Work and Allan Stewart for Industry and Education. The fact that the duties of ministers are cross-departmental may have certain advantages in terms of promoting a breadth of outlook, but it may also weaken ministerial control within individual departments, especially when it is borne in mind that politicians have to spend much of their time in London on parliamentary business.

It is, however, extremely difficult to characterise the precise division of responsibility that exists between ministers and senior civil servants, whether in Edinburgh or London. As Sir Toby Weaver, former Deputy Secretary at the DES, has commented:

> Many attempts have been made to devise a formula by reference to which the respective spheres of ministers and officials can be demarcated. Ministers, it is sometimes said, deal with values, officials with facts; ministers determine ends, officials settle means; ministers make policy, officials apply it; ministers make important decisions, officials unimportant ones; officials propose, ministers dispose. These neat formulations state only partial truths, each subject to many exceptions.[8]

In the case of the SED, there are grounds for thinking that a very substantial amount of authority is assumed by officials (although, as will be shown, there are some exceptions to this general pattern). Part of the explanation is that education tends to assume a lower priority than economic and industrial matters, which often require more urgent and immediate attention by the minister. Furthermore, the level of interest in education among politicians, especially Conservative politicians, is not noticeably high.[9] Even on the Labour side, the amount of informed comment — as distinct from emotive rhetoric — is very limited. In 1981, Tony Worthington, himself a Labour councillor in Strathclyde, remarked on the poor level of educational input from Scottish councillors and MPs. He referred to his fellow politicians as a 'group of educational under-achievers' and posed the question:

> Who can name one national or local politician who is contributing anything original or thought-provoking to the Scottish educational debate? Unless things change, I could (sadly) write the educational part of the Labour Party manifesto for the next election in 10 minutes. It would mention the divisiveness and privilege-maintenance of Tory policies; aim for equality of educational opportunities; support comprehensives; and promise more nurseries, teachers and so on. Only in one respect would it have changed since the mid-1950s, when support swung firmly behind comprehensives — there would be a reference, justly, to the Open University.[10]

Unable to resist a party point, Worthington continued: 'The Conservative and SNP manifestos would take five minutes each and show even less serious thinking about the contemporary education needs of our society'.[11] Recent developments in Scottish education — in particular, curriculum and examination reforms — may seem to cast doubt on Worthington's analysis, but it would be difficult to argue convincingly that the impetus for these reforms has come from politicians. They are not the brainchild of Allan Stewart or Alex Fletcher or any of their Labour predecessors as Under Secretary of State with responsibility for education. Rather they have emerged from the cumulative pressures of professionals and administrators, working through educational quangos such as the CCC. To express the point this way may give a misleading impression of the purity of educational motivation of professional as compared to political interests. It will be argued in succeeding chapters that the impulse for 'reform' has had more to do with professional aggrandisement than with educational principles. For the moment, however, what needs to be stressed is that Scottish politicians, whether Labour or Conservative, have tended to leave a policy vacuum in the field of education, and this has meant that initiatives have been pursued by others.

Where there has been direct political intervention in education, it has not been peculiarly Scottish in character. For example, perhaps the two major developments in the post-war period, the replacement of a selective system of secondary education with a comprehensive system, and the raising of the school leaving age to 16, have applied to the whole of Britain, not just Scotland. The reason for this is quite simple: 'the same political party governs on both sides of the border and its philosophies are inevitably reflected in legislation for both territories'.[12] A more recent example of a policy development which has derived from London rather than Edinburgh is the Assisted Places Scheme, designed to provide financial support for parents of limited income who wish to send their children to private schools. In the Scottish context, this provision must be regarded as a marginal development, given the very small proportion of pupils attending schools outside the state sector. Its introduction can be seen as an indication of the extent to which Scottish ministers have to carry out decisions determined in London, regardless of their relevance north of the border.

All this is not to suggest that Scottish education ministers make absolutely no impact on policy matters, but those issues in which they do intervene personally rarely seem to have anything to do with a vision of the way Scottish education ought to be developing. On the contrary, they often seem to depend on fairly idiosyncratic impulses. For example, Allan Stewart's predecessor, Alex Fletcher, was responsible for the attempt, initiated in 1983, to close a social science degree course at Paisley College of Technology. The course was quite highly regarded in academic circles and the number of students seeking entry had steadily increased.[13] Fears about Scottish central institutions expanding too much on the arts and social science side, allied to the government's concern to develop science and technology, were presumably part of the explanation for the intervention (though it is worth pointing out that Scottish students have a much poorer range of options in the area of liberal arts education outside the university sector than their English counterparts). However, another consideration seems to have been the fact that the left-wing political affiliations of the Head of the Politics and Sociology Department were viewed with disapproval. In the event, a face-saving compromise, whereby the course was allowed to continue but with reduced numbers, was arrived at. Another instance of Mr Fletcher's erratic performance — his role in the sale of Hamilton College — will be used as a case study later in the chapter to illustrate the relations between politicians, officials and external bodies.

If it is the case that the education portfolio in the Scottish Office receives the attention of the Minister responsible on a somewhat intermittent and arbitrary basis, the question arises, 'How is policy actually formulated?' The political manifesto of the government party may provide a starting point but, in the light of Tony Worthington's remarks, it is unlikely to offer much beyond general guidelines. In any case, both the major political parties have shown themselves capable of a fairly cavalier attitude towards manifesto promises: their continuing neglect of pre-school education, to which they have been nominally committed for decades, is possibly the best example of the gap between advance publicity and actual performance. Where political will is lacking, power tends to devolve to officials who are inclined to deal with policy questions on a reactive basis, rather than out of principle: that is, they respond to pressures from within the educational world, pressures which serve to create a policy agenda. It will soon become apparent that this is only part of the explanation and that it needs to be qualified in important ways but, for the moment, it is worth looking at the 'reactive' process a little more closely. On initial inspection, there seems to be something to be said for an arrangement which involves the utilisation of consultative machinery that appears open and democratic. SED officials are in regular contact with representatives of many bodies — e.g., the Association of Directors of Education, the Educational Institute of Scotland, the Convention of Scottish Local Authorities, the Headteachers' Association of Scotland, the GTC, the CCC, the SEB, etc. Representatives of 'non-professional' groups — such as the Church of Scotland, the Roman Catholic Church, the Scottish Parent-Teacher Council — are also consulted. In addition, members of the inspectorate provide a steady flow of information to New St. Andrew's House — the principal location of the SED in Edinburgh — about matters that seem worthy of attention at the level of policy-making. It thus seems that the policy agenda is constructed on the basis of topics that have been identified as of real importance by those who are genuinely concerned about education.

There are, however, a number of serious disadvantages in evolving policy options in this way. Too much reliance on the views of pressure groups can lead to a situation where those who know how to operate the system, rather than those who have the best case, are taken most seriously. All pressure groups have their own particular interests to pursue, and these are unlikely to correspond to the interests of the educational service as a whole. The point has been forcefully put by Sir Douglas Wass, a former Permanent Secretary to the Treasury:

> The pressure group . . . is often quite unrepresentative of the people as a whole. The costs of deferring to it are rarely evaluated in terms of the impact on the entire community. It is much easier politically for governments to come to terms with some special interest than to oppose it. Those who suffer from the compact are often unorganised, and their protests — if they are ever articulated — go unheard.[14]

In order to arbitrate between competing claims, officials need to be able to refer to criteria other than the priorities of those who are lobbying: in other words, they need a framework of policy aims which only the government can provide. Where this is lacking, they tend to operate on an unsatisfactory *ad hoc* basis, which usually involves taking decisions that are politically expedient rather than educationally desirable.

Furthermore, the competence of SED officials to draw up policy options on an entirely open and fair-minded basis must be questioned. Undoubtedly they like to think that their perspective is more detached than that of others in the world of Scottish education, but they themselves can be considered as constituting a pressure group, an internal pressure group, with their own particular priorities which they are concerned to protect. Policies which might threaten their position are unlikely to be received enthusiastically. To portray SED officials as disinterested arbiters is thus to misunderstand the nature of bureaucracy. Those who have acquired power do not give it up lightly. They may seek to disguise the way in which their authority is exercised, or present it in some other light (such as democratic partnership), but they will seek to ensure that, whatever happens, their own role is not weakened.

One of the principal ways in which this is achieved within the SED (and, indeed, the Scottish Office generally) is through the use of patronage. The Secretary of State has power to appoint people to many outside bodies — committees, councils, boards, etc. — and he relies on his officials for recommendations. That this is regarded as an important exercise has been freely acknowledged by Sir William Kerr Fraser: 'A lot of very senior people spend a great deal of time on these appointments'.[15] Criticisms of the system are expressed from time to time, though hard information about the internal processes is difficult to come by. One commentator has observed that 'Charges of 'cronyism' are not unknown',[16] and an ex-Minister is quoted as saying:

> The civil servants do tend to come up with the same kind of people . . . Sometimes they would be quite determined to get their nominees appointed, and the same names would come up for a dozen different jobs.[17]

In the field of education, a scrutiny of appointments to bodies such as the CCC, SEB, SCRE, SCET, SCOTEC and SCOTBEC — the last two now superseded by SCOTVEC — undoubtedly suggests that certain individuals are particularly favoured. (The case of the CCC will be examined in detail in Chapter 5.) This may, of course, be because they are especially talented but, equally, it may be because they can be relied upon to take a line that is generally acceptable to the SED. Beneficiaries of patronage who serve on a number of bodies may reasonably expect, in due course, to receive some recognition in the Honours List. The prospect of such recognition may, in certain cases at least, serve to condition the nature of their contributions, not always in ways that benefit the organisations concerned or Scottish education as a whole.

It is not hard to see how the patronage system can be used to neutralise criticism by placing people who are susceptible to the blandishments of the SED in influential positions within the major educational bodies in Scotland. In so far as this actually happens, it suggests a need to qualify the role assumed by some 'pressure' groups. If certain groups have, in effect, been 'infiltrated' by SED sympathisers, they are not likely to be especially robust in their dealings with the Department. Further, the more extensive the network of patronage, the less convincing the idea of developing educational policy on a reactive basis becomes, for if the input to SED thinking comes largely from groups that perceive the political and educational world in a similar way, then the likelihood of genuinely new insights and ideas is greatly reduced. What will happen, in fact, is that existing ways of conceptualising problems will be confirmed. There will be little to challenge the conventional wisdom. Indeed, the whole exercise can easily become an extended sham, whereby a process of mutual reinforcement masquerades as democratic consultation.

It would, however, be wrong to push the argument too far because the stage-management of the SED is, fortunately, not totally successful. There *are* conflicts and disagreements in Scottish education, and sometimes they do come to the surface. But the SED is rarely directly in the firing line. The target of teacher dissatisfaction, for example, is usually the education authority which formally employs them. Even although the authority may simply be carrying out national policy, it receives the brunt of the attack. In other words, the SED's mode of operation allows it to use external bodies as shields, and this enhances its claim to be acting in a detached and disinterested manner. The fact that the very existence of these bodies can be adduced as evidence on the part of the Department to remain conveniently above the fray usually goes unnoticed. It is merely one illustration of the tendency of all government administrations to engage in a strategy of 'damage limitation'; that is, to provide targets other than themselves for critics to aim at.

## Personnel

If, echoing Worthington (p.39), it is accepted that political dereliction, together with the use (or abuse) of patronage, combine to give officials within the SED a disproportionate amount of influence in policy matters, what are their credentials for the role they assume? Are they well qualified, in terms of background and commitment, to advance the interests of Scottish education? What is the relation between the values they hold and the structural characteristics of the SED previously identified? In seeking to answer these questions, it is necessary to refer to particular individuals. Of critical interest in this respect are those at the very top of the SED hierarchy — that is, those who hold the rank of Under Secretary or Secretary — for it is officials in such positions who are likely to set the standards and shape the attitudes of their subordinates. Four examples will be given.[18]

The present Secretary of the SED is James Scott. He assumed office only in 1984 so it is too early to form a judgement of his actual performance. It is, however, possible to provide some information about his previous career. He is the son of a British civil servant, who served in Palestine, and was educated at Dollar Academy and St. Andrews University. Spells in the RAF and the Commonwealth diplomatic service were followed by varied experience in the Scottish Office: he acted as private secretary to two Secretaries of State, was head of the police division in the Scottish Home and Health Department, and served as Under-Secretary in the Industry Department for Scotland. All this suggests that he is an able and adaptable man, though it is not clear how these various posts have prepared him for his responsibilities in the SED. He himself has observed, 'I don't know why I was appointed to this job . . . '[19] Scott's background in the Industry Department may provide one explanation, especially in view of recent developments in the field of vocational preparation and skill training. More mischievously, Neil Munro has noted that 'promotions to deputy secretary grade require the approval of the Prime Minister and she is not known to be favourably disposed to those who are not 'one of us' '.[20] But perhaps the most damaging fact that Scott will have to overcome is 'his decision not to educate any of his four children in the system he is now in charge of',[21] a decision that seems to raise questions concerning the extent of his commitment to Scottish state education. He may, however, not be unduly concerned about this apparent disadvantage since it is one that he shares with the Secretary of State for Scotland.

Scott's immediate predecessor as Secretary of the SED was Angus M. Mitchell who was appointed in 1976. Mitchell's father served in the Indian Civil Service, and Mitchell himself was educated at an English public school, Marlborough College, and at Brasenose College, Oxford. He had a distinguished military record and was awarded the Military Cross in 1946. He entered the Scottish Office in 1949, and his subsequent career took him to several departments: in addition to the SED (1949–58; 1959–65; 1969–75; 1976–84), he served in the Secretary of State's office as Private Secretary (1958–59 and 1968–69), in the Department of Agriculture and Fisheries (1965–68), the Scottish Development Department (1968) and the Scottish Home and Health Department (1975–76). On his retirement Mitchell gave an interview to Willis Pickard, editor of the *Times Educational Supplement Scotland*, in which he offered limited insights into both the work of the SED and his own character. He declined to answer questions referring to his relations with politicians and remarked, 'My nature is to be self-effacing'. However, he went on: 'I have tried to overcome this by going out and talking to those in the field, to our partners in the service — the Convention of Scottish Local Authorities, the directors, the unions, and I think I am on first name terms with the leaders in all these areas'.[22] The appeal to the notion of partnership and to personal friendship with other members of the educational leadership class should be noted. At the same time — and this indicates that reticence and assertiveness can be found in the same person — Mitchell's response to a suggestion that all was not well in Scottish education was vigorous in its denial: 'There is no continuing crisis in Scottish education, as some people claim'.[23] Since he had been responsible for the service for eight years, his reluctance to countenance criticism is perhaps not surprising. In his retirement, he will continue to be actively involved in educational matters. It was announced in October 1984 that he had been appointed Chairman of the Court of Stirling University, a move which the *Glasgow Herald* described as a 'coup' for the University but which might equally well be described as a 'coup' for the SED.[24]

The most senior rank beneath that of Secretary is Under Secretary. Under Secretaries supervise the work of several divisions (the remits of which will be described in detail in the next section). Until 1985 the person in charge of matters pertaining to school education was Miss P.A. Cox (in May 1985 it was announced that she would be moving to the Scottish Home and Health Department): her name is, therefore, familiar to many people in the Scottish educational world as for several years her signature appeared on circulars and other documents sent by the SED to education authorities. Miss Cox is the daughter of Sir G.E. Cox, a former Professor of Chemistry at Leeds University and later Secretary of the Agricultural Research Council. She was educated at Leeds Girls' High School and Newnham College, Cambridge. In 1953 she joined the Scottish Office as an Assistant Principal, and her early experience was mainly in the Home and Health Department. Interestingly, however, her civil service career also included spells in London, most notably at the Treasury (1962–65). She was appointed Assistant Secretary of the SED in 1967 and promoted to Under Secretary in 1976.

Another Under Secretary is Ian M. Wilson whose main responsibilities are in the fields of higher education and teacher supply. He was educated at George Watson's College and Edinburgh University. He joined the Scottish Office in 1950 at the age of 23 and has served in various capacities in the Home and Health Department, as Private Secretary to the Permanent Under Secretary of State and as an Assistant Under Secretary of State. He became Under Secretary at the SED in 1977.

What is interesting about these four examples is the uniformity of their backgrounds and careers. Scott, Mitchell and Miss Cox all belong to families with a record of public service at a senior level: there are, for example, entries for the fathers of Mitchell and Miss Cox in *Who's Who*. The education of all four is also similar: none attended an ordinary state grammar or secondary school, and indeed two (Mitchell and Miss Cox) received all their secondary and higher education outside Scotland. The Scottish schools that Scott and Wilson attended cannot be regarded as representative, as both are grant-aided institutions. And even their universities (St. Andrews and Edinburgh) might be described as less than aggressive in their Scottishness: St. Andrews is sometimes regarded, no doubt unkindly, as a refugee camp for Oxbridge rejects, and the Anglophile tendencies of Edinburgh are well established. The backgrounds of all four could not unreasonably be described as educated, professional, financially secure, upper middle class.

It is frequently insisted that recruitment patterns to the civil service have been changing, and it may well be that middle-ranking and junior staff are more diversified in terms of their educational and family backgrounds. Nevertheless, the fact remains that in recent years the SED has been headed by people with a particular, relatively privileged, kind of pedigree. That fact does not, in itself, disqualify them from carrying out their duties with intelligence and efficiency, but it does prompt questions about the extent of their understanding of state education in Scotland and the suitability of the characteristic assumptions they will bring to bear on the problems they encounter. It might be contended that the issue at stake is their general competence as administrators, not their first-hand experience of Scottish schools. However, in so far as senior administrators are concerned with policy matters it would seem desirable that their advice to ministers should be based on a sound knowledge of the conditions to which their recommendations refer. They can, it is true, draw on information from the inspectorate, but that is likely to be transmitted in the form of official reports and cannot be regarded as an adequate substitute for direct personal experience. Manifestations of serious administrative ignorance are certainly not unknown. For example, at a meeting with a body representing parental interests, one senior administrator, seeking to illustrate a point with reference to 'a typical Scottish secondary school', chose the Royal High School in Edinburgh. The extent of the error was quickly pointed out.

These problems regarding the adequacy of SED officials' grasp of educational matters can be related to wider issues to do with the nature and limitations of bureaucratic thinking. The four officials mentioned above have spent all, or nearly all, of their working lives in the civil service. Inevitably, therefore, they will have been subject to a socialisation process. The characteristic styles of officials can be described in several, mutually supporting, ways: in terms of their relative remoteness from the situations to which their advice refers; in terms of a greater interest in procedural than in substantive questions; in terms of a disposition to reach decisions in private rather than in public; in terms of resistance to change; in terms of a preference for a particular kind of impersonal, formal language. These tendencies are likely to be picked up incidentally and will not be considered remarkable by those who share them. Where signs of deviance occur they are likely to be discouraged in the normal course of institutional absorption. For example, a recruit to the administrative ranks of the SED was informed by a superior that her early progress had been extremely satisfactory, save in one respect. She had a tendency to use written language too simply and directly: it would be wise to cultivate a certain judicious indirectness of style.

To the extent that pressures to conform to certain approved models, whether of language or anything else, tend in a uniform direction throughout the civil service, the claimed distinctiveness of practices within the Scottish Office will be further weakened. Indeed, Keating and Midwinter suggest that it is at the civil service level that links between Edinburgh and London are strongest[25] and, assuming they are correct, the most important factor in seeking to understand the people who occupy senior positions within the SED may be their willingness to accept the approved bureaucratic norms. This line of argument is sometimes dismissed as a distortion which relies too heavily on the exaggerations of the television programme 'Yes, Minister'. Indeed, Sir William Kerr Fraser tried to make light of such imputations when he addressed the annual conference of the Law Society of Scotland at Gleneagles in 1983. He employed self-deprecating irony — a disarming form much favoured by senior civil servants — in anticipation of criticism: 'I know we are sometimes depicted as clutching our little buff files to our bosoms in order to inflate our sense of self-importance or to conceal from the public things which the public is entitled to know. I hope this is a caricature'.[26] Sir William defended the traditional bureaucratic virtues of silence and anonymity on four main grounds: the need (a) to preserve national security, (b) to respect secret information supplied by others, (c) to ensure the political neutrality of the civil service, and (d) to maintain the confidence of government ministers. His development of this argument indicated what might be regarded as an undue concern for appearance and image-projection rather than truth and accountability. Civil servants, he said, 'are concerned that whoever is their political master for the time being makes a good impression — on Parliament, on the public and on his Ministerial colleagues. They will seek to ensure that his policies and decisions are presented in as favourable a light as possible. They will seek to discover and, if possible, neutralise the opposition which his proposals may encounter in Cabinet or Parliament or the country at large'.[27] Furthermore, an important criterion of a civil servant's success, according to Sir William, is the ability to contribute to the further advancement of his political master. Presumably if this is accompanied by the implementation of effective policies, so much the better, but this would not seem to be an essential requirement. Illusion rather than reality seems to be what ultimately matters. In Sir William's own words: 'There has to be a bit of an actor in all successful politicians and our role as civil servants is to write bits of the script, to prompt now and again and to move the scenery around between the scenes'.[28] For an audience of lawyers, this view of political life may have been considered witty and sophisticated: in other circles it might have been regarded as chillingly cynical.

Although the limitations of bureaucratic thinking manifest themselves equally north and south of the border, there are some grounds for thinking that Scottish education is in a marginally worse position than English education. The DES has few admirers, but there has at least been some serious public debate about its shortcomings. Following the appearance of a critical study by the Organization for Economic Co-operation and Development in 1975,[29] the Expenditure Committee of the House of Commons responded with a detailed investigation of the powers of the DES.[30] On the process of consultation and the dissemination of information, the Committee had this to say:

> We believe that the habit of secretiveness — the instinct to withhold rather than voluntarily to share information — lies at the root of most of the criticisms of the DES' consultative processes. We realize that this attitude is common throughout the British Civil Service and that it is created by the conventions of government confidentiality which successive administrations have been content to sustain. These conventions, which are traditional, and for the most part unwritten, grew up when government was more autocratic and public opinion less well-informed; they served to 'prevent embarrassment'. We recognize that to alter the rules would require radical change in the working of the whole Civil Service and that it would be unrealistic of us to make this a recommendation for the DES alone and beyond our remit to advocate it formally for all Government departments. *We therefore reluctantly accept the present conventions while trying to make their application more flexible.* At the same time we put on record our belief that the weight of public opinion which is beginning to form will in due course bring about a more open form of government in Britain to which the Civil Service will have to conform.[31]

Official recognition of the problem led in turn to some useful academic studies of the activities of the DES.[32] As yet, it would be over-optimistic to claim that there has been any significant improvement, but the issue has received some serious attention, which is a necessary first stage.

In Scotland, there has been nothing comparable. A few polemical articles have identified some of the critical issues,[33] but no sustained examination of them has been undertaken. Part of the explanation, to be discussed more fully in a later chapter, is the collusion that exists between the academic community and other members of the leadership class, not least SED officials themselves, about what constitutes legitimate research. Another factor is that the inspectorate within the SED arguably have taken a less independent line in relation to administrators than their counterparts in the DES,[34] and there has, therefore, been insufficient internal pressure to complement external concern and so promote public discussion. When the various factors that have been identified in this section are combined — the absence of a proper forum for debate, the patterns of socialisation within the civil service, and the uniformity of backgrounds of senior SED officials — the prospects of making a significant impact on the prevailing orthodoxies seem decidedly bleak.[35]

## Departmental Organisation

The work of the SED is carried out in a series of divisions, each headed by an Assistant Secretary (or, in the case of the Educational Statistics division, by a Chief Statistician). Precise remits are subject to change as policies evolve and new issues emerge. At present, however, the allocation of responsibilities is officially described as follows:[36]

PUBLIC SCHOOL ORGANISATION; PRIVATE SECTOR SCHOOLS; SPECIAL EDUCATIONAL NEEDS
(This division deals with nursery, primary and secondary school organisation; parental choice of school; school councils; denominational education; school closures; discipline in schools; school meals, milk, transport and clothing; independent schools; grant-aided secondary schools; assisted places scheme; education of children with special needs; child guidance service.)

SCHOOL CURRICULUM AND ASSESSMENT; EDUCATION FOR 16–18s
(This division deals with the curriculum in schools; the Consultative Committee on the Curriculum; school links with industry and the careers service; national examinations; the Scottish Examination Board; standards of attainment and educational disadvantage; co-ordination of reforms of education for the 16–18 age group; educational aspects of sex discrimination and race relations.)

VOCATIONAL FURTHER EDUCATION
(This division deals with the development of vocational further education; educational aspects of Manpower Services Commission programmes; the Scottish Technical and Business Education Councils; approval of advanced courses.)

ARTS; SPORT; COMMUNITY EDUCATION
(This division deals with (a) arts, museums, galleries and libraries, including the Royal Scottish Museum, the National Museum of Antiquities of Scotland, the National Library

of Scotland and the Scottish Film Council; Gaelic cultural issues. (b) sport and physical recreation; the Scottish Sports Council. (c) community education; the Scottish Community Education Council; grants for village halls and recurrent grants to voluntary organisations.)

HIGHER EDUCATION
(This division deals with (a) higher education policy; the Scottish Tertiary Education Advisory Council; Central Institutions. (b) student awards; educational endowments.)

EDUCATIONAL STATISTICS; SUPPLY OF TEACHERS
(This division deals with the collection, analysis and publication of educational statistics; educational planning models; teacher demand and supply.)

ADMINISTRATION OF COLLEGES OF EDUCATION; TRAINING OF TEACHERS; TEACHERS' SALARIES AND CONDITIONS
(This division deals with (a) the administration of colleges of education. (b) the training of teachers; the General Teaching Council for Scotland; overseas exchanges. (c) teachers' salaries and conditions; the National Committee for the In-Service Training of Teachers.)

BUILDING, RESEARCH, PLANNING, ETC.
(This division deals with the school building programme; educational building approvals; design guidance, standards and costs; educational research and technology; micro-electronics in schools; broadcasting; departmental planning, co-ordination and expenditure policy; industrial relations.)

This description indicates the immense scope of the work conducted within the SED. But it does not end there. The Secretary of the SED also has responsibility for social work, including children's panels, the probation service, 'List D' schools, the elderly, physical and mental handicap, voluntary sector policy, child care, advice to local authorities in the development of their services, not to mention the research, training, finance and manpower implications of all of these fields. The primary concern of the present volume is with education, but it is important to recognise that the SED has other concerns. Indeed, Angus Mitchell, on his retirement as Secretary, remarked, 'The Scottish Education Department is a bit of a misnomer'. He went on to argue for greater recognition of the department's involvement in the arts, sport and social work — 'not least because of the opportunities they afforded for contact with other departments, in Whitehall and in the Scottish Office'.[37]

All this refers to the administrative, as distinct from the inspectorate, side of the SED. It is apparent, however, that liaison between senior administrative officials and members of the inspectorate is required — otherwise problems could easily arise with regard to the consistency of departmental policy. Nevertheless, some criticism has been expressed about the inadequacy of links between administrators and inspectors. In an official report into the work of HMIs it is stated: 'There is an apparent lack of well developed lines of communication between the Inspectorate and the administration at all levels . . . '[38] The report acknowledges that there is a Departmental Planning Committee chaired by the Secretary of the SED which is intended as 'a prime forum for joint discussion of future issues by administrators and Inspectors', but states that 'it appears in practice to be too limited a foundation for the necessary degree of collaborative peering into the future . . .'[39] Although Chief Inspectors are 'to a greater or lesser extent, in touch with their opposite number Assistant Secretaries',[40] there is scope, it is suggested, for much greater collaboration.

There are several possible explanations for the existence of this problem, assuming the official report gives a fair account of it. It may be that the areas of responsibility between administrators and inspectors are sufficiently clearly demarcated to obviate the necessity for close consultation. This, however, is unlikely: it is hard to see, for example, how a coherent policy on curriculum and assessment matters could be implemented without regular contact between HMIs and administrative officials. An alternative explanation might be that both groups seek to maintain a degree of autonomy and try to protect their territorial independence. There may even be an element of unfriendly rivalry in this, with attempts on occasion to conceal and even mislead. Such developments are certainly not unknown in large organisations which, by their very nature, often breed mutual suspicion among members, especially where different groups have rather different backgrounds.

Yet another explanation — in some ways the most likely — is that administrators regard inspectors as service personnel, whose main function is to provide them with information and to carry out instructions. If this is correct, administrators would not be particularly concerned with the internal workings of the inspectorate and would certainly not feel the need to invite HMIs on a regular basis to contribute to high-level deliberative discussions. In other words, to put it rather pejoratively, senior administrators might look upon HMIs as well-paid field workers, whose prime function is to do the leg-work on which their own more elevated activities depend. The official report referred to above includes a statement which gives some credence to this interpretation. It says that 'The Department naturally trades on the excellent provision of 'eyes and ears' which the Inspectorate comprises, resources it can effortlessly tap for information to help reply to PQs [Parliamentary Questions] or Ministerial correspondence and to advise on visits, Honours proposals and so on . . . '[41] This suggests an important, but subsidiary, role for HMIs and, in Chapter 4, further evidence will be presented to support this view.

A large part of the Department's executive work is carried out by means of statutory instruments in the form of regulations or codes which carry the force of law. It also issues circulars and memoranda to education authorities and schools to intimate departmental policy, explain new regulations, request information, offer advice and guidance, etc. Much of this work, of necessity, is routine in nature. Of greater interest, from an interpretative point of view, is the conduct of the Department in relation to non-routine matters which raise important issues of principle and test the efficiency of senior officials. In the next section, a concrete illustration which lends support to the interpretative line that has been advanced regarding the SED's mode of operation will be offered.

## The Sale of Hamilton College — A Case Study in SED Administration

Detailed evidence of the internal workings of the SED is hard to come by. Officials are constrained both formally, by their conditions of employment, and informally, by the bureaucratic ethos which they inhabit, from giving detailed information to outsiders about the conduct of business within the Department. Only rarely do public disclosures occur and, when they do, they provide valuable insights into relations between ministers and officials, and between the Department and other educational bodies. A recent example concerns the sale of Hamilton College of Education, a transaction which became the subject of a House of Commons enquiry by the Committee of Public Accounts in 1983. The report of this committee is a particularly useful source as it includes verbatim accounts of evidence given by SED officials.

The background to the enquiry was as follows. A decision to close Hamilton College of Education was taken by the Secretary of State, amidst some considerable public controversy, in August 1980. The buildings were relatively new, having been erected in the mid-1960s at a cost of about £2 million. They consisted of a main college block, offering teaching accommodation for 900 students, and residences for 600 students. The site as a whole covered 51 acres and included extensive playing fields. Following the closure decision, ownership of the property was transferred from Hamilton's Board of Governors to the Board of Governors of Jordanhill College, Glasgow, which was to absorb staff and students from Hamilton. The Jordanhill governors were instructed to sell the land and buildings subject to the consent of the Secretary of State. In the words of the report of the Public Accounts Committee: 'A joint Jordanhill/SED Committee was set up to deal with the disposal and to ensure that SED were a party to all decisions'.[42]

Late in 1982 separate agreements were reached for the sale of the main college buildings (together with the playing fields) and the halls of residence. The total amount realised was £680,000 — approximately one-third of the original cost of construction and a fraction of the probable replacement cost at the time of the enquiry (calculated at £20 million). When the figures were revealed, considerable political and public disquiet was expressed and an enquiry was initiated. The disquiet centred on three main areas.

First, the extent to which established procedures regarding the sale of public property were followed was questioned: 'Scottish Office Departments are expected, under guidance issued by the Scottish Solicitor's Office in 1981, to adopt the procedures recommended by the Halliday Committee in 1980 in a report on their enquiry into how the purchasers of Robroyston Hospital in 1977 had made substantial profits after developing the site'.[43] The report of the Halliday Committee made specific recommendations about the desirability of taking professional advice from the Chief Valuer (Scotland) and the Solicitor's Office about using properly qualified and experienced selling agents. These requirements, claimed critics, had been disregarded.

Secondly, concern was expressed about whether a strenuous enough attempt had been made to secure a good price for the land and buildings, and about whether the SED had kept other relevant departments (notably the Treasury) adequately informed about what was happening.

And thirdly, the role of the then Minister responsible for Scottish education, Mr Alex Fletcher, was subject to criticism. It was suggested that the government, because of the controversy surrounding the decision to close the college in the first place, wanted to secure a quick sale to reduce their embarrassment. Further, it was alleged that the intention of the purchaser of the main teaching block and playing fields, Mr Charles Oxley, to open a private school was viewed with approval for doctrinaire party political reasons.

With regard to the first point — that proper procedures had not been followed — the Public Accounts Committee fully endorsed the criticisms. Although the advice of the Chief Valuer (Scotland) had been sought by the SED, the Department decided that the sale should be handled by Jordanhill College's solicitors before his considered recommendation had been received.[44] The Chief Valuer suggested that a commercial selling agent, who would be likely to have specialist knowledge of this kind of transaction, would be more appropriate. Another reason for the desirability of not using Jordanhill College's own solicitors emerged during the submission of oral evidence. A member of the Board of Governors was also a partner in the firm of solicitors which handled the sale. The Secretary of the SED at that time, Mr Mitchell, accepted that the Department had 'contributed to this situation'.[45] The person concerned did not, however, take part in the transaction and there was no suggestion of any impropriety on his part.

Of greater interest is Mr Mitchell's defence of the SED's failure to take proper account of advice from the Chief Valuer and the Solicitor's Office. In response to a question from the Chairman of the Public Accounts Committee, Mr Robert Sheldon —'Do you consider that in disregarding that advice you were still complying with the Halliday procedures?' — Mr Mitchell stated:

> The Halliday Report was concerned with the sale of hospital property by the Secretary of State, in other words it was Crown property. In the case of Hamilton College it was not Crown property, it had been transferred by order from the ownership of the governors of Hamilton College to the governors of Jordanhill College of Education. It was the governors of Jordanhill who were accordingly responsible for its disposal.[46]

This reply, while it displays a certain skill in forensic footwork, is less than fully convincing. The existence of the joint SED/Jordanhill committee immediately casts doubt on the extent to which the College was an independent party in the transaction. Despite Mr Mitchell's insistence that 'the board of governors of Jordanhill is a responsible public body set up under statute, it is not simply a creature of the Secretary of State',[47] the Public Accounts Committee concluded:

> In our view the Board of Governors were not and could not be considered as independent of SED in this matter since SED officials act as assessors to the Board, SED officials were members of the working party, the College's main source of

> income is SED and many of the Board's members are appointed by the Secretary of State. The original cost of the property and its running costs had been met from public funds, the proceeds of sale were to go to the Exchequer, and SED ultimately had power to determine how the sale was handled.[48]

The role of Jordanhill College in the whole exercise has not received the attention it deserves, either in the Report of the Committee of Public Accounts or in subsequent press comment. Perhaps the major issue is why the members of the Board allowed themselves to be used to facilitate the sale and to shield the SED. An unflattering explanation would be that the Boards of the Scottish Colleges of Education have a long history of willing capitulation in the face of SED pressure, a point that will be developed more fully in Chapter 7. Less severely, it might be said that since almost all developments in the colleges depend on SED approval and support, the Jordanhill governors felt that they had to cooperate for the sake of good relations in the future. Whatever the precise motivation, the politicians on the Public Accounts Committee failed to probe this aspect deeply enough. Indeed, John Maxton MP, a former lecturer at Hamilton College, managed to let an SED official off the hook at a critical moment. Referring to the joint SED/Jordanhill committee, Mr Maxton asked Mr J. Keeley, Assistant Secretary in the SED: 'Could you tell me who were the Jordanhill people on that [committee]?'[49] Mr Keeley failed to answer the question directly and, surprisingly, Maxton did not pursue the matter. It would seem that the Jordanhill governors escaped rather lightly. Some realisation of this seems to have penetrated the College, for in a subsequent internal minute of a Jordanhill committee an almost audible sigh of relief can be detected:

> With regard to the hearing before the Public Accounts Committee of matters related to the sale of the former Hamilton College the Committee was pleased to note that no criticism had been made of the College.[50]

The second area of criticism — that alleging a degree of laxity in the efforts to secure a good price — can be dealt with more briefly. It was estimated by the Chief Valuer that, in favourable conditions, the property might fetch £6 million. In the event, the total selling price was £680,000 (£270,000 for the main block and playing fields, £410,000 for the residences, which were to be converted to private housing by the purchaser, Miller Homes). Adverse comment was made by the Public Accounts Committee on the timing and placing of advertisements, on the nature of approaches to potential purchasers, and on the seemingly insufficient regard to the interests of taxpayers in view of the fact that the money accruing from the sale would return to the Treasury. On this last point, Mr C.H.A. Judd, a Treasury Officer of Accounts, gave evidence to the effect that the Treasury 'was not actually involved either in the marketing of the property or in the decision to accept or reject any of the offers received. The Treasury was informed in August 1982 of the amounts of those offers, though not of the Chief Valuer's advice or the original or current replacement costs of the buildings'.[51] One MP on the Committee, William O'Brien, expressed the view that the transaction represented 'the sale of the century'.[52] Despite this, Mr Mitchell said he was satisfied that the very best had been done to get as much money for the property as was possible in the circumstances.[53] The conclusion of the Committee was less confident. It criticised the SED for being 'much less frank than they should have been' with the Treasury and continued:

> There can ... be no certainty what price would have been obtained for Hamilton College if SED had sought to have its sale handled in accordance with the Chief Valuer's and Solicitor's Office advice. But SED adopted a more casual approach to the sale than the recommendations of the Halliday Report demanded ... We consider that in taking this approach SED failed to ensure that everything possible was done ... to market the property adequately.[54]

The third area of complaint regarding the sale of Hamilton College — the role of the Minister — is, in some respects, the most interesting, though it is also the most difficult in terms of securing firm evidence on which to base a judgement. There is a parliamentary convention whereby Ministers are not normally called before select committees in order to account for their actions: indeed, it is not usually considered appropriate to put probing questions to officials about the part played by Ministers. It would seem, in fact, that the rules governing most select committees have been drawn up to ensure that politicians can escape detailed scrutiny. Even opposition parties normally acquiesce in this convention, presumably because they realise that if they themselves ever assume office it might afford useful protection. In the case of the Hamilton College enquiry, the questioning of officials was rather more rigorous than usual, and some questions were actually directed at the extent of ministerial involvement. The following exchange between John Maxton MP and Mr Mitchell came near the end of the oral evidence:

> Mr Maxton: Was it not to the Minister's advantage to get rid of that college as fast as possible?
>
> Mr Mitchell: Only the Minister can answer that question.
>
> Mr Maxton: Surely you can answer whether the Minister applied any pressure upon yourself, the department and Jordanhill College of Education in the sale?
>
> Mr Mitchell: Out concern was to get the best price that we could, at whatever time.
>
> Mr Maxton: Are you telling me that the Minister had no involvement whatsoever in any of this?
>
> Mr Mitchell: Not at all. I am sorry but I cannot answer detailed questions as to the involvement of Ministers at any particular stage of this.
>
> Mr Maxton: Would you not accept that getting rid of it stopped the continuing political embarrassment that this property had in terms of that particular Minister?
>
> Mr Mitchell: I cannot answer questions about political embarrassment.[55]

This exchange is a testimony to Mr Mitchell's powers of stone-walling and perhaps also to his sense of loyalty to the Minister. But it is an even more eloquent testimony to the investigative limitations of House of Commons select committees which supposedly meet to serve the public interest. By any reasonable standards, the extent of ministerial involvement in the Hamilton College sale was a critical issue which ought not to have been evaded.

In the absence of conclusive evidence, two possible explanations of Mr Fletcher's role suggest themselves. First, it may be that he was not deeply involved in the arrangements that were made and that the errors that occurred can be attributed largely to officials. This would be consistent with that part of the argument advanced earlier in the chapter which drew attention to the range of duties assumed by Scottish Office Ministers and the pressures to delegate authority to senior civil servants. Alternatively, it may be that Mr Fletcher was deeply involved — perhaps the prime mover in the exercise — and that officials simply found themselves in the unfortunate position of having to carry the can. This would be in line with that part of the argument advanced earlier in the chapter which suggested that ministerial involvement often seems to be erratic and wilful. In the case of either interpretation, it is difficult to see how Mr Fletcher could avoid a measure of blame for what happened: in the first case, the charge would be neglect and, in the second, defective judgement. However, events following the publication of the Public Accounts Committee Report conveyed the impression that Mr Fletcher had a rather underdeveloped sense of ministerial responsibility. By that time he had moved to another post as Minister for Consumer and Corporate Affairs in the Department of Trade and Industry in London.

In a television interview Mr Fletcher seemed to take comfort from the fact that he was not named in the Public Accounts Committee Report (a curious basis for consolation since he is clearly referred to as 'the Minister'). Despite calls for his resignation in parliament and the press, and despite subsequent statements by both the Treasury and the Scottish Office admitting that serious errors had been made, he did not deem it appropriate to give up public office. In this he had the support of no less a person than Mrs Thatcher who stated in the House of Commons on March 13, 1984 that she saw 'no reason to condemn Mr Fletcher'.[56] The writer of a leader in the *Glasgow Herald* some three weeks earlier had reached a different verdict:

> There are two constructions that can be placed on that sorry performance [the sale of the college]: first there was administrative lethargy amounting to gross incompetence; or alternatively there was a predilection for a sale to a private educationist at all costs. The first charge is serious enough; the second is really grave. But it needs to be emphasised that Mr Fletcher ... is not charged with corruption. Incompetence is excusable in a minister; corruption is not ... It is now clear that in any future reshuffle he will no longer be a credible candidate for a promoted post at the Scottish Office. His political reputation and career in Scotland have been dealt a grievous blow, which is just, for he presided over an appalling sequence of administrative ineptitude.[57]

The Hamilton College episode reflected badly on the SED at both administrative and political levels. In this respect, it lends some support to the view, often privately expressed by civil servants themselves, that the SED is one of the weakest departments in the Scottish Office. There is, however, a wider and more important conclusion to be drawn from what happened. It concerns the extent to which parliamentary procedures are adequate to ensure the public accountability of officials and politicians. The Committee of Public Accounts is a Select Committee of parliament. Its investigation of the SED's performance is generally reckoned to have been more robust than is usual in such cases. Even so, it failed to determine the extent of ministerial responsibility. In one of his 1983 Reith lectures, Sir Douglas Wass commented:

> ... the actual performance of the Select Committees has not to my mind been very impressive. The examination of witnesses has been superficial. The Committees have allowed themselves to be sidetracked by evidence which was not relevant to their enquiry.
> Officials who wanted to stonewall have rarely had difficulty in doing so and they have been surprised to encounter so little forensic skill.[58]

In another lecture Sir Douglas remarked on the slow progress which Britain appeared to be making, in comparison with other mature democracies, towards a more open system of government and referred, in particular, to lukewarm attitudes towards the possibility of a Freedom of Information Act.[59]

In the Scottish context, the mechanisms for monitoring the performance of government ministers and officials are certainly inadequate. There are, it is true, four committees which are concerned with purely Scottish affairs — the Scottish Grand Committee, two Scottish Standing Committees, and the Select Committee on Scottish Affairs. The first three are principally concerned with the progress of legislative proposals. Only the last (established as recently as 1979) has significant investigative potential. 'It has powers to summon ministers and take evidence from civil servants and private individuals, to examine written evidence and to travel.'[60] To date, however, it has not made a very significant impact, save perhaps in the area of local government finance. And Donald Dewar, the Select Committee's first Chairman, has expressed the view that, as a watchdog, it is helpless in the face of the sheer diversity of the Scottish Office's functions.[61]

Even on the floor of the House of Commons, opportunity for proper debate, as distinct from a ritualistic exchange of insults. is limited, not least because of the sheer pressure on parliamentary time. Moreover, sometimes full advantage of the opportunities that do arise is not taken. In the Hamilton case, for example, after strenuous and finally successful efforts by George Robertson, MP for Hamilton, to gain parliamentary time to debate the issue, only three other Labour MPs remained in the chamber to support him (against ten Conservatives).[62] It is true that the sitting took place at a late hour but, even so, the level of attendance must be judged poor. All this reinforces the argument that an adequate understanding of the political context within which the SED operates is essential to a proper evaluation of the Department's performance. In important respects, both the context and the performance have been shown to be unsatisfactory.

## Conclusion

The activities of the SED take place within a political and bureaucratic framework that is inimical to the development of coherent educational policies. The quality of leadership by politicians is weak and erratic, and this creates a policy vacuum which officials are obliged to fill as best they can. By background and training senior civil servants within the SED are not especially well-equipped to tackle the problems they encounter. As a consequence, policy is formulated partly on a reactive basis which allows self-interested pressure groups to exert too much influence on the decision-making process, though that influence is subject to manipulation by SED officials through the patronage system. Further, administrators (and inspectors) can themselves be regarded as constituting a powerful *internal* pressure group which is well placed to shape events since, ironically, it is expected to arbitrate between competing external claims. The general quality of performance of SED personnel cannot be regarded as satisfactory. As a case study, the sale of Hamilton College illustrates the Department's failure to follow Scottish Office guidelines designed to protect the public interest and the attempted use of an outside institution (Jordanhill College) to shield the SED from legitimate criticism. The episode also highlights the limitations of parliamentary select committees in establishing ministerial responsibility.

### *Notes and References*

1. SIO, *Factsheet 20*, 'The Scottish Office', April 1984, pp. 9–10.
2. SIO, *Factsheet 15*, 'Scottish Education', n.d., p. 16.
3. For a variety of perspectives on the political context, see J.M. Ross, *The Secretary of State for Scotland and the Scottish Office*, Centre for the Study of Public Policy, University of Strathclyde, 1981; J.G. Kellas, *Modern Scotland*, 2nd ed., Allen and Unwin, London, 1980; and T. Nairn, *The Break-Up of Britain*, 2nd ed., Verso, London, 1981.
4. SIO, *Factsheet 20*, p. 6.
5. *Ibid.*, p. 13.
6. *Ibid.*, p. 6.
7. M. Keating and A. Midwinter. *The Government of Scotland*, Mainstream, Edinburgh, 1983, p. 17.
8. Sir Toby Weaver, *Department of Education and Science; 'Central' Control of Education?*, Unit 2, Course E222, Open University, Milton Keynes, 1979, p. 13.
9. This point was made by Mrs Anna McCurley, MP for Renfrew West and Inverclyde, in an address on 'The Conservative Party and Scottish Education' given to Glasgow University Educational Colloquium on March 30, 1984. See also Bruce Millan, 'No danger from England', *TESS*, February 8, 1974.
10. Tony Worthington, 'A profession can colonise the mind', *TESS*, February 20, 1981, p. 16.
11. *Ibid.*, p. 16.

12. Alastair Macbeth, 'The Government of Scottish Education: Partnership or Compromise?', in D. McCrone (ed.), *The Scottish Government Yearbook 1984*, Unit for the Study of Government in Scotland, Edinburgh 1983.

13. See 'Social science degree axed', *THES*, April 22, 1983 and subsequent letters in the *THES* by Ian Carter (May 6), Walter Humes and Terry Cox (both May 13).

14. Sir Douglas Wass, 1983 Reith Lectures, Lecture VI, 'Participation — the sole bond', reprinted in *The Listener*, December 15, 1983, pp. 15–17.

15. Quoted by Douglas Reid in 'Who Runs Scotland?', *Sunday Standard*, October 3, 1982, p. 13.

16. *Ibid.*, p. 13.

17. *Ibid.*, p. 13.

18. The four examples given represent all the entries for SED staff of Under Secretary and Secretary level in the 1983 edition of *Who's Who.* It should be noted, however, that two other Under Secretaries in the SED, I.L. Sharp and D.A. Leitch, are not listed.

19. Quoted in Neil Munro, 'Out with the old, in with the new', *TESS*, August 31, 1984, p. 4.

20. *Ibid.*, p. 4.

21. *Ibid.*, p. 21.

22. Quoted in Willis Pickard, 'Out with the old, in with the new', *TESS*, August 31, 1984, p. 4.

23. *Ibid.*, p. 4.

24. See 'University move yet another coup', *GH*, October 9, 1984, p. 8.

25. Keating and Midwinter, *op. cit.*, p. 18ff.

26. Quoted in 'Top civil servant tells of "silent" role', *GH*, April 25, 1983, p. 5.

27. *Ibid.*, p. 5.

28. *Ibid.*, p. 5.

29. *Educational Development Strategy in England and Wales*, OECD, Paris, 1975.

30. *Policy Making in the Department of Education and Science*, HC 621, Tenth Report from the Expenditure Committee, Session 1975–76, HMSO, London.

31. *Ibid.*, para.87. Expenditure Committee's italics.

32. See, e.g., Denis Lawton, *The Politics of the School Curriculum*, Routledge and Kegan Paul, London, 1980, especially Chapter 2, 'The growing power of the mandarins and the secret service'.

33. See, e.g., Walter M. Humes, 'Scotland's "Decaying Educational Mandarinate"', *Chapman*, Vol. VIII, No.2, 1984, pp. 10–13.

34. See Alastair Macbeth, *op. cit.*, p. 173 and Sheila Browne, 'The Accountability of HM Inspectorate (England)', in J. Lello (ed.), *Accountability in Education*, Ward Lock, London, 1979, pp. 35–44.

35. On possible strategies for civil service reform, see J.M. Ross, *What Next, Minister? Another Way of Looking at the Civil Service*, Centre for the Study of Public Policy, University of Strathclyde, 1984.

36. This information is taken from the *Civil Service Year Book 1984.* Other useful sources —though they are not always entirely consistent with the *Civil Service Year Book* — are the *Education Year Book 1984*, Longman, London, 1983; the *Education Authorities Directory and Annual 1984*, School Government Publishing Company, Redhill, 1984; and *Scotland's Regions 1983–84*, Wm. Culross and Son, Coupar Angus, 1983 (in association with the Scottish Council Development and Industry).

37. Willis Pickard, *op. cit.*, p. 4.

38. P. Rendle, *Scrutiny of HM Inspectors of Schools*, Report to Mr Alex Fletcher MP,

Parliamentary Under Secretary of State for Industry and Education, Scottish Office, July 1981, para.8.2.

39. *Ibid.*, para.8.3.

40. *Ibid.*, para.8.4.

41. *Ibid.*, para.8.9.

42. *Hamilton College of Education: Disposal of Land and Buildings*, Ninth Report from the Committee of Public Accounts, Session 1983-84, HMSO, London, p. v.

43. *Ibid.*, p. v.

44. *Ibid.*, p. vi.

45. *Ibid.*, para.301.

46. *Ibid.*, para.313.

47. *Ibid.*, para.399.

48. *Ibid.*, pp. viii–ix.

49. *Ibid.*, para.351.

50. Jordanhill College, *Minutes of the Finance, Property and Law Committee*, December 5, 1983, para.IIb.

51. *Hamilton College of Education: Disposal of Land and Buiuldings*, para.440, Note by witness.

52. *Ibid.*, para.502.

53. *Ibid.*, para.457.

54. *Ibid.*, p. x.

55. *Ibid.*, paras. 539–542.

56. See reports in *GH*, March 14, 1983, p. 8 and *Scotsman*, March 14, 1983, p. 5.

57. 'College fiasco', *GH*, February 23, 1984, p. 8.

58. Wass, *op. cit.*, Lecture IV, 'Critical opposition: part of the polity', reprinted in *The Listener*, December 8, 1983, pp. 24–27.

59. *Ibid.*, Lecture V, 'Opening up government', reprinted in *The Listener*, December 15, 1983, pp. 12–14.

60. Keating and Midwinter, *op. cit.*, p. 83.

61. See Douglas Reid, *op. cit.*, p. 13.

62. See 'Younger admits errors were made over college', *GH*, March 13, 1984, p. 11.

# 4
# *Her Majesty's Inspectorate*

## 'Friendly, helpful and very intelligent men and women'?

The Education (Scotland) Act of 1980, in line with previous legislation, granted power to the Secretary of State 'to cause inspection to be made' of schools, colleges and other educational establishments: 'such inspections shall be made by Her Majesty's Inspectors or other persons appointed by the Secretary of State for the purpose'.[1] This form of words, not least the term 'inspector' itself, suggests a rather forbidding function for HMIs and, indeed, at certain points in the history of Scottish education, such an interpretation would not have been disputed. In the nineteenth century, for example, the award of a government grant to a school depended on the results of inspection, and so the visits of HMIs were viewed with some trepidation. Again, until relatively recently, HMIs acted as the Secretary of State's agents in deciding whether or not to grant prospective teachers a certificate of competence. From the 1960s, however, partly under the influence of J.S. Brunton, who was Senior Chief Inspector from 1955 to 1966, the image of the inspectorate began to change. In 1968, in its evidence to the Select Committee on Education and Science, the SED stated:

> The Inspectors more and more regard themselves and appear more and more to be accepted by the teachers as friendly advisers and helpers rather than as official watchdogs.[2]

This self-perception is supported by Dr T.R. Bone in the only detailed study of the development of the Scottish inspectorate:

> Authoritative control has given way to persuasive leadership; prescription and enforcement have been replaced by consultation and guidance. No longer regarded as pedants and detectives, the inspectors today are generally considered friendly, helpful and very intelligent men and women, neither to be elevated above all human failings, nor to be bitterly attacked for the slightest slip they make. Their suggestions are often accepted because they are seen to be imaginative and sensible, hardly ever just because it is the inspector, a kind of Orwellian Big Brother, who makes them.[3]

Bone also writes of the inspectorate ceasing to be regarded as 'the enforcing instrument of a remote and paternalistic authority'[4]: relations between inspectors and teachers, he maintains, have improved immeasurably because of 'the relaxation of central control, the sharing of responsibilities and the partnership in development work'.[5]

These remarks refer to the period up to 1966, the end-point for Bone's study. However, a much more recent commentator, Dr W.A. Gatherer, himself a former inspector, presents a similar picture and identifies the inspectorate as perhaps the principal influence for good in the advancement of Scottish education:

> In Scotland HMIs have played the major role in shaping and reshaping our curricula, developing the subjects, creating new methodologies, new approaches to school management, teacher training, staff development, assessment, cultural transmission. The Inspectorate has done more than any other single body to exercise a beneficent, creative influence on Scottish education.[6]

These panegyrics make substantial claims about the value and quality of the contribution made by HMIs. Dr Bone states that he is keen to avoid 'an attitude of complacency or self-congratulation',[7] but it must be said that it is hard to find evidence of any other attitude in his analysis. What needs to be looked at closely and critically is the extent to which the received wisdom about the inspectorate is justified. Are its members quite as benevolent, intelligent and creative as Bone and Gatherer suggest? Have they indeed abandoned the paternalism of the past in favour of a more democratic and cooperative style of working? Do teachers, in fact, regard them with respect, as sources of informed advice? Is the power that they exercise always used constructively for the benefit of Scottish education? These questions are especially important in view of the very considerable influence that HMIs undoubtedly enjoy. As a recent official report into their work puts it:

> The Inspectorate pervades the educational scene in Scotland, excluding the universities: they are members or assessors of well over 400 external bodies, committees and panels ... Scotland's relatively small size and its long tradition of a centrally organised system have led to the involvement of the Inspectorate in virtually every educational body of note in Scotland.[8]

A much less favourable view than that of Bone and Gatherer has been expressed by Lionel Griffiths, a teacher of English at Hawick High School, at a meeting of the national council of the EIS in November 1983.[9] The members of the council were discussing draft notes of guidance for teachers prepared by EIS officials following the decision to publish inspectorate reports on schools (a development that will be considered later in the chapter). The draft version stated that 'the EIS has always valued the traditional independence and professional approach of the Inspectorate' and referred to 'the happy relationship which has hitherto existed between the Inspectorate and the teaching profession'. Griffiths challenged this view and described the flattering comments as 'false, servile and insincere'. He went on to dispute the alleged independence of the inspectorate and claimed that they have 'never shown the moral courage or capacity to act independently of the education authorities, of the Scottish Education Department, or of their political masters'. Griffiths also questioned the professionalism of the inspectorate on the grounds that their credibility as expert advisers on teaching was severely compromised by their remoteness from the classroom and by their failure to live up to a professional code of ethics. Finally, he cast serious doubt on the claimed happy relationship between teachers and inspectors: this, he suggested, was a myth which inspectors themselves liked to believe but which teachers would dispute. His speech was well received by council members and he succeeded in having the notes of guidance amended.

It is clear that these criticisms were made from a value position that is itself open to argument. Griffiths was speaking as an EIS delegate, and plainly his definition of professionalism centres on the interests of teachers, which may or may not coincide with the interests of pupils, parents and the community at large. As was shown in Chapter 2, the whole question of professionalism is highly complex and it will be discussed more fully in Chapter 7. Again, the sort of independence on the part of the inspectorate that Griffiths would welcome seems to be confined to a support of EIS policy (on such matters as class size) in the face of 'attack' from the SED and regional authorities. Real autonomy would not guarantee that sort of alignment, and sometimes the consequences would be uncomfortable for the EIS as well as for other groups involved in education.

Nevertheless, Griffiths' criticisms serve to raise further interpretative issues of some importance. He suggests, in effect, that HMIs adopt an acquiescent role within the SED while exercising a good deal of authoritarianism in relation to classroom teachers. How justified is this charge? And he raises the vexed issue of the degree of credibility achieved by the inspectorate in view of the fact that they are distanced from the situation — the classroom — to which much of their professional advice relates. Does this nullify their recommendations, or does it, on the contrary, give them a breadth of vision and a measure of objectivity which individual teachers in individual schools cannot possibly achieve?

In approaching these questions, several lines of investigation will be employed. First, some remarks about recruitment to the inspectorate and promotion within it will be offered. These will be followed by a detailed consideration of the structure, organisation and priorities of the inspectorate, drawing principally on the 1981 Rendle Report, *Scrutiny of HM Inspectors of Schools in Scotland.* Reactions to the proposals of Rendle will then be examined and the contents of the policy statement by the Secretary of State in 1983 about the future role of HMIs will be reviewed. Finally, the quality of inspectorate reports will be assessed.

## Appointment and Promotion

Formally, HMIs 'are appointed by HM The Queen on the recommendation of the Secretary of State'.[10] In practice, however, they are recruited through the normal procedures of the Civil Service Commission. Vacancies are advertised publicly, usually for specialists in particular subject areas. Candidates are expected to have good academic qualifications together with several years' successful teaching experience: the normal age of appointees is 30—45. Interviews are held in Edinburgh by a selection board consisting principally of senior members of the inspectorate, with a representative of the Civil Service Commission acting as chairman. Appointments are probationary in the first instance: the period of probation is two years and, assuming satisfactory performance, appointees are confirmed in post until retirement at 60.

This description makes the process sound more open that it actually is. As part of their general 'talent spotting' work, established inspectors are on the look out for likely candidates to join their ranks. Inspectorial patronage includes 'encouraging' favoured teachers to apply when HMI vacancies occur. It is all done subtly and indirectly, of course, and anyone who is incapable of reading the signs is, by definition, unworthy of elevation. In recent years, the Munn/Dunning development programme has provided a very effective means of testing the suitability of prospective appointees. The piloting of Standard Grade material, and the frequent conferences and workshops associated with the development programme, have allowed the inspectorate ample opportunity to assess the willingness of teachers to 'cooperate' in national developments. Academic ability and professional competence are undoubtedly sought-after characteristics, but so too are 'political' awareness and a suitably supportive attitude towards bureaucratic conventions. Sometimes the prelude to appointment can produce an entertaining degree of anxiety. One aspirant who had been privately advised by his HMI patron that he was in line for appointment when the next vacancy in his subject area occurred was alarmed when the patron, who had previously carried responsibility for that subject area, was promoted and moved to other duties of a more general kind. He need not have concerned himself: he was duly clutched to the bosom of the department some months later.

There is another sense in which the process of appointment is less open than it may appear at first sight. It has been argued by Andrew McPherson that, certainly until recently, the career patterns of inspectors and other senior figures in Scotland's educational leadership class indicates a preference on the part of the SED for a particular kind of background. A disproportionate number of appointees have had their main educational experiences (both as pupils and teachers) in small towns outside the West-Central belt which are unrepresentative of the backgrounds of the majority of the population but which serve to perpetuate many of the traditional assumptions about democracy and classlessness. McPherson calls this the 'Kirriemuir career' and remarks that it 'produced the sort of person that could be invited into the councils of the state'.[11] This interpretation lends support to some of the arguments advanced in Chapter 1 about the reasons for the continuing potency of the idea of a Scottish educational tradition.

On initial appointment, an HMI is likely to be involved in routine inspecting work within one of the three territorial divisions (Western, Eastern and Northern). He will, however, make regular visits to St. Andrew's House in Edinburgh to attend briefing sessions and training programmes, and to take part in national committee work. HMIs are expected not only to monitor standards in schools but also to contribute to educational change, especially in the area of curriculum. Thus, for example, an inspector with a background in mathematics will seek to contribute to the development of that subject by advancing new ideas and by passing on information about good practice that he has observed in schools. This can be done *via* his fellow inspectors, advisers, education officers and college of education lecturers, as well as classroom teachers. Sometimes this aspect of HMI work is referred to as the 'multiplier effect', a term used to signify the network of communication which inspectors use to spread approved ideas. This strategy also has the advantage of providing HMIs with a series of contacts within the educational world who can serve as useful sources of information to be fed back into St. Andrew's House in Edinburgh.

At more senior levels the task of providing guidance on policy matters to administrators and politicians tends to assume greater importance than ordinary inspection and development work, although there is no formal division between these various functions: tendering advice presupposes a sound grasp of what is happening on the ground and the prospects for successful innovation. The flow is not all one-way, for sometimes politicians, acting in response to external pressure groups, will come up with proposals on which the inspectorate are asked to comment. A fairly recent example was the move by Alex Fletcher to introduce legislation on parental choice of school. It seems, in fact, that he had to push the idea through in the face of opposition both within the SED and from the local authorities.

The new recruit to the inspectorate will naturally be concerned about the possibility of advancement within the service. What are the prospects? Of 112 staff in post in July 1981 (out of an official complement of 118), 99 occupied the rank of Inspector (HMI), 10 Chief Inspector (HMCI), 2 Deputy Senior Chief Inspector (HMDSCI), and 1 Senior Chief Inspector (HMSCI),[12] Approximately one-third of the 99 inspectors were classified as 'Higher Grade'; this grade is used 'to provide a reasonable promotion outlet from the broad initial grade base'.[13] Both the total number of HMIs and the proportion of promoted posts were subject to steady increases until 1976, as can be seen from the following table:[14]

| | *HMSCI* | *HMDSCI* | *HMCI* | *HMI(HG)* | *HMI* | *TOTAL* |
|---|---|---|---|---|---|---|
| 1948 | 1 | — | 4 | 9 | 87 | 101 |
| 1964 | 1 | — | 6 | 25 | 75 | 107 |
| 1970 | 1 | — | 7 | 28 | 77 | 113 |
| 1976 | 1 | 2 | 11 | 35 | 76 | 125 |
| 1979 | 1 | 2 | 11 | 35 | 69 | 118 |

Since 1976 'staffing restrictions have reduced the complement to 118 and more recent bans on recruitment have brought the staff actually in post down to 112 [at July 1981]'.[15] The fact remains, however, that in the post-war period 'a generally upward trend in the size of the complement of the Inspectorate'[16] can be detected. This, together with the proliferation of promoted posts, is a marked feature of developed bureaucracies, but expansion need not, by definition, mean that unnecessary jobs are being created. There may be a need for more staff because there is genuinely more work to do. Significantly, however, HMIs formally *shed* work in the 1960s (with the setting up of the GTC, the CCC and the SCEEB), but their numbers continued to increase. It is difficult to resist the conclusion that an element of empire-building was taking place, especially in view of the fact that there were already proportionately more HMIs in Scotland than in England, relative to the number of pupils, schools and teachers — a situation that still applies.[17]

Assuming that an HMI is untroubled by these features of what might be called bureaucratic drift — that is, the tendency of large and powerful organisations to display a measure of self-aggrandisement — and is keen to do well within the service, what pattern should his (or, much less commonly, her) career follow? The present Senior Chief Inspector, Mr John A. Ferguson, provides a useful example. Following one year as a school teacher (1950—51), Mr Ferguson worked in further education from 1951 to 1961 before joining the inspectorate. For the next eleven years he gained experience in the range of work carried out by HMIs; then in 1972, in an extremely interesting move, he switched over to the 'career civil service' side of the SED as an Assistant Secretary. He held this post until 1975 when he returned to the inspectorate as HMDSCI. He was appointed HMSCI in 1981.

The significance of Mr Ferguson's spell as Assistant Secretary should not be underestimated. It is sufficiently unusual not to be a matter of chance, and the career of at least one former HMSCI followed a similar pattern. J.S. Brunton, HMSCI from 1955 to 1966, served as an Assistant Secretary in the SED in the early 1950s. Several interpretations suggest themselves. It might simply be that those picked out for secondment to the administrative side are regarded as high-fliers and likely to benefit from the experience. The exercise might even be mutually beneficial, with administrators gaining insight into 'professional' problems as well as *vice versa*. Again, the transfer of people like Brunton and Ferguson might be looked on as a small gesture aimed at reducing any incipient hostilities between HMIs and career civil servants: HMIs have to gain the cooperation of administrators, and it would seem important, therefore, to understand their problems (for example, in relation to politicians) and to learn the art of the possible. Equally, however, administrators might easily resent the occupation of a senior post by someone other than a career civil servant: some of them might even regard HMIs as unwelcome outsiders. Thus the arguments about reducing hostility and promoting cooperation are evenly balanced.

The most likely explanation is that experience on the administrative side is regarded as a testing ground, a means of assessing those who are considered suitable material for high advancement within the inspectorate. The exercise has as much to do with completing the process of assimilation into the approved value system of the civil service as with any direct benefits to the Department. If this is so, it reinforces the extent to which career civil servants call the tune within the SED: in effect, they are invited to give the stamp of approval to future HMSCIs, and approval would seem to require preparedness to play second fiddle to the Permanent Secretary. The lesson, as far as the ambitious new recruit is concerned, is that ability, hard work and extensive experience of routine HMI duties are all important, but the unwritten rules of organisational behaviour may be more important than any of these.

Mr Ferguson's career highlights the significance of the political context of inspectorate work. The successful HMI is one who learns to conduct himself according to the bureaucratic conventions of the civil service. Discretion and confidentiality are particularly important elements of the approved model. Indeed HMIs, rather comically, have to sign the Official Secrets Act. The implication that defeating the enemy depends on what goes on within the SED is, on the face of it, difficult to take seriously. It is, of course, fashionable in certain quarters to speak of 'the enemy within', and perhaps the requirement is aimed at anyone who dares to criticise the SED. More importantly, however, some of the effects of progressive initiation into such a secretive atmosphere are likely to be unhealthy as far as the general climate of educational debate is concerned. If senior HMIs reach their positions partly because of their political acceptability, their powers of *educational* percipience are likely to be severely compromised. They will tend to promote those ideas and those people who share their values and assumptions, and will seek to suppress proposals and individuals that present a challenge. When it comes to the crunch, there is no doubt that successful HMIs, like senior career civil servants, owe their first loyalty not to education, nor even to Scotland, but to the machinery of the British state.

## The Rendle Report

The fullest source of recent information on the work of the inspectorate is the report of the Rendle enquiry, which commenced in December 1980. This document, written by Mr Peter Rendle, a former Under-Secretary at the Scottish Office, was submitted to Alex Fletcher MP, then Parliamentary Under Secretary of State for Education and Industry in July 1981, but was not released to the public until 1983. The reasons for the delay will become apparent later.

Rendle's remit was as follows:

> To consider and report on the role, organisation, staffing and effectiveness of Her Majesty's Inspectorate of Schools in the Scottish Education Department, including the main priorities of work to be undertaken, and arrangements for collaboration between the Inspectorate and the rest of the Scottish Office, taking account in particular of the following:
> 1. The responsibilities and policies of the Secretary of State;
> 2. The present and prospective needs of all components of the education service;
> 3. The role of education authorities and their staffs and of other educational agencies;
> 4. Government statements of policy relating to the quality of education and to the Inspectorate; and
> 5. The Government's plans to reduce public expenditure and civil service manpower.[18]

In carrying out his remit, Mr Rendle sought the views of over eighty people, a majority of whom came from within the SED. More than forty HMIs were consulted, and more than ten administrators. In addition, a number of 'outsiders' were interviewed: directors of education, advisers, head teachers, college principals, the head of a university education department, directors of two educational quangos, plus some others. All of the responses, it should be noted, came from within the educational world, and most of the informants were themselves members of the leadership class. 'No general invitation was issued for persons or organisations to submit evidence, though 2 unsolicited papers were received and noted.'[19]

Despite the evident bias of the data base on which Mr Rendle relied, his report does succeed in identifying a number of critical issues. Indeed, as will be seen, it provoked a considerable measure of hostility within the inspectorate, and this suggests that he did not accept everything he was told at face value. As in so many official reports, the actual recommendations are fairly modest, and it is the argument leading up to them that is of most interest. First, however, it will be useful to provide some further factual information about the organisation of the inspectorate.

Rendle states that 'the Inspectorate is a highly complex organism: it operates in practice in several planes. Because it is a professional body the Inspectorate is only partly hierarchical: and the Inspectors comprising it work both as individuals and in teams or groups ... '[20] The suggestion that professional bodies are not notably hierarchical might well be challenged, but the general point that the organisation of the inspectorate is fairly flexible can be accepted. Underlying this flexibility, however, there is a basic structure which can be described in terms of four 'dimensions'. First, there is a geographical or territorial dimension. Well over half the total number of HMIs work in one of the three divisions — Eastern, Western and Northern — which provide the management framework for the national work of inspecting education authority schools. Each division is headed by a Chief Inspector. The divisions are further subdivided into districts, with local offices throughout Scotland, for purposes of liaising with particular authorities. Indeed, a good deal of the work of HMIs assigned to divisional duties involves contact with directors of education and their staffs on matters such as the quality of individual schools, of subject departments within schools, and of buildings and other facilities.

The second organisational dimension of inspectorate work relates to the different stages of education, each supervised by a Chief Inspector. At the time of Rendle this meant primary education, secondary education, etc. However, a number of changes have since been made and the duties of some HMCIs reallocated. The present position is that there is now an HMCI for Basic Education (0–10 year olds) and Special Education; one for 10–16 year olds; one for 16–19 year olds; and one for Further Education, including community education and adult education.[21] The duties of HMCI (Higher Education), HMCI (Teacher Education and Supply) and HMCI (Research and Intelligence) continue as before.

The third dimension concerns subject specialisms. Certain HMIs are designated national specialists in particular subject areas — for example, English or Modern Languages — and are responsible for coordinating developments in these fields. In a time of curricular change, this is obviously an important function and, in recent years, the involvement of national specialists in planning the piloting of Foundation course materials has been considerable. The subject dimension is also significant with regard to the ordinary work of inspection. Rendle notes that there is a convention, as far as secondary school inspections are concerned, 'that HM Inspectors do not inspect subjects they are not qualified to teach'.[22] This, however, does not apply in primary, further or higher education. In the case of FE and HE 'the range of subjects ... is so wide that it is ... impracticable for the Inspectorate to be expert in and to have had teaching experience of each'.[23] And in the primary field 'A substantial proportion of inspection ... is carried out by Inspectors who have no primary teaching training[*sic*] or experience'.[24]

The final organisational dimension relates to special aspects of inspectorate work, such as educational research, which exists as a separate unit — the Research and Intelligence Unit — with its own Chief Inspector. The Development Unit Executive Group set up to coordinate the Munn/Dunning programme could also be classified under this heading. It was managed by a team of four HMCIs together with an Assistant Secretary from the administrative side of the SED.[25] Rendle refers to the work of this group as illustrating 'perhaps to a more than usual degree, the potential power of central influence in Scotland and the widespread involvement of the Inspectorate'.[26]

This account is inevitably simplified. In addition to the four broad (and overlapping) dimensions identified there are a whole series of committees, panels, working groups, etc. which serve to complicate the organisational structure even further. For example, Rendle lists HMCI committees dealing with such topics as micro-electronics, educational broadcasting, environmental education, guidance and health education, and panels and development groups covering a wide range of primary and secondary school subjects.[27] Probably only a senior member of the inspectorate itself could give a clear and comprehensive account of all the organisational complexities and, viewed from the outside, it is difficult to form a definite judgement about whether they constitute a cumbersome mixture of management forms or a suitably flexible response to the variety of tasks HMIs have to perform.

Overall responsibility for the work of HMCIs and HMIs rests with the Senior Chief Inspector (Mr Ferguson) and his two Deputies, Mr H.F. Smith, who deals with post-school education, and Mr W.R. Ritchie, who deals with school education. There are major planning groups, consisting of Chief Inspectors, relating to these two areas of command and chaired by the HMDSCIs. Mr Ritchie only became an HMDSCI in 1984, succeeding Mr A.D. Chirnside, having previously been responsible for the progress of the 16–18 Action Plan. His appointment, viewed in conjunction with Mr Ferguson's own background in FE, and Mr Smith's responsibility for post-school education, can perhaps be regarded as signalling a shift in perspective from the traditional institutional categories of primary and secondary education.

All this refers to the structure of the inspectorate. What about its overall role within the Scottish educational system? On this, the Rendle Report has a number of extremely interesting things to say. It states, for example, that 'It is important ... for the Inspectorate's role to be clearly understood by the teaching force (as well as by the Inspectors themselves and the Department)' and goes on, 'This is not the case at the moment'.[28] In effect, Rendle suggests that HMIs try to do too much and fail to establish a clear sense of priorities. He observes: 'The Inspectorate has long prided itself on being the eyes and ears of the Department and has tended to aim at omniscience'.[29] They justify this approach on the grounds that they need 'to maintain their standing and credibility as a force which is accepted as being familiar with what actually goes on in classrooms'.[30] Rendle is unconvinced and remarks that 'some teachers discount the credibility which inspectors can gain from formal inspections, which often create artificial conditions . . . '[31] He might have added that there is an inherent tension between credibility within the Department and credibility within the teaching profession. Being effective as the 'eyes and ears' of the Department may mean engaging in activities of an information-gathering and, more contentiously, of an evaluative kind that some teachers are likely to resent. If, for example, a teacher holds views which he knows are at odds with currently approved policies but which he is honestly convinced are right, he might well perceive inspectors as departmental spies, intent on identifying heretics and forcing them to accept, or at least accede to, the established faith. This may seem exaggerated but certainly, with regard to Munn and Dunning, HMIs tended to engage in a degree of proselytising that could be regarded as undesirable. It must also be borne in mind that, as HMIs with divisional responsibilities are in regular contact with Directors of Education and their staffs, they are in a position to influence the promotion prospects of classroom teachers. The pressures to conform can, therefore, be considerable. Rendle puts the point with some delicacy but the message is plain. An inspector, he suggests, may be perceived in a variety of ways: 'from one who, with his colleagues, spreads to one and all the true and accepted gospel, to the helpful co-professional giving useful tips to an individual teacher'. He adds: 'there is a danger that some recipients might regard such advisory activities as warranting rather less flattering descriptions than these'.[32]

Similar expressions of caution occur in relation to the inspectorate's influence over such bodies as the CCC, the GTC and the SEB, and also the education authorities. Referring to development work, the report questions the degree of involvement of the inspectorate and states that '*it is important to avoid any undue reluctance to hand over the reins to those who are more appropriately placed . . . to achieve effective results*'.[33] Again, 'A degree of dependence on the Inspectorate has been built up (even where, as with the CCC, formal responsibilities have been devolved elsewhere) which might ultimately be regarded as debilitating to other parts of the system. This tendency is also suspected among some education authorities . . . '[34] Such reservations constitute a recurring theme in the report and, although they are voiced with the characteristic restraint of official documents, their general drift is unmistakable. They are summed up in the following important passage:

> While it is effective in terms of influence for HMIs to play a due part as members, assessors or observers . . . in the deliberations of . . . many bodies it is important for

> them not to exert too tight a grip on the system, the various components of which might operate with more self reliance given modest encouragement. At present, the willingness of the periphery in Scotland to look to the centre for a lead and the commanding position of the Inspectorate which derives from their almost universal participation in and knowledge of the educational field both combine to give HMIs what some might regard as a disturbingly powerful influence . . . [H]ere and there one discerns mild misgivings as to the almost automatic precedence given to the views of an HMI among a committee or other group of educationists . . . [I]t is important that Inspectors do not trade too much on the respect they have gained. It would be unhealthy for the system if too tight a grip were exerted at too many points throughout it. What these reservations amount to, therefore, is that care should be taken not to be stifling to initiative, enterprise, new or different ideas which could emerge from other agencies.[35]

These remarks, notwithstanding the careful qualifications, are extremely perceptive. They serve to cast doubt on the enlightened self-image that members of the inspectorate have of themselves. Their comfortable assumption that the pervasiveness of their influence in Scottish education is invariably beneficial is, in effect, being questioned. Likewise, Rendle is less than fully convinced that the powers of penetration of HMIs are exceptional: good ideas, he suggests, can arise from many sources provided the channels of communication are not monopolised by one centralised group. Underlying these observations is the hint that the inspectorate may operate in a more authoritarian manner than is often supposed. Certainly they prefer to work through advice and persuasion if at all possible but, should the need arise, they are undoubtedly capable of using more directive methods. These are most likely to be triggered by action that is perceived to be threatening to the status and authority of members of the inspectorate, or to the favoured policy of the moment, especially where it derives from a source that cannot be dismissed as wilfully maverick or subversive. An example will illustrate the point.

It concerns the experiences of an east coast headmaster who wrote a series of articles in 1980–81 for a regional teachers' magazine. The articles contained some critical comments about the SED in general and the inspectorate in particular. Reference was made, for example, to the uniformity of background of HMIs, the élitism of the civil service and the unquestioning acceptance of SED authority on the part of most Scottish teachers. These remarks, it should be said, represented only a very small part of the overall argument that was being advanced, an argument which dealt with an impressive range of educational issues (social, psychological and epistemological) based on an informed awareness of recent research. The proposals of the Dunning Report on assessment came in for detailed comment and, although he rejected some of the recommendations, the headmaster stated that the report contained much of value. Nevertheless, despite the general context in which the critical remarks occurred, and the constructive response to important policy questions exhibited in the articles, the headmaster found himself the object of unfavourable attention. He received a formal visit from a senior HMI who read from a prepared statement which indicated the extent of official displeasure. It was suggested that the headmaster might consider it wise to publish a retraction. This, to his credit, he declined to do and, in fact, indicated that another article containing some critical comments would shortly be appearing in a different journal. It was then intimated, subtly and indirectly, in a manner that could not be construed as constituting an overt threat that, in the absence of a retraction, certain consequences might follow. First, the director of education for the region might come to hear of the headmaster's 'misdemeanour'. Secondly, his school might be withdrawn from the Munn/Dunning pilot studies that were proceeding at the time. (That this should have been regarded as a punishment rather than a reward indicates a decided failure of judgement on the part of the senior HMI.) And thirdly, the headmaster might find that his school would gain early, first-hand experience of the rigours of a full inspection. The first and third of these possible consequences did actually occur. The second did not because, ironically, it would have caused more inconvenience to the SED officials concerned with the pilot studies than to the school. Throughout the exchange between the headmaster and the senior HMI the formal courtesies were observed: the subsequent directness of action on the part of the latter was not anticipated by directness of utterance.

This case suggests over-reaction on the part of the inspectorate to what was, after all, a little local difficulty. At the very least, it serves to undermine the claim that they act as 'friendly advisers and helpers rather than official watchdogs'. It is, of course, impossible to say how frequently such over-reaction manifests itself. Almost certainly there will be many instances where official displeasure is conveyed in a less heavy-handed fashion and where the wisdom of 'retraction' is quietly accepted by headteachers with a more pragmatic and less principled view of their position. Such pragmatism is perhaps not admirable but it is comprehensible. It has already been pointed out that contact between HMIs and Directors of Education is frequent. A headteacher who is careful to maintain good relations with the inspectorate thus goes a long way to maintaining good relations with the directorate, as the latter regard inspectors as an important and generally reliable information service. Keeping divisional HMIs sweet is, in fact, a sound investment for the headteacher who hopes to secure his fair share of teaching and other resources from his education authority. It is yet another instance of the way in which institutional and bureaucratic pressures help to encourage a high measure of conformity.

The Rendle Report raised many vital issues, but its impact at the level of educational debate has been minimal. This is partly because its actual recommendations were modest in comparison with the depth of analysis which was exhibited in the main body of the text. It proposed, among other things, a small reduction in the number of HMIs, a degree of disengagement from traditional inspectorial functions, better communication between inspectors and administrators, and improved liaison with education authority advisers. But perhaps a more important reason for the limited impact of Rendle was the strenuous effort made to discredit it within the SED. The motives for this will be examined in the next section.

## Responses to the Rendle Report

The Rendle Report was completed in July 1981. It did not become available to the public until 1983, and even then it was not published under an HMSO imprint but as an 'in-house' document which could be obtained from the SED only after persistent enquiries. In the interim, a draft policy statement by the Secretary of State, arising out of Rendle, was prepared and became the subject of much internal lobbying before a final policy statement was issued in March 1983. Particularly active in the lobbying process was the HMI section of the Association of First Division Civil Servants, a kind of upmarket trade union (though no doubt its members would deplore such a downmarket description). An examination of the Association's reaction to both Rendle and the Secretary of State's draft policy statement is of considerable interest in respect of establishing its members' order of priorities.

In a letter dated November 15, 1982 addressed to the Manpower Services Division of the Scottish Office and signed by Douglas W. Duncan, Honorary Secretary of the HMI section of the Association of First Division Civil Servants, a thoroughgoing denunciation of Rendle is offered. It is stated that 'a detailed critique would be unproductive' but that 'the following general criticisms should be made':

> The report reveals a lack of perception of what HM Inspectors really do; it is demonstrably inaccurate in places; there is, throughout, a lack of evidence to support the conclusions and recommendations and so these are merely unsubstantiated assertions. The report therefore provides a poor basis for developing proposals and this is starkly revealed in the wide divergence of the Draft Policy Statement from the report. We are consequently very firmly of the view that the report should not be published. To do so would simply attach ill-repute to the whole process of Rayner Scrutinies and would vitiate its future use as a weapon in the battle for efficiency.[36]

As an illustration of the considered reaction of 'very intelligent men and women' this statement is quite remarkable. It accuses Rendle of demonstrable inaccuracy but fails to provide any examples: in this it exemplifies precisely the kind of 'unsubstantiated assertion' it complains of. The attempt to suppress publication betrays a fear of open scrutiny, an unwillingness to explain and justify the work of the inspectorate within the context of public debate. Moreover, the reference to 'the battle for efficiency' is self-evidently an attempt at evasion, a crude appeal to the favoured dogma of the government of the day in the interests of avoiding substantive issues to do with the nature and quality of the work of inspectors.

All this is bad enough, but the letter goes on to comment on the draft policy statement — which it claims to find 'generally acceptable' and 'much more positive and helpful than the Rendle document'[37] — in terms which reveal an unhealthy degree of touchiness. The draft policy statement describes the work of inspection as 'basic'. Mr Duncan's letter objects that this 'is open to misinterpretation as 'elementary or low level' whereas what is meant is 'supremely important'. The word 'basic' should be deleted'.[38] A reference to recruitment to the inspectorate is also found unacceptable. It 'could be construed as saying that the Inspectorate does not, at present, attract teachers and others who are leaders in their field. This is plainly not so'.[39] Evidently this remark is not offered as another example of 'unsubstantiated assertion' but as a justified statement of self-confidence. There are, however, definite limits to the self-confidence of HMIs, for another proposal of the draft policy statement, that the reports resulting from inspections should be published, provokes alarm: 'We would require to know the legal position where a statement in such a report led to action against any HMI ... Legal Aid is not available in defamation cases'.[40] Finally, on the question of manpower savings, the inspectorate recommends, with a disarming degree of frankness, that proposals for cuts in particular areas should simply be fudged: 'It would be better to avoid the issue by indicating that manpower savings have been achieved by a re-allocation and re-grouping of tasks within the Inspectorate'.[41]

Further insight into the collective sensitivity of the First Division Association can be gained from its Annual Report for 1982. Concern is expressed that 'an outsider' — presumably Mr Rendle — should have been charged with making a survey and helping to determine policy. It is surmised that the intention was 'to provide objectivity' but, in the event, he succeeded in 'merely providing ignorance'.[42] With a delightful disregard for consistency, in view of the attempt to suppress both the Rendle document and the results of inspections, the report goes on: 'The ingredient missing is that of informed discussion which we keep being told is the basis of democracy'.[43] And, in a less than elegant transition, the next paragraph reads:

> This is not to conclude that we are opposed to Rayner-type exercises. On the contrary, there should be more of them but better done. A sound principle is that it is the inside of the shoe which knows where the pressure is on the foot.[44]

In other words, inspectors should be allowed to monitor their own performance and should not be subject to external scrutinies carried out in the name of efficiency and accountability.

Fortunately the government was not fully persuaded by these protestations. In his final policy statement of March 24, 1983 the Secretary of State not only released the Rendle Report (albeit two years after its completion), but also confirmed the proposal to publish inspectors' reports.[45] Rendle was far from being fully endorsed, however, for the value of the traditional inspectorial function of HMIs was restated and the recommendation that the number of inspectors should be reduced to 100 was rejected: a figure of 112 was deemed appropriate. Some, but not all, of Rendle's proposals for structural reform were accepted. The reallocation of HMCI duties, previously described, was confirmed but a suggestion that the number of territorial divisions should be reduced from three to two was turned down.

Of particular interest in the Secretary of State's final policy statement is the redefinition of the function of the inspectorate and the best ways of carrying it out. Six aspects of their role are identified:

i. to provide information, assessment and advice to Ministers, the Scottish Education Department, other Government Departments and agencies and the other central bodies involved in education;
ii. to provide an audit by assessing and reporting on the quality of education and training provided to make available to those responsible for taking action the advice and assistance considered necessary to effect an improvement;
iii. to identify and make known the educational needs of the nation having taken account of the perceived needs and wishes of parents and pupils;
iv. to identify cost-effective ways of meeting these needs and to influence the responsible bodies and agencies to meet them;
v. to indicate desirable and attainable norms of quality and to advise on the actions required to achieve them;
vi. to give a lead in development work in the various sectors of education, formal and informal, and to work with directors of education, heads of schools and colleges, advisory and executive bodies and others through appropriate forms of liaison to bring about necessary changes in the system.[46]

This statement provides a nice example of linguistic counterpointing. First, the use of language commonly employed in commerce and industry ('audit', 'cost-effective', 'norms of quality') reveals the adherence of the government to an investment-return model of education. However, an attempt is made to balance some of the less attractive associations of this model by introducing a human element — 'the perceived needs and wishes of parents and pupils'. Then the traditional task of information-gathering by inspectors is reasserted and related to their responsibility to offer advice to politicians and officials. This too is balanced by the more 'progressive' and 'innovative' requirement to 'give a lead in development work'. Inspectors are thus expected to be informers and assessors, planning agents and channels of influence.

How are these expectations to be translated into practice? The policy statement identifies three interrelated tasks. First, 'a programme of general inspections of a sample of schools and other educational institutions [including central institutions and colleges of education]'[47] is to be carried out. This work, in the view of the Secretary of State, remains fundamental in the interests of accountability and the maintenance of standards. Secondly, and partly arising out of the routine work of inspection, HMIs will be responsible for 'a programme of tasks resulting in reports on aspects of education of national importance, reports to Ministers and SED, discussion papers, etc.'[48] Recent examples under this heading include *The Education of Pupils with Learning Difficulties*,[49] *Learning and Teaching in Primary 4 and Primary 7*,[50] *Teaching and Learning in the Senior Stages of the Scottish Secondary School*,[51] and *Learning and Teaching in Scottish Secondary Schools: School Management*.[52] Such reporting helps to ensure that 'the Inspectorate ... act[s] as a catalyst for change throughout the system'.[53] Thirdly, inspectors will be required to participate 'in a national development programme which comprises a series of longer-term objectives derived from the policies of the Secretary of State'.[54] The work associated with Standard Grade courses, the Action Plan and the development of micro-computers in schools would come into this category.

The transition from the Secretary of State's definition of the role of HMIs, with its careful balancing of 'traditional' and 'progressive' functions, to his account of this role in operational terms involves a subtle shift of emphasis. It is clear from the specification of tasks to be carried out that HMIs are to remain agents of central control. They are, first and foremost, to be at the disposal of ministers and officials, gathering, sifting and evaluating information, rendering palatable policies that have received the stamp of approval from government, and preparing the database for future policies. What is not clear is what scope, if any, remains for the exercise of their independent judgement, assuming they have both the capacity and the inclination to generate ideas of their own. This, of course, may not be perceived as a problem by HMIs themselves, especially if the process of bureaucratic assimilation is as comprehensive as has been suggested. In effect, they can look forward to increased authority in relation to other sectors of the educational system. The fact that this will require them to adopt a subservient position within the SED is something they are probably willing to settle for. After all, their initiation into the ways of government is essentially an initiation into the benefits to be gained from playing by the rules and accepting the 'realities' of power.

## The Quality of Inspectorate Publications

It is one of the many ironies of the inspectorate's position that while its members are required to assess the effectiveness of other sectors of the educational service, their own accountability for the quality of their performance is minimal. What formal scrutiny they are subject to is almost invariably internal to the SED, and the level of public, and even professional, awareness of what they do is not such as to encourage careful evaluation. The sort of monitoring and advisory role which occupies HMIs for much of their time is, of course, difficult to assess with any degree of precision. But evaluation is not entirely impossible for, as Rendle notes, 'The output of HM Inspectors can be considered in terms of what they say and to whom; and what they write, what is published and what is not; and who reads or benefits or is influenced by it'.[55] A distinction must, however, be made between individual inspectors and the service as a whole. Inspectors as individuals manage to remain fairly anonymous, partly because their conditions of service discourage them from giving public lectures and publishing written work, save in special circumstances and with the previous sanction of the Department. This injunction is presumably intended to enhance their 'credibility' by minimising the opportunity for public gaffes. At a collective level, the position is different. As well as reports on individual schools, HMIs produce a number of significant documents on a wide range of educational topics, and these can form the basis of a tentative judgement of their work.

The results of school inspections became available in the course of 1983, and an initial appraisal suggests that they are extremely uneven in quality. Some consist of little more than bland generalities. The following examples convey the level of penetration that is often the norm:

> Textbooks and other teaching materials were in good supply for the most part.[56]

> Teachers were diligent in their correction of written work and set appropriate standards of presentation for pupils to reach.[57]

> The overall balance of the curriculum is sound. Pupils are organized so that group and individual approaches may be employed. There is good collaboration between full-time staff and visiting teachers.[58]

> Priority should be given to the planning of the curriculum and the devising of guidance for the teachers.[59]

The last example is typical of a common fault — a recommendation that is so vague as to be positively unhelpful. In another report it is stated that 'senior staff should review arrangements for pupils with learning difficulties'[60] without any indication of the particular issues that should be addressed. Similarly, a recommendation in a primary school report that 'A review of school policy for language should seek to extend the good practice which is available within each stage'[61] is offered without clear identification of what constitutes 'good practice'.

A few reports do manage to rise above this level to make specific and helpful recommendations. One example is that on Grove Academy, Tayside.[62] Although it is actually quite critical of a number of aspects of the school's performance, the report succeeds in specifying the areas that need attention and makes detailed suggestions for improvement. The points that are covered relate not only to the curriculum and management of the school but also to the responsibilities of the education authority for deficiencies in accommodation and safety. By drawing attention to the latter, the report should have strengthened the headteacher's hand in his dealings with the Director of Education.

But reports of this quality have, to date, been relatively rare, and the general verdict must be that they do not present the inspectorate in a good light. Dr W.A. Gatherer, who, as has already been shown, is a stout defender of HMIs, has been particularly severe in his comments. He refers to the reports as 'crude and ineffectual' and goes on:

> The on-the-spot, quick judgements incorporated in inspection reports must be recognized for the crude, subjective, inadequate observations they are.
> It should be obvious that they are virtually useless: to the teachers since they are too brief and superficial to help them improve the service they proffer; to the managements since they are based almost wholly on observations of teachers and do not include analysis of provision; and to the public since they give an inadequate and often misleading view of what the education system is supposed to be doing. They merely give the impression that the state is vigilantly supervising the schools. They do not even begin to offer satisfactorily the accountability we owe to society.[63]

Dr Gatherer would prefer to see HMIs encouraging a process of self-evaluation, which would allow each school to look at the various aspects of its service in a critical and constructive manner. This is close to the view held by the late William Boyd, a former Head of the Education Department at Glasgow University, that 'school inspection [is] not compatible with the dignity of a learned profession'[64] — a position that could only be sustained if there was greater public confidence in the quality of the educational service than exists at present. In any case, it is worth pointing out that HMIs resisted the publication of school reports not on the grounds that they could do their job better in other ways but on the very self-interested grounds that they were afraid of defamation suits. This, incidentally, may help to explain the relentlessly bland character of many of the reports. The essential point, however, is that high-principled ideas about the best means of securing effective public accountability have not featured in the inspectorate's attempt to defend its own anonymity. On the contrary, its response could not unfairly be described as *un*principled and designed to ensure the accountability of everybody but the inspectorate.

A major part of the problem with HMI reports is the inexplicitness of the criteria on which they are based. It is apparent that commitment to certain approved ideas underlies the assessments that are made, but these are rarely made explicit and are certainly not defended at a conceptual level. Instead, an implicit value system is conveyed as a distillation of 'good practice'. There is no real effort to justify the designation of certain forms of teaching as representative of 'good practice', and the suspicion arises that HMI approval depends on adherence to the latest fashions. What is lacking is an appreciation of the very simple fact that good teaching comes in a variety of forms, both 'traditional' and 'progressive', and that intelligent, reflective teachers will seek to capitalise on, and extend, their own particular strengths rather than mimic an approved model that may not suit their personalities or their educational principles.

When it comes to HMI reports on specific topics, as distinct from those on individual schools, the problem of the criteria on which judgements are based is intensified by the fact that often members of the inspectorate are evaluating the results of policies that they themselves were responsible for introducing. That this is an undesirable situation is fully appreciated by Rendle:

> The Inspectorate's close involvement at all levels of the educational system does mean that it may be concerned with the assessment of standards of performance in the setting of which it played a large part in the first place ... The situation is open to the theoretical objection ... that the Inspectorate's involvement in the recommendation and development of new standards might conflict with their eventual judgement of the suitability of those standards, as achieved, for meeting the requirements of pupils, students and the nation at large.[65]

A sceptic might extrapolate from this the likelihood that, when the Munn and Dunning reforms come to be evaluated in a few years, the inspectorate will have a very strong vested interest in ensuring that the report presents a favourable picture, whatever is actually happening on the ground. That, however, is speculative. A more reliable view can be formed from looking at the experience of the past. Two examples will have to suffice.

In 1965 the SED published a report entitled *Primary Education in Scotland*, the product of the deliberations of a committee of teachers, HMIs, college of education lecturers, and others. This document, which came to be known as the *Primary Memorandum*, is usually regarded as a watershed publication, in the sense that it seemed to give official departmental support to 'progressive' and 'child-centred' teaching methods and advocated a move away from more formal didactic techniques. In fact, this view has recently been challenged by Frank McEnroe, himself a primary headteacher. McEnroe argues that 'the *Memorandum*, in spite of frequent references to liberal sentiments, envisages education as an instrument for promoting the value system of a reified society'.[66] Nevertheless, in the years following 1965, the *Memorandum* was projected as a progressive document, with HMIs acting as the principal propagandists on its behalf. In 1980 an HMI report on *Learning and Teaching in Primary 4 and Primary 7* appeared. Although it was not specifically designed as a review of the effects of the *Primary Memorandum*, it makes a number of direct references to the earlier publication and concludes:

> Since 1965, 'the Memorandum' has materially influenced the primary school system and much of its approach has become a fact of our educational lives . . .
> HM Inspectors have reported a steady advance and improvement in the state of our primary schools since 1965, and the survey now underlines that message.[67]

The P4-P7 Report is not, however, entirely uncritical. Indeed, it suggests that, while primary teachers are very competent at promoting literacy and numeracy, they are less successful in creative and aesthetic fields. The result is that the curriculum of many children is not as broad as it ought to be. In other words, many of the 'progressive' recommendations of the *Primary Memorandum* have not made as much impact as is often supposed. What is interesting about this conclusion, apart from the doubt it casts on the inspectorate's capacity for consistency of argument, is that it raises a series of critical, interpretative questions which are blithely ignored. It is assumed that teachers 'still feel threatened by the changes of recent years'[68] and are therefore less adventurous than they ought to be. There is no serious evaluation of the continuing validity of the recommendations of the *Primary Memorandum*, no assessment of the effectiveness of the inspectorate in convincing teachers of the soundness of its principles, and no exploration of the underlying reasons for the inherent conservatism of the teaching force. The final section of the report, which consists of five lines, refers vaguely to 'the need to preserve breadth in the curriculum; and the importance of maintaining and supporting a teaching force of quality and imagination'.[69] What is implied is that, where blame is to be apportioned, it is the teachers who are at fault, not the policy-makers or their agents. Evidently the 'progressivism' of the *Primary Memorandum* does not extent to shared responsibility for failures by the leadership class.

A similar exercise in inspectorial hand-washing combined with proprietorial self-esteem can be seen in the 1984 report, *Learning and Teaching in Scottish Secondary Schools: School Management*. This reviews the effects of a 1971 Green Paper and a 1972 Circular which led to a new structure of promoted posts in secondary schools.[70] There was a general increase in the number of promoted posts, partly brought about by the rapid development of the guidance system, which was intended to provide for vocational, curricular and personal counselling for pupils throughout their school career. Both at the time and subsequently criticisms of the new arrangements were expressed: on the grounds, for example, that they had little to do with educational motives, that they were used as a means of avoiding a general salary increase for all teachers, and as a way of covering shortages in particular subjects by promoting people for reasons of expediency rather than ability. Despite this the 1984 report concludes that 'the structure introduced by Circular 826 was well conceived and is operating satisfactorily'.[71] Reservations are, however, expressed about the tendency among promoted staff to view 'management' purely in routine, organisational terms instead of as a continuing process of policy generation and refinement, especially with regard to the curriculum. Interestingly, the report is careful to distance HMIs from both the cause of, and the responses to, this situation: 'As employers, education authorities have a unique responsibility to take a lead in these matters'.[72] Teacher associations and colleges of education are also identified as parties who ought to devote attention to the problem. Nevertheless, there are definite limits to the preparedness of the SED to distance itself from future developments. The passing on of responsibility is one thing. The passing on of power is quite another. Thus the final sentence of the report reads: 'The Department might be the most appropriate agent for bringing together the interested parties to establish a programme for action'.[73]

## Conclusion

The members of Her Majesty's Inspectorate can be regarded as powerful and important figures in Scotland's educational leadership class. Their power and importance depend on a number of things: their willingness to conform to the established conventions within the SED and the Scottish Office; their skill in avoiding situations where they might have to justify their actions in public; their capacity to manipulate the patronage system to ensure that like-minded individuals are appointed to key positions in major educational bodies. As a consequence, they have been generally successful in projecting an image of themselves as extremely able and enlightened men and women. That reputation is not fully justified. A close examination of the evidence reveals that the 'democratic' and 'progressive' policies which they advocate for others are often directly in conflict with the role they themselves assume within the government machine and exercise within Scottish education. Moreover, a study of their published writings suggests that their contribution to Scottish educational policy and practice has been less distinguished than is often supposed. Undoubtedly the inspectorate contains men and women of talent. Their intelligence, however, is often misused. It is directed as much at trying to maintain the secure position which they themselves enjoy as at the advancement of the educational service as a whole. The process whereby their ostensible functions are subverted needs to be understood in relation to the exercise of political power and the tendency of well-established bureaucracies to place the interests of members above those of the public.

*Notes and References*

1. *Education (Scotland) Act*, 1980, section 66. The wording of the relevant section (section 67) in the *Education (Scotland) Act*, 1962, is almost identical, but whereas the earlier statute refers to inspection as a 'duty' of the Secretary of State, the later one describes it as a 'power'.
2. Quoted in S. Leslie Hunter, *The Scottish Educational System*, 2nd edition, Pergamon, Oxford, 1972, p. 34.
3. T.R. Bone, *School Inspection in Scotland 1840–1966*, SCRE, Edinburgh, 1968, p. 248.
4. *Ibid.*, p. 242.
5. *Ibid.*, p. 235.
6. W.A. Gatherer, 'The boss's job', *TESS*, May 25, 1984, p. 16.
7. Bone, *op. cit.*, p. 247.
8. P. Rendle, *Scrutiny of HM Inspectors of Schools*, Report to Mr Alex Fletcher MP, Parliamentary Under Secretary of State for Industry and Education, Scottish Office, July 1981, para. 3.7. Hereafter referred to as the *Rendle Report*.
9. See 'HMIs criticized as reports go public', *TESS*, December 2, 1983, p. 1. and 'Who inspects the Inspectorate', *TESS*, December 9, 1983, p. 6. The second article is an extract from Mr Griffiths' speech, and all quotations are taken from it.
10. Scottish Information Office Factsheet 15, *Scottish Education*, n.d., p. 16.
11. Andrew McPherson, 'An Angle on the Geist: Persistence and Change in the Scottish Educational Tradition', in W.M. Humes and H.M. Paterson (eds), *Scottish Culture and Scottish Education 1800–1980*, John Donald, Edinburgh, 1983, p. 231.
12. See *Rendle Report*, Appendix F.
13. *Ibid.*, para. 5.4.
14. *Ibid.*, Appendix D.
15. *Ibid.*, para. 6.1.
16. *Ibid.*, para. 6.1.
17. *Ibid.*, para. 3.5.
18. *Ibid.*, para. 1.1.
19. *Ibid.*, Appendix A, para. 1.
20. *Ibid.*, para. 5.1.
21. See 'SED appointments hint at radical change of emphasis', *TESS*, July 2, 1982, p. 1.
22. *Rendle Report*, para. 6.13.
23. *Ibid.*, para. 6.15.
24. *Ibid.*, para. 6.14.
25. *Ibid.*, Appendix E, para. 7.
26. *Ibid.*, Appendix E, para. 1.
27. *Ibid.*, Appendix H.
28. *Ibid.*, para. 4.28.
29. *Ibid.*, para. 4.23.
30. *Ibid.*, para. 4.23.
31. *Ibid.*, para. 4.24.

32. *Ibid.*, para. 4.40.
33. *Ibid.*, para. 4.43. Rendle's italics.
34. *Ibid.*, para. 4.45.
35. *Ibid.*, para. 11.14.
36. Letter from the Executive Committee of the HMI (Scotland) Section of the Association of First Division Civil Servants, dated November 15, 1982, to Mr W.B. Ritchie, Manpower Services Division, Scottish Office, para.1. The process by which a copy of this letter was obtained is not without interest. A report by Neil Munro in the *TESS* of May 20, 1983 referred to its contents and stated that the letter had 'been lodged in the library of Old St. Andrew's House in Edinburgh. Under new rules introduced last year, the public has access to certain restricted Government papers'. An enquiry by the present writer to the Scottish Office Library, requesting a copy of the letter, at first produced no response. A second enquiry elicited a reply from Ms. E.M. Macdonald (designation unspecified) which contained the statement: 'The document is no longer in St. Andrew's House Library'. She suggested, however, that Mr J.G. Morris, HMCI, Chairman of the inspectorate section of the Association of First Division Civil Servants, would be able to supply the information required. A letter to Mr Morris produced a very prompt and helpful response, including a copy of the elusive document. His reply ended: 'I am sorry that you have had this difficulty in gaining access to the material which you require'.
37. *Ibid.*, para. 2.
38. *Ibid.*, para. 2.
39. *Ibid.*, para. 2.
40. *Ibid.*, para. 2.
41. *Ibid.*, para. 2.
42. Association of First Division Civil Servants, *Annual Report*, 1982, para. 188.
43. *Ibid.*, para. 188.
44. *Ibid.*, para. 189.
45. *Scrutiny of HM Inspectorate: Policy Statement by the Secretary of State for Scotland*, March 1983. Hereafter referred to as *Secretary of State's Policy Statement on HM Inspectorate.*
46. *Ibid.*, para. 2.2.
47. *Ibid.*, para. 3.1.
48. *Ibid.*, para. 3.1.
49. SED, *The Education of Pupils with Learning Difficulties*, HMSO, Edinburgh, 1978.
50. SED, *Learning and Teaching in Primary 4 and Primary 7*, HMSO, Edinburgh, 1980.
51. SED, *Teaching and Learning in the Senior Stages of the Scottish Secondary School*, HMSO, Edinburgh, 1983.
52. SED, *Learning and Teaching in Scottish Secondary Schools: School Management*, HMSO, Edinburgh, 1984.
53. *Secretary of State's Policy Statement on HM Inspectorate*, para. 3.1.
54. *Ibid.*, para. 3.1.
55. *Rendle Report*, para. 7.2.
56. SED, St. Roch's Secondary School, Glasgow, Strathclyde Region, Report of an Inspection in October/November 1983, para. 3.07.
57. *Ibid.*, para. 4.06.
58. SED, Newbigging Primary School, near Carnoustie, Tayside Region, Report of an Inspection in September 1983, p. 1.
59. SED, Rockfield Primary School, Oban, Strathclyde Region, Report of an Inspection in September 1983, para. 5.00.

60. SED, Newbattle High School, Lothian Region, Report of an Inspection in October 1983, para. 6.1.

61. SED, St. Thomas's RC Primary School, Wishaw, Strathclyde Region, Report of an Inspection in October/November 1983, para. 2.01.

62. SED, Grove Academy, Tayside Region, Report of an Inspection in November 1983.

63. Dr Gatherer's remarks first appeared in the Newsletter of the Association of Educational Advisers. They were reported in the *TESS*, April 13, 1984, p. 1.

64. See Bone, *op. cit.*, p. 248.

65. *Rendle Report*, para. 4.46.

66. F.J. McEnroe, 'Freudianism, Bureaucracy and Scottish Primary Education', in Humes and Paterson (eds), *op. cit.*, p. 244.

67. *Learning and Teaching in Primary 4 and Primary 7*, p. 54.

68. *Ibid.*, p. 54.

69. *Ibid.*, p. 55.

70. SED, *The Structure of Promoted Posts in Secondary Schools in Scotland*, 1971, and Circular 826, *The Structure of Promoted Posts in Secondary Schools in Scotland*, 1972.

71. *Learning and Teaching in Scottish Secondary Schools: School Management*, p.38.

72. *Ibid.*, p.38.

73. *Ibid.*, p.38.

# 5
# *The CCC — Consultation or Control?*

The aim of this chapter is to examine in some detail the role assumed by one of the most important educational quangos in Scotland, the Consultative Committee on the Curriculum (CCC). A proper appreciation of the position the Committee now occupies, and in particular its relation to the SED and to classroom teachers, requires an account of its origins and development as well as an analysis of its present structure. In addition, the system through which people are appointed to key positions within the CCC needs to be investigated. It should be said in advance that the picture that will emerge is complex, for the CCC is not an organisation marked by simplicity of form and function. That complexity must, however, be confronted directly if the influence exerted by the Committee is to be understood.

## Origins and Early Development

The CCC was set up as an advisory body by the Secretary of State for Scotland in October, 1965. Its creation can be regarded as part of a wider process designed to restructure and redirect work formerly undertaken by the Advisory Council on Education in Scotland. The first Advisory Council was established under the Education (Scotland) Act of 1918, but it was not until after its reconstitution in 1942 that it began to have a significant impact on educational thinking, if not on practice. Its 1947 report on *Secondary Education* is still regarded by many as possibly the most impressive document ever to have been published under an SED imprint.[1] As a strategy for action, however, it was consistently ignored, and Leslie Hunter has remarked that 'the work of the Council seemed to be gradually edged out in favour of reports written by panels of Inspectors'[2] — for example, the 1950 report on *The Primary School in Scotland*[3] and the 1955 report on *Junior Secondary Education.*[4] No new Advisory Council was appointed after 1961. It was against this background that the CCC appeared.

As is to be expected, the structure and function of the Committee have been subject to change and development. Its initial remit required it to maintain a general oversight of the whole school curriculum (both primary and secondary); to draw the Secretary of State's attention to any aspect of the curriculum which seemed to call for consideration by specialist bodies; and to give the Secretary of State its comments on the recommendations of working parties appointed by him on the advice of the CCC.[5] Towards these ends, a number of sub-committees and working parties on particular aspects of the curriculum were established and a series of reports and curriculum papers published. Increasingly, however, it was felt that a standing committee system, with powers to follow through the impact of reports and to promote curricular development in specific areas, was necessary.[6]

By 1976 there were nine such committees — called Central Committees — on English, Modern Languages, Mathematics, Science, Technical Education, Religious Education, Social Subjects, Physical Education and Primary Education. The work of some, but not all, of the Central Committees was supported by four curriculum development centres set up between 1967 and 1971 and by the Primary Education Support Service established in 1975.[7]

As an example of the sort of activities undertaken, reference can be made to the first Central Committee on English under the chairmanship of W. A. Gatherer, then an HMI, later Chief Adviser to Lothian Region. Between 1967 and 1972 the Committee published a series of five Bulletins on various aspects of English teaching.[8] These were widely discussed by teachers, a process which was facilitated by the creation of a system of local development committees throughout the country. The Bulletins quickly became required reading for prospective English teachers in the colleges of education. In addition, a Centre for Information on the Teaching of English was established at Moray House College of Education in September, 1967; this was, in fact, the first of the curriculum development centres to be set up, designed 'to facilitate the exchange of information on English teaching and the promotion of research and development by teachers themselves'.[9]

The system of Central Committees up to 1976 certainly provided a stimulus to development work, but their precise relation to the CCC itself and to the development centres came to be regarded as unsatisfactory. In the words of the Fourth Report of the CCC:

> The growth of standing committees and their supporting services proved to be somewhat arbitrary. There was no provision to help central committees to develop their subjects unless they were associated with a development centre. Significantly, the CCC was not formally responsible for the standing committees or for the allocation of funds to the supporting services. As a consequence the CCC appeared to be detached from the interpretation of its recommendations by the policy making committees and implementation by the development centres.[10]

These concerns led to a review of the whole structure and a reconstitution of the CCC, with a much wider remit, in 1976. 'In effect, this remit gave the new CCC control over the existing agencies for curriculum development, power to appoint new committees (subject to the approval of the Secretary of State) and authority to distribute the resources made available as it saw fit.'[11]

Three features resulting from the 1976 reconstitution are worthy of particular mention since they remain important in the present structure. The first was the setting up of two major policy committees, accountable to the full CCC, with responsibility for a sub-structure of committees in their respective fields. The Committee on Secondary Education (COSE) assumed general oversight of Central Committees covering subjects taught in secondary schools, while the Committee on Primary Education (COPE) took over from the former Scottish Central Committee on Primary Education and became responsible for the work of a number of sub-committees dealing with particular topics (for example, language arts, environmental studies, assessment). Both COPE and COSE met for the first time in 1977.[12]

The second important feature was the coordination of the work of the formerly independent development centres and the Primary Education Support Service under the umbrella of the Scottish Curriculum Development Service (SCDS), often described in official publications as the 'executive arm' of the CCC.[13] One of the aims behind this move, apart from a desire to give the main CCC body more authority, was a concern to involve the centres in a wider range of tasks and reduce their identification with particular subjects.

Thirdly, a full-time secretariat was appointed, consisting of permanent officers of the SED and headed by a member of the inspectorate, Mr D. R. McNicoll, specially seconded for this purpose. Later in the chapter it will be suggested that the role played by the secretariat is worthy of close scrutiny in relation to the CCC's perception of its functions and its links with the SED.

What significance can be attached to the establishment and early development of the CCC? As with many new institutions, it had a certain liberating effect at the outset, and the results can be seen in an extensive list of publications, a substantial amount of in-service activity at local level (made easier by the rapid growth of the advisory service in the late '60s and early '70s[14]) and an increased awareness of the importance of curriculum issues in the educational process as a whole. Indeed, the most widely discussed curriculum document in recent years — the report on *The Structure of the Curriculum in the Third and Fourth Years of the Scottish Secondary School* (the Munn Report)[15] — was the work of a sub committee of the CCC appointed in 1974. All of this can be made to sound impressive, and some commentators have even gone so far as to locate the growth of the CCC within a wider movement of democratic reform in Scottish education. It was noted in Chapter 1 that James Scotland has argued that the setting up of the CCC in 1965, when viewed in conjunction with a number of other developments — such as the establishment of the SCEEB (now the SEB) under the Education (Scotland) Act of 1963 and the GTC under the Teaching Council (Scotland) Act of 1965 — marked 'the beginning of an overt process in which [the Secretary of State] devolved many of his duties to other authorities, effecting an appreciable redistribution of power'.[16] Mr Scotland's optimism may have seemed justified when he offered this analysis in 1969, but only three years later, in 1972, another observer, Leslie Hunter, remarked that, notwithstanding the use of 'advice, suggestion, persuasion' rather than heavy-handed direction, 'control from the centre is a reality'.[17] This difference of interpretation highlights the way in which potentially liberating institutions can, under bureaucratic pressures, quickly become agents of restriction. The CCC's recurring concern with questions of structure and organisation can be seen as symptomatic of a desire to ensure that curriculum development proceeded in a way that was acceptable to policy-makers. No doubt some of the motives underlying the reconstitution of 1976 were benign and reflected a feeling that an overall, coordinated strategy was required. But other motives can also be detected — most notably, a feeling that the Central Committees had become too autonomous and ought to be subject to clear lines of authority and responsibility. As the Fourth Report states; 'The terms of new remits made these committees' relationships with other committees, and in particular COSE, unequivocal'.[18] COSE and COPE, in turn, became agencies for 'the implementation of the parent body's decisions'[19] (that is, the decisions of the CCC itself). As will be seen shortly, the interrelationships between the different parts of the CCC turned out to be less unequivocal than was hoped, but the intention was plain enough — to establish a firmly demarcated hierarchy. An unhealthy corollary was a growing preoccupation with procedural rather than substantive issues. Such a preoccupation is characteristic of bureaucracies, and it can easily have a deadening effect on initiative and innovation. As organisations expand and become more complex, so the strategies of control exercised by the leadership class develop in style and sophistication. This process has continued up to the present, but before an analysis of the current position is offered, reference has to be made to a further review of the CCC's work conducted in 1979–80.

## The Rayner Study

In July, 1979 the Conservative government announced that, as part of its stated policy to increase efficiency and reduce costs, the Scottish Office would carry out a study of the Secretary of State's involvement in curriculum development. The study was directed by the Earl of Mansfield, Minister of State at the Scottish Office, and was undertaken in consultation with Sir Derek Rayner, Joint Managing Director of Marks and Spencer Limited. Its precise terms of reference were as follows:

> To consider and make recommendations on the Secretary of State's involvement in curriculum development and on the constitution, terms of reference and organisation of the Consultative Committee on the Curriculum (CCC), its committee structure and the Scottish Curriculum Development Service (SCDS), having particular regard to the costs and resources involved.[20]

Provisional conclusions were published in a consultative paper dated February, 1980 and, after a period of further consideration, a final statement was issued in September, 1980.[21]

It will be instructive to mention some of the issues which were identified as important before outlining the principal changes which resulted from the Rayner study. Three main problems were noted at the outset: the size and apparent complexity of the CCC structure; its inflexibility of structure, in terms of standing committees and permanent staff; the costs involved, especially the potential demand for additional finance if the structure continued to develop along existing lines. There was an implicit recognition of the tendency of all institutions to seek to assume more authority, and doubt was expressed about whether central government 'should continue to take responsibility for services which might more appropriately be provided by education authorities, colleges of education, or even associations of subject teachers'.[22] Considerations of economy doubtless lay behind these observations, but the question of the relative contribution of different parts of the system is an important one, especially if principles like democracy and decentralisation are to mean anything. Unfortunately, however, this brief (and probably accidental) foray into the realm of social theory was not sustained: the actual recommendations were relatively modest and subsequently became even more modest in the light of CCC and other representations.

Membership of the CCC was broadened to include parental, industrial and commercial interests, but educationalists remained very much in the majority. The status of SED officials within the CCC was altered, although the precise significance of the change is open to argument. Before 1980, the Chairman of the CCC had been the Secretary of the SED. It was felt, however, that 'the CCC should be seen to be in a position to give [the Secretary of State] entirely independent advice'.[23] and so, henceforth, the Chairmanship would be occupied by someone from outside the Department. The phrase 'seen to be' would appear to be critical. The first external Chairman was Dr James Munn, who was subsequently reappointed for a second term of office. SED representatives (whether career civil servants or HMIs) on the CCC would no longer serve as ordinary members but as 'assessors';[24] in other words, they would clearly be present 'on behalf of the Secretary of State'.[25] They could, however, continue to serve as full members within the sub-structure. These reforms have sometimes been presented as evidence of Scottish Office enlightenment and liberality of outlook, but they need to be understood in relation to the whole system of appointments, a topic which will be examined later in the chapter.

The SCDS was pruned, though not dramatically. It had originally been proposed that it should be located in a single centre but, in the event, the decision was that its activities should be concentrated at three centres instead of five. Callendar Park College of Education was to be closed anyway, and its work in the primary field was transferred to Moray House. Also to be transferred to Moray House was developmental work in modern languages and music previously carried out at the Aberdeen centre (in fact, music was subsequently transferred to Dundee). The two other remaining centres were at Jordanhill and Dundee Colleges of Education. Complete centralisation was still said to be 'a principal consideration'[26] in the longer term but, in a delightful piece of officialese, the September 1980 statement managed to point in both directions at once: the Secretary of State considered 'that a gradual approach is necessary at this stage which, while evolving towards centralisation, would not rule out the possibility that some elements of dispersal might eventually be retained'.[27]

There were some changes in the relation between the CCC and its satellite committees but, again, these were relatively minor. A proposal that membership of COPE and COSE should be restricted solely to members of the CCC was withdrawn. Furthermore, 'the Secretary of State ... accepted the view that a standing structure of small committees and consultative panels covering main subjects and aspects of the primary and secondary curricula should be maintained ... '[28] Approval was given for the setting up of new committees on Special Educational Needs and Gaelic which would be responsible to both COPE and COSE, and on Expressive Arts in the Primary School, while reconsideration of the need for committees on Classics, Art, Drama, Nautical Subjects and Guidance was urged.

If these changes are assessed in the light of the three principal problems identified at the outset of the Rayner exercise, it is hard to see how any significant advance was achieved in relation to any of them. There was, it is true, a reduction in the number of top-level committees — for example, the previously existing Appointments and Steering Committees were replaced by a smaller Executive Committee — but the main effect of this, as will be shown, was to concentrate power in the hands of a few people and increase opportunities for behind-the-scenes decision-making. Furthermore, at lower levels of the structure the framework of standing committees emerged relatively intact, and the reduction in the number of permanent staff required for curriculum development purposes was small (SCDS staff are, in any case, formally employees of colleges of education and can, therefore, be assigned to other duties). As for the desire to achieve savings, the success of the exercise can be measured against the published figures. In 1979/80, the total cost of all CCC activities — including SCDS, but excluding the secretariat — was £467,250.[29] It should be noted, however, that because of uncertainty arising from the Rayner study, a number of developments were postponed, and the full amount of grant available for that year (£536,000) was not used. By 1982/83 the figure had risen to £739,680, which, even allowing for inflation, represents an increase in real terms.[30] Expenditure on SCDS is the biggest single item by far, and it is certainly true that, with the closure of the Callendar Park centre in 1980 and the Aberdeen centre in 1982, its costs began to level off. Against this, however, it should be noted that during the period 1980–83 general committee expenses doubled and primary committee expenses almost trebled.

The important point to emphasise is that, by the criteria which the Rayner study itself established, the exercise could hardly claim to have been a startling success. Now, of course, those criteria can be challenged, a response which opens up a general argument about the best means of promoting curriculum development. Some comments on that issue will be offered later. For the moment, however, two related questions remain. What did the Rayner study achieve? And what did it show about the response of the Scottish educational bureaucracy to a potential threat?

Despite the fact that the Rayner enquiry was a failure in terms of its stated aims, it performed a useful *political* function as far as the SED was concerned. Existing arrangements were publicly validated by the study. The Minister responsible for education could now say that the CCC had been closely scrutinised and had emerged with credit from the exercise. As the final paragraph of the September, 1980 paper states:

> Since the CCC was set up in 1965, it has given valuable advice on various aspects of the curriculum and has laid a secure foundation for further development. The Secretary of State is confident that the changes set out in this paper will strengthen the work of the CCC and enable it to meet the curricular needs of schools in the 1980s.[31]

Such statements of confidence are enough to sustain an organisation for several years, no matter how much the facts may point to another conclusion. What is 'seen to be' the case is, for most governments, more important than what actually *is* the case. By these alternative political standards, then, the Rayner study did everything that was expected of it.

Similarly, for the members of the CCC, the enquiry seemed to provide a complete vindication. Mr McNicoll, the Secretary, observed in November, 1980: 'The fact that the CCC and its structure have survived relatively unscathed is a tribute to the principles on which the CCC is based and to those persons who have worked within its organisation over the years.'[32] That is one interpretation. Another is that the review represented a 'tribute' to the institutional inertia of the upper levels of Scottish education. When it was first set up, the Rayner study threatened to undermine the position of CCC members, particularly the full-time staff in the secretariat and SCDS. There was, however, a successful mobilisation of forces against any attempt at major reconstruction. Naturally, the counter-attack was not mounted in a crude or strident fashion; tactics of that kind would have been unproductive. Instead, the CCC reacted in the 'positive' and 'constructive' way which characterises successful lobbying in most areas of government activity; in this, the members were probably well advised by the secretariat. Thus, for example, in responding to the consultative document of February, 1980, it was conceded that 'there is some justification in the criticism that our structure is complex and inflexible', and selective 'pruning' and 'redeployment of resources' were considered possible.[33] Again, it was suggested that 'one secret of cost effectiveness lies in the careful fashioning of remits and the creation of sensible time limits',[34] a statement in which the term 'fashioning' seems to carry resonances beyond those intended. The general tenor of the response was 'interpretative and supportive'[35] rather than combative, and this strategy clearly paid dividends. Overall, then, the episode provided an interesting illustration of bureaucratic 'defence mechanisms', in both the literal and psychological senses of that term. Whether it did anything to help the supposed beneficiaries of the educational process — pupils, their parents, and the community at large — is another matter.

## Structure and Organisation

The present organisational pattern of the CCC is indicated in the table given below.[36] Apart from a tendency to acronymania, several features invite comment. First, the most important functions, in terms of decision-making and policy implementation, are carried out by the main body of the CCC together with COPE and COSE, all of which have small executive committees that are designed to ensure continuity between formal meetings and that are empowered to act on behalf of the membership as a whole. This executive function is significant and raises the question of whether, in practice, power resides with a relatively small inner circle of members. Between 1980 and 1983 the full CCC met on eleven

## ORGANISATION OF THE CCC

| CONSULTATIVE COMMITTEE ON THE CURRICULUM | | |
|---|---|---|
| COMMITTEE ON PRIMARY EDUCATION (COPE) | EXECUTIVE COMMITTEE (CCC) | COMMITTEE ON SECONDARY EDUCATION (COSE) |
| EXECUTIVE COMMITTEE (COPE) | | EXECUTIVE COMMITTEE (COSE) |

**SCOTTISH (PRIMARY) COMMITTEES OR ADVISORY GROUPS**

- LANGUAGE ARTS (SCOLA)
- MICRO COMPUTING
- LEARNING AND TEACHING
- HOME/SCHOOL/COMMUNITY (SCHSC)
- EARLY EDUCATION (from 1986)

**COMMITTEES OR ADVISORY GROUPS REPORTING TO CCC, COPE and/or COSE**

- EDUCATION/INDUSTRY (SEIC)
- SPECIAL EDUCATIONAL NEEDS (COSPEN)
- COMPUTING (MEC)
- EDUCATION 14–18
- GAELIC (COG)
- TECHNOLOGY (COT)

**NATIONAL PROJECTS AND DEVELOPMENT PROGRAMMES**

- FOUNDATIONS OF WRITING
- ENVIRONMENTAL STUDIES
- EXPRESSIVE ARTS
- SCOTTISH RESOURCES
- INTERNATIONAL AND MULTI-CULTURAL EDUCATION
- EQUAL OPPORTUNITIES FOR THE SEXES
- EDUCATION 10–14
- EDUCATION 14–16 (MUNN/DUNNING)
- EDUCATION 16–18 (ACTION PLAN)

**CENTRAL (SECONDARY) COMMITTEES OR ADVISORY GROUPS**

- ART
- BUSINESS SUBJECTS
- CLASSICS
- COMPUTING
- DRAMA
- ENGLISH
- GUIDANCE
- HOME ECONOMICS
- MATHEMATICS
- MODERN LANGUAGES
- MUSIC
- PHYSICAL EDUCATION
- RELIGIOUS EDUCATIO
- SCIENCE
- SOCIAL SUBJECTS
- TECHNICAL EDUCATIO

| EXECUTIVE AND DEVELOPMENT SERVICES | |
|---|---|
| SECRETARY (CHIEF OFFICER) | |
| SERVICE LIAISON GROUP (SLG) | |
| CCC SECRETARIAT | SCOTTISH CURRICULUM DEVELOPMENT SERVICE |
| Administrative, Executive and Clerical Officers from SED | Directors, Curriculum Officers, Information Officers, Graphic Artists, Administrative and Clerical Officers |
| New St. Andrew's House, Edinburgh | Curriculum Development Centres, DUNDEE, EDINBURGH, GLASGOW |

occasions (including two two-day conferences), COPE on ten occasions (including one two-day conference), and COSE on eleven occasions (including one two-day conference). This represents an average of less than four meetings per year for each committee and, given the range of responsibilities to be carried out, it would be surprising if, in practice, many decisions were not taken by the executive committees and simply approved by the full bodies at a later date.

The creation of the Executive Committee (CCC) had been recommended in the Secretary of State's consultative paper of February, 1980. Previously the same tasks had been carried out by standing sub-committees (including a Steering Committee and an Appointments Committee), and it may have been thought that a single committee would be more efficient. Possibly it was also felt that the term 'Steering Committee' carried certain undesirable connotations. The intention was that the new Executive Committee 'would be competent to act and to ratify actions taken by the Secretariat between meetings of the main body and ... would also take over the work of the ... Appointments Committee'.[37] In an interesting form of words, suggestive of a commendable spirit of self-sacrifice, the Fifth Report of the CCC, covering the period 1980–83, states: 'the Executive relieves the main body of many of the burdens relating to finance, appointments and administrative references'.[38] It is unclear what exactly is meant by 'administrative references', but the lack of clarity may not be deliberate. It would seem, however, that the powers assumed by the Executive Committee of the CCC are considerable. The lack of detailed information about its activities in the Fifth Report does not serve to undermine this interpretation. Experience readers of minutes and other official documents will appreciate that such items are often as interesting for what they conceal as what they reveal.

The sub-structure of the CCC now includes 'Scottish Committees' on various aspects of primary education, which are responsible to COPE, and 'Central Committees' which are responsible to COSE. In addition, there are a number of Project and Development Programmes which have their own committees and which often cut across the conventional primary/secondary division. This aspect of the work of the CCC has increased in recent years and reflects a move towards cross-sector and multi-disciplinary enquiries, as well as a concern to respond to social change, evident, for example, in the programme on equal opportunities for the sexes.

The extent to which the Project and Development Programmes enjoy the benefit of what the Fifth Report calls 'devolution of authority'[39] is questionable. Several of the studies — for example, 'Education 14–16' and 'Education 16–18' — were undertaken as part of government programmes in which the CCC acted as functionary rather than primary agent. The remit of the 'Education 14–16' committee was quite explicit about its functions and subordinate role:

(i) To advise the CCC and the Committee on Secondary Education on matters related to the responsibilities of the CCC under the Government's Munn and Dunning Development Programme;

(ii) To carry out related tasks in co-operation with the Department's Development Unit and other agencies.[40]

As an additional insurance against any incipient delinquency on the part of members, there was unusually strong representation from the secretariat, the SED and SCDS. The whole process by which people are appointed to serve at the various levels of the CCC structure is central to an understanding of its mode of operation, and a separate section is devoted to this later in the chapter.

Two other aspects of the present structure invite comment — liaison with other bodies and the work of SCDS. Reference is made in Fifth Report to a 'considerable strengthening of links'[41] between 1980 and 1983 with, among others, the Scottish Examination Board, the Scottish Council for Educational Technology, the Scottish Council for Research in Education, the Scottish Council (Development and Industry) and the Manpower Services Commission. Evidently it takes more than two to quango. Contact also takes place on a fairly regular basis with a number of professional associations, such as the Association of Educational Advisers in Scotland, the Headteachers' Association of Scotland, the Educational Institute of Scotland and the Association of Directors of Education in Scotland. Add to this the 'various patterns of co-operation'[42] with local education authorities, colleges of education and the inspectorate, and the extensiveness of the network of connections becomes apparent. These links undoubtedly make it easier for certain developments to take place and may improve communication within the system as a whole, but they are also likely to reinforce the rather incestuous character of the leadership class in Scottish education. Furthermore, it tends to be assumed that links are, by definition, a good thing: their value, however, depends primarily on the quality of the ideas that are being promulgated and not on the simple fact that they exist.

On the SCDS front, the structural consequences of the Rayner review have led to the three remaining centres extending their roles. At present, the subject and area responsibilities are distributed as follows:

| | |
|---|---|
| Dundee Centre | Art, Mathematics, Music, Science, Technical Education, Nautical Studies, Microelectronics and Computing |
| Edinburgh Centre | Primary Education, English, Physical Education, Modern Languages, Gaelic, Drama, Education 10–14 |
| Glasgow Centre | Social Subjects, Business Subjects, Religious Education, Guidance, Home Economics, Special Educational Needs, Classics, Education/Industry, Equal Opportunities for the Sexes.[43] |

Despite the hope of simplifying the organisation of SCDS, it has been admitted that its responsibilities 'have become at once more extensive and more complex'.[44] The perceived solution to these problems is revealing with regard to the value system of the decision makers:

> To meet the needs of this changing situation and at the same time to provide a career structure for members of the SCDS, the CCC has created a small number of Principal and Senior Curriculum Officer posts intermediate between the Curriculum Officer and Director grades.[45]

The extremely hierarchical character of Scottish education has already been noted. It appears that the elaboration of hierarchies is seen by the CCC as an effective way of coping with increasing complexity of function within SCDS, although the basis of this confidence is not explained. Perhaps more fundamentally, the establishment of a career structure, with sharply defined levels of responsibility and reward, provides a good means of containing any potential disaffection within the ranks. The promise or prospect of advancement is likely to encourage a cautious attitude to the expression of criticism and a commitment to the structure as a whole. There seems, however, to be little awareness of the extent to which these consequences undermine much of the rhetoric which surrounds the CCC — most notably, its alleged commitment to a philosophy of equal partnership with classroom teachers. Moreover, by creating an élite cadre of permanent staff within SCDS, that flexibility of response which is said to be a mark of the new, improved CCC, is compromised. Ideas which represent a challenge to the dominant interest groups are unlikely to make their way through the sub-strata of working parties and development committees to see the light of day in the CCC itself. If, by any chance, they do, and, even more improbably, if they manage to capture the attention of some members of the CCC, there is always the filtering mechanism of the Executive Committee.

There is a further escape clause which serves to protect the 'integrity' of the whole structure. Formally, the CCC is only an advisory body. It has no statutory powers and, should anything go seriously wrong, the blame would lie elsewhere. The point was made very plainly in the First Report and, although subsequent reports have played it down — presumably because the increasingly interventionist and directive role adopted by the CCC (under the 'guidance' of the SED) has reduced its credibility — it would doubtless be restated with vigour should the need arise:

> While the Committee provides advice to the Secretary of State which he may publish and commend to education authorities and teachers, neither the Secretary of State nor the Scottish Education Department has any direct responsibility for the school curriculum. Education authorities ... acting with the advice of the heads of their schools and their teachers decide what shall, or shall not, be taught in their schools ... and it is for them to decide whether or not to accept any advice which is offered to them.[46]

## Present Remit and Priorities

At the time of writing the CCC was the Sixth to have been appointed, serving until August 31, 1986, its precise terms of reference requiring it to:

i. Keep under review the curriculum of schools in Scotland;

ii. Identify any aspects of the curriculum which call for investigation and development; with the agreement of the Secretary of State establish committees, including committees established jointly with other bodies, to carry out such investigations; consider the reports of such committees and advise the Secretary of State on further action;
iii. Promote and keep under review a programme of curriculum development within funds made available by the Secretary of State;
iv. Issue guidance on the curriculum to education authorities;
v. Advise the Secretary of State on any other matters relating to the curriculum which he may refer to the Committee, or which it wishes to consider;
vi. Maintain appropriate liaison with Government Departments, education authorities and other bodies;
vii. Have regard to the effects of economic and social changes, to the links between schools and further education, and to the implications for the organisation of schools, for accommodation and other resources and for teacher training; and
viii. Act in accordance with any direction which the Secretary of State may from time to time make.[47]

This remit is very similar to that of the Fifth CCC, though clause vi is entirely new. Its inclusion would seem to lend support to the view that CCC activity has, increasingly, been heavily circumscribed by government initiatives: the Munn/Dunning Development Programme, the 16–18 Action Plan and the Youth Training Scheme have all reduced its room for manoeuvre. In February, 1984 this was freely acknowledged in relation to secondary education:

> For the new few years the work of COSE will be firmly related to existing Government and CCC initiatives spanning the whole secondary curriculum and beyond: the CCC 10–14 Programme and the Government's 14–16 and 16–18 Programmes.[48]

In the primary sector, too, the field has been largely mapped out by a publication issued by the present COPE's predecessor, *Primary Education in the Eighties.*[49] A start has been made on 'the task of building on the Position Paper *Primary Education in the Eighties* ... and of considering the shape of a sub-structure which can take up and develop some of the issues raised in the Position Paper'.[50]

There are other signs of the Sixth CCC having had its priorities determined for it. The Fifth CCC had identified three issues requiring urgent attention:

(i) The need to rationalise the overcrowded curriculum;
(ii) The identification and development of knowledge and skills appropriate to future generations;
(iii) The definition and organisation of social education.[51]

In its initial review of its role, the Sixth CCC considered that 'redefined and expanded ... these areas should continue to represent its main priorities'.[52] Under (i) the importance of early education, including the pre-school years, will receive particular attention: under (ii) technology, microelectronics and computing will represent major themes; and under (iii) projects on international and multicultural education, and police and community issues will feature prominently.

All this suggests that continuity is now a major priority for the CCC, a view supported by the Chairman, Dr James Munn, who is on record as favouring a 'Steady as you go' policy.[53] There is obviously a case for a measure of continuity, as frequent changes of strategy would be confusing for teachers and would cause serious implementation problems, especially as there is always a time-lag between the adoption of a plan and its effective communication to the wider educational community. Too much emphasis on carrying through existing programmes does, however, have certain disadvantages. It tends to restrict the role of new members to a consideration of operational questions and limits their contribution to substantive policy discussions. If they happen to disagree with the views of their predecessors, they are likely to find the emphasis on operating within existing guidelines rather frustrating. This objection does, however, depend on two assumptions that may not be justified: first, that the CCC is actually intended by the SED to make a significant contribution to policy formulation; and secondly, that the people appointed to serve are selected because of their capacity to generate ideas. If, as some critics would maintain, the CCC is merely a 'front' organisation, which is designed to provide a cloak of respectability for SED-inspired directives, then questions of freedom of action will not be perceived as problematic, and those who are selected will be chosen for qualities other than creative thinking. This leads directly to a consideration of precisely how and why particular people are appointed and to an assessment of their adequacy for the tasks with which they are charged.

## Appointments and Personnel

The First CCC had twenty-four members. The Sixth, appointed after the streamlining Rayner exercise, has twenty-eight, not including SED, secretariat or SCDS representation. From the beginning there has been an insistence in official statements that members are appointed for their individual qualities rather than as representatives of particular interests. For example, in a Scottish Information Office publication of August, 1982 it is stated:

> Members of the main body of the CCC have been appointed by the Secretary of State on the basis of their personal knowledge and experience and in such a way as to give him independent advice which nevertheless reflects opinion in the education service as a whole and in the wider society. The Chairman and members (who are unpaid) are selected for their individual contribution and not as delegates of associations or other bodies.[54]

This system may be contrasted with those of the SEB, which consists largely of delegates of different sectors of the educational world (with the universities, teachers' organisations and COSLA being represented most strongly), and the GTC, to which members are elected on a constituency basis. On the face of it, the CCC method seems quite attractive: members apparently represent only themselves and are not under any obligation to speak on behalf of some external body. In practice, however, it is evident that some notion of representation is brought to bear on the composition of the Committee. The current membership,[55] for example, can be categorised as follows:

| | |
|---|---|
| Secondary Education | 7 |
| Primary Education | 3 |
| Higher Education | 5 |
| Further Education | 1 |
| Industry (Management) | 4 |
| Industry (Trades Unions) | 1 |
| Directorate | 3 |
| Advisory Service | 2 |
| Psychological Service | 1 |
| Parental Interests | 1 |

The principle of representativeness is also apparent in the geographical distribution of members: there is plainly an attempt to ensure that the different regions of Scotland have a voice in CCC discussions. This, it should be said, is a perfectly defensible position but, once again, it serves to qualify the claim that membership is entirely dependent on individual ability.

However, even if that claim is taken to mean simply that, within the constraints dictated by the need to reflect opinion 'in the education service as a whole and in the wider society', appointments are made on merit, certain questions arise which call for examination. How is merit defined, and who is responsible for identifying it? With regard to the first of these questions, several possible criteria might be postulated: academic achievement; successful teaching experience; previous involvement in curriculum work; relevant research and publications. Given that a good many people in Scottish education are likely to satisfy one or more of those criteria, some further requirements would seem to be called for. The history of CCC appointments suggests that these include recommendation from a reliable source, satisfactory service in part of the CCC sub-structure prior to appointment to the main body, and a reputation as someone who can work constructively and cooperatively within a committee framework. As soon as these additional qualities are brought into consideration, however, it is apparent that merit is being defined in terms of organisational as well as intellectual and professional virtues: dependence on 'reliable' sources, assessments of 'satisfactory' service, and of a capacity to work 'constructively' and 'cooperatively' presuppose a value system which attaches considerable weight to political acceptability. In other words, it assumes a consensus model of policy formulation and implementation in which the smooth running of the bureaucratic machine is a prime consideration. Whether such a model is conducive to the kind of independent, critical thinking which would seem to be a necessary prerequisite of worthwhile educational reform is open to doubt, but the key figures in the present set-up are not lacking in confidence about its success. Mr McNicoll, for example, has claimed:

> By bringing together on its committees and working parties individuals of proven wisdom and experience from every level of the education system the CCC provides a focus for the formulation of advice and guidance which is likely to be both constructive and palatable.[56]

It might be observed that 'palatability' would seem to be a somewhat limited criterion in assessing the *quality* of advice, but its invocation does lend support to the putative value system suggested above.

Recommendations for appointment come from a variety of 'reliable' sources (such as directors of education and college of education principals), but appointments to the CCC itself rest with the Secretary of State. In effect, this means that he relies on the patronage system managed by SED officials. As Secretary, Mr McNicoll is in a critical position in respect of communicating advice to his colleagues within the SED. Two other SED officials can be assumed to have played a leading part in the machinery of appointments. These are Miss P. A. Cox, a senior civil servant, who has been associated with the CCC, first as a full member, then as one of the Secretary of State's assessors, since May, 1976, and Mr A. D. Chirnside, Her Majesty's Depute Senior Chief Inspector of Schools, who, like Miss Cox, started as a member of the CCC (in his case in January, 1975) and then became an assessor after the Rayner exercise. Both Miss Cox (who moved from the SED to the Scottish Home and Health Department in 1985) and Mr Chirnside (who retired in 1984) have, in fact, had CCC connections for longer than Mr McNicoll, who commenced as Secretary in June, 1978.

Only one member of the CCC has had a longer association than Miss Cox and Mr Chirnside, and that is the present Chairman, Dr James Munn, whose service stretches as far back as 1968. In a 'Profile' article published in February, 1984 it was stated that Dr Munn's 'background has fashioned him to be Consensus Man'.[57] a role which accords well with the desired characteristics of CCC personnel. He served in the Indian Civil Service, taught modern languages in Glasgow and Stirlingshire schools, eventually becoming Rector of Cathkin High School, Glasgow in 1970, a post which he held until his retiral in the summer of 1983. He was also a member of the University Grants Committee for ten years. Early in 1984 he assumed a major additional responsibility as Chairman of the Manpower Services Commission in Scotland, an appointment which prompted one sceptical headteacher to speculate that 'perhaps Munn's job is to give the MSC respectability in educational circles'.[58]

That Dr Munn has a generally favourable view of the way of the world in Scottish education is to be expected, but he has explained his satisfaction in an interesting and revealing way:

> One of the reasons Scotland has been able to get ahead with so much educational change is the tradition of partnership between the SED or CCC and the education authorities which you can't always say exists south of the border. Scotland is also fortunate in its size and geography which makes it a cohesive unit for educational development. Most people in positions of influence know each other and meet regularly.[59]

Leaving aside the question of the inferences that might be drawn from the use of the conjunction 'or' to link the SED and the CCC, and the familiar appeal to a complacent form of nationalism — a form of nationalism that actually does a disservice to Scotland — the significant feature of this statement, as far as appointments are concerned, is its uncritical belief in the virtues of the enclosed network of communication which characterises the leadership class. In a context of this sort, one probable consequence is that those selected for advancement are likely to possess similar characteristics to the selectors. A measure of continuity of personnel may have something to commend it, but this type of continuity can very easily develop into a tradition of entrenched mediocrity.

When it comes to the sub-structure of the CCC, the Executive Committee is the channel through which recommendations are filtered and appointments proposed. Decisions are then presented to the full CCC for ratification. The Executive Committee (CCC) consists of the Chairman (Dr Munn), the Secretary (Mr McNicoll), the Chairmen of COPE and COSE (Mr D. L. Fulton and Sister Maire Gallagher) and three other members, plus one SED assessor and two SCDS officers. No detailed account of the work of this committee is available, as all matters relating to staffing and appointments are regarded as confidential. There is, however, some evidence to suggest that, even within the Executive Committee, not all members are actively involved in the business of making appointments. A former Chairman of COPE, Mr George Paton, has said that even he did not fully understand the process by which certain names 'emerged'.[60] If this is so, then authority for appointments may effectively be confined to the Chairman and Secretary in consultation with SCDS officers and the SED assessor.

It would perhaps be an exaggeration to say that all those appointed to the CCC and its sub-structure are consensus men and women. Many are undoubtedly hard-working and well-meaning, and concerned to make a worthwhile contribution to curriculum development. At the lower levels of the structure they will have been appointed in the first place for their experience, if not their expertise, in a particular subject area, and, provided they do not show any propensity to challenge the mechanisms by which 'agreed' policy is reached, they are unlikely to feel especially constrained. Should they be tempted in the direction of rebellion, the wisdom of self-restraint will undoubtedly be borne in upon them. While career prospects would certainly be enhanced by a successful spell on a CCC committee — 'successful' being defined in social rather than academic terms — a willingness to display nonconformist behaviour could be seriously damaging. The culprit would soon merit the description 'forthright', which in Scottish education is a widely recognised codeword for 'troublemaker'.

Skilful selection of appointees can, however, ensure that deviance is minimal. Belief in what Mr McNicoll has called the 'partnership principle' — 'a system of checks, balances and influence on the control of the schools and the curriculum'[61] — can thus be sustained. This view is assiduously publicised by the leadership class, but the Panglossian optimism which underlies it is not shared by everyone. Early in 1984 two headteachers, Tom O'Hagan of Glenlivet School and J. F. Kirk of Tain Royal Academy, expressed their contempt for 'the gravy train'[62] of committee membership and the endless production of jargon-ridden reports. Mr O'Hagan commented with some bitterness on the processes whereby mediocre men and women achieve 'distinction':

> ... greatness is usually conferred ... by their contemporary self-seekers, whose reputations are enhanced by proximity to this greatness, or by their successors who

admired and emulated the route to eminence . . . Self-seekers are by their very nature birds of passage. A couple of years of self-advertisement here, volunteer for the right committees to make the acquaintance of those with promotion clout and then off to dress windows elsewhere. The frantic and very public activities these people stir up are for themselves, and sensed to be so.[63]

In more restrained vein, Mr Kirk remarked on the damaging effects of a situation in which 'committee work is preferred to dedicated classroom teaching when a teacher is being considered for promotion', an order of priorities which makes teachers 'professionally insecure' and 'cynical about the motives of promoted colleagues'.[64]

There is little doubt that these comments accuately reflect the views of many classroom teachers but, if they are noticed at the upper levels of the CCC, they are unlikely to be taken very seriously. After all, the sources from which they emanate are not especially high on the educational hierarchy and so can be safely ignored. The valuations which really count are those of the leadership class itself, and its members need look no further than the Secretary of the CCC for reassurance about the worth of their contribution: 'Scottish education, as well as the CCC, is well served by its membership, associates and staff'.[65]

## Symptoms of Malaise

The CCC is now a well-established part of the educational landscape and, no matter how attractive the prospect of its removal may seem to some classroom teachers, it is unlikely to disappear in the near future. From the point of view of the decision-makers, it serves a number of important functions: its sub-structure makes a useful contribution to the effective working of the patronage network by providing a testing ground for potential recruits to the higher levels of the system; it acts as an intermediary body between the SED on the one hand and education authorities and teachers on the other, thereby disguising the extent of control exercised by Scottish Office officials; and, more generally, it plays a part in helping to sustain those elements in Scottish educational mythology which stress 'partnership' and 'democracy'. These are necessary *political* functions which help to protect the decision-makers from public scrutiny and which provide them with legitimacy of a kind.

Nevertheless, there are several indications which suggest that dissatisfaction with the CCC is likely to increase, and there may well come a time when its role will be questioned more rigorously than it has been hitherto. Three points, in particular, invite comment: continuing structural difficulties; problems relating to the production and dissemination of publications; and concern with the confidentiality of CCC proceedings. These issues will be looked at in turn.

Organisational questions have surfaced at several places in the foregoing account and they continue to be a source of difficulty. Most notably, there have been examples of discontent within the CCC about the precise relation between the major committees — the CCC itself, COPE and COSE — and the numerous satellite bodies which they supervise. Both the Central Committee on Mathematics and the Central Committee on Technical Education have objected — albeit not very publicly and with a proper concern for decorum — about decisions being taken without sufficient consultation on matters for which they are nominally responsible. In the case of the Central Committee on Technical Education, the circumstances surrounding the issue of SED Circular 1107 on Technical/Technological Education in S3 and S4 provoked quite lengthy internal rumblings.[66] The principal complaint was that the secretariat and the Executive Committee did not give the members of the Central Committee adequate opportunity to discuss the merits of proposals for new courses but simply rubber-stamped the SED line. In a letter to the Secretary of the SED,[67] Mr McNicoll acknowledged that some members had asked for more time to discuss the issues involved, but he went on to say that the Executive Committee judged that their formal response to the proposals represented a consensus of views within the main body of the CCC and, moreover, that the urgency of the matter did not admit of delay.

An attempt has recently been made to forestall the development of such minor crises by having a member of the CCC attend the meetings of subject committees. The Central Committee on Mathematics, for example, now has Professor R. R. Burnside of Paisley College of Technology acting as a link with the main body. Professor Burnside's own discipline is mathematics and he is, therefore, well qualified to communicate the views of the Central Committee to his colleagues on the CCC. It is unlikely, however, that similar expertise is to be found for every area of CCC activity, and so the potential for friction between the main body and the sub-structure remains. Problems of this sort are inherent in any organisation possessing the Byzantine characteristics of the CCC, and further instances of conflict can be anticipated, despite efforts to devise more efficient strategies of containment.

The second sign of malaise is associated with the never-ending avalanche of publications produced by the CCC and the SCDS.[68] It is obviously important that those involved should be 'seen to be' busy, and the production of reports, bulletins, discussion papers, memoranda and guidelines serves to justify the existence of committee members and full-time staff. In fairness, it should be said that some of these publications are worthwhile and, used selectively, they could make a useful contribution to the work of the classroom teacher. But the point has now been reached where they are being produced at such a rate and in such quantity that it is quite impossible for members of the CCC itself, let alone teachers in schools, to read, absorb and reflect on their contents. The process is, in fact, beginning to become self-discrediting because it is apparent that visibility rather than quality has taken over as a principle of operation. There is, it is true, some glimmering of awareness that this is happening by leading figures in the CCC. The present Chairman of COPE, Mr Les Fulton, has observed with nice understatement, 'I know that many teachers have reservations about what they consider to be a rather prolific output of curricular publications',[69] a comment echoed by his counterpart on COSE, Sister Maire Gallagher — 'There must be many people in schools who are hoping that the Committee on Secondary Education ... will produce no reports for the next three years'.[70] This awareness is, however, extremely unlikely to halt the flow of documentation for, if it were to stop, questions might begin to be asked about the need for those who authorise it.

The third sign of malaise concerns the question of confidentiality. The publication of 'definitive' documents is one thing: access to the process by which they emerge is quite another. If the rhetoric of partnership and involvement and communication were to be taken at its face value, then it might be assumed that the CCC would seek to encourage the widest possible interest in its internal policy discussions on important matters of educational principle and practice (assuming discussions of this kind do sometimes take place). After all, the security of the nation hardly depends on keeping the *bons mots* of Dr Munn and Mr McNicoll a secret. But from the beginning of the CCC's existence, there has been an unhealthy preoccupation with problems which might arise from the premature disclosure of information. Some mild expressions of disquiet on this subject actually managed to surface briefly in *CCC News* during 1978 and 1979 when a short-lived series of 'Profiles' of 'People in the System' was published. Mrs Marion Blythman, a member of both the CCC and of COSE from 1976 to 1980, referred to the need 'to combat the view ... that the CCC is some sort of secret society'.[71] And Miss Dorothy Smart, a member of the Central Committee on Modern Languages from 1976 to 1980, feared that 'an obstacle to the work and aims of the CCC might be the question of confidentiality'.[72] In a helpful editorial parenthesis, Miss Smart was reassured that 'The CCC has now issued appropriate guidelines on this subject to all concerned'. (It may be remarked in passing that the word 'appropriate' is invoked with such a degree of frequency in official CCC statements that even the least suspicious reader may be forgiven for wondering, 'Appropriate for whom?')[73]

That the subject continued to be regarded as sensitive is evident from the issuing of new guidelines in 1983.[74] These appeared, with the unerring sense of timing characteristic of Scottish educational officialdom, only a few weeks before the launching of a national campaign for freedom of information. They bear all the marks of Orwellian newspeak, in which mutually contradictory statements can be expressed without any sense of embarrassment or conflict. To begin with, there is a familiar ritualistic appeal to the *amour propre* of those involved in high-level deliberations: 'In considering questions of confidentiality, the Consultative Committee on the Curriculum relies on the professional discretion and responsibility of members of the CCC and its committees and the members of the curriculum development service.'.[75]

Having disarmed *via* flattery, the document then proceeds to reassure: 'In principle a policy of open communication should be adopted. Matters will therefore be regarded as within the public domain and open to public discussion unless they fall within the restrictions set out below or have specifically been deemed to be confidential'.[76] This sounds promising, even bold, but the hopeful reader is quickly disillusioned when the list of exceptions to the 'principle' of openness is examined in detail. There are seven of these. First, 'Matters relating to appointments and staffing should always remain confidential'.[77] In view of the uncertainties surrounding the criteria for CCC appointments, this is no doubt prudent. Second, 'Minutes and papers should not normally be released beyond the CCC':[78] where abnormal release is contemplated, 'approval should be obtained from the chairman of the committee concerned'.[79] Third, 'if an item is judged to be confidential, committee papers should be marked accordingly by the committee secretariat and members asked not to discuss the matter outwith the committee'.[80] This particular injunction is expressed in the much-favoured impersonal mode and the quesion again arises, 'Who does the judging?' Fourth, 'the contents of CCC publications should not normally be divulged outwith the CCC structure in advance of publication'.[81] Fifth, 'The content of estimates not yet approved by Parliament should not be divulged outwith the CCC structure until such time as the Parliamentary estimates are published'.[82] Sixth, 'It should be assumed that advice given by the CCC to the Secretary of State for Scotland is confidential and should not be revealed or discussed in public until he has indicated that he has reached a decision, unless the chairman of the CCC specifically indicates otherwise'.[83] This particular clause was invoked by the Secretary of the CCC during the correspondence relating to Circular 1107 referred to earlier in this section. Seventh, 'At all levels of the CCC structure advice on confidentiality should be sought from the committee chairman. In particular members are asked to consult their chairman or their parent committee about any article or talk they have been invited to prepare if they are in any doubt about confidentiality. The status of any topic may be clarified by the Secretary of the CCC'.[84]

These seven modest constraints on the general principle of frankness and openness are unlikely to be remarkable in the context of government. Doubtless the members of other quangos are issued with similar documents which also invite ridicule. What they indicate is an unedifying mixture of self-importance and fear among those who govern. Membership of an élite group is personally gratifying to those selected, and procedures designed to confirm their exclusiveness are likely to enhance that sense of well-being. At the same time, however, anything which detracts from the weighty eminence of the elect — such as an informed public discussion of the issues — is perceived as a threat. Insofar as fears of this kind exist, they are likely to indicate the mediocre quality of the leadership class. People of real ability, who are confident of the merits of what they propose, will welcome wide dissemination of their ideas and will not seek to control the channels and arenas of debate.

The CCC's preoccupation with the confidentiality of its proceedings is closely related to its desire always to be seen to reach a consensus — a feature already noted in passing — and its insistence on its own representativeness in this respect. The Fourth Report, for example, asserts that the CCC 'reflects the national consensus on the major issues facing Scottish education'.[85] Although there is much talk of consulting widely within the educational world, the outcome is invariably expected to be an agreed statement of policy, enshrined in an official publication. If there are serious disagreements among CCC personnel, these are not aired in public, and the stress on confidentiality ensures that a seemingly united front can be presented. There is little awareness of the dangers in assuming that the result of deliberations should always be a consensus: these include the encouragement of the view that there is a 'right' answer to all educational problems and the failure to appreciate the potential in allowing alternative, even conflicting, curricular strategies to proceed at the same time. Furthermore, the importance attached to the presentation of an agreed position on every subject leads to the bland elision of many substantive issues in the interests of administrative smoothness. Naturally, this is an interpretation that would be denied by CCC officials. Referring to 'the current social and economic situation against which its advice on the curriculum has to be offered', Mr McNicoll assured his readers in November, 1981 that 'the CCC structure is chiselling at many of the issues'.[86] 'Chiselling' is presumably intended to convey an impression of rugged intellectual engagement.

Finally, what can be said about the significance of the CCC as far as the quality of teaching in Scottish schools is concerned? After all, its ostensible function is to facilitate curriculum development, and undoubtedly it promotes a great deal of activity under that heading. But as Sydney Smyth, Director of the Edinburgh centre of SCDS, remarked in 1979: 'The 'Curriculum Development' that really matters happens inside the heads of practising teachers, alertly reflecting upon their own aims and procedures . . . '[87] It is extremely doubtful whether a strongly centralist organisation like the CCC, closely identified with government policy, and locked into a system of bureaucratic constraints, can contribute usefully to the process of self-development which lies at the heart of good teaching. Teachers may comply with its directives because they feel they have no alternative, or because it is in their interests to do so, but the only real results will be cynicism among those who are prepared to play by the unwritten rules, and anger or despair among those who are not. The attitude of Scottish teachers to central direction is undoubtedly ambivalent, and it has often been remarked that they both want to be told what to do and resent being told when someone actually obliges them. Whatever their feelings, in the end they usually comply. Some SED and CCC personnel certainly see their role as giving a lead to teachers by promoting developments which might not take place otherwise. But that response merely reinforces the problem of professional uncertainty, a problem which has its roots in the training and induction of teachers and which will be examined in more detail in Chapter 7. There is no evidence to suggest that the CCC has seriously addressed the question of how far its own mode of operation — from the centre to the periphery — actually undermines those critical, reflective qualities to which Mr Smyth referred. Instead, it continues to give priority to internal bureaucratic matters. Ample confirmation of this can be found in a statement issued in October, 1984:

> The CCC has recently undertaken a review of its sub-structure and has, after internal negotiation, proposed a three-stage restructuring. This will comprise: the establishment of small 'caretaker groups' for those Committees now or shortly due for reconstitution; the reconstitution of all Central Committees for a period of 18 months from early 1985; and the establishment of a significantly revised structure

thereafter. Proposals for the new structure will be brought before the main Committee by February 1986 and will be implemented by the Seventh CCC which assumes office in August 1986.[88]

*Notes and References*

1. SED, *Secondary Education: A Report of the Advisory Council on Education in Scotland,* HMSO, Edinburgh, 1947.
2. S. Leslie Hunter, *The Scottish Educational System,* 2nd edition, Pergamon, Oxford, 1972, p. 37.
3. SED, *The Primary School in Scotland,* HMSO, Edinburgh, 1950.
4. SED, *Junior Secondary Education,* HMSO, Edinburgh, 1955.
5. See SED, *CCC: First Report, 1965–68,* HMSO, Edinburgh, 1969, p. 5.
6. See SED, *CCC: Second Report, 1968–71,* HMSO, Edinburgh, 1972, p. 7.
7. See SED, *CCC: Fourth Report, 1974–80,* HMSO, Edinburgh, 1980, p. 9.
8. SED, *English in the Secondary School: Early Stages* (Bulletin No. 1), HMSO, Edinburgh, 1967; *The Teaching of Literature* (Bulletin No. 2), HMSO, Edinburgh, 1968; *English for the Young School Leaver* (Bulletin No. 3), HMSO, Edinburgh, 1970; *English in the Secondary School: Later Stages* (Bulletin No. 4), HMSO, Edinburgh, 1971; *The Teaching of English Language* (Bulletin No. 5), HMSO, Edinburgh, 1972.
9. Bulletin No. 5, p. 3.
10. *CCC: Fourth Report,* p. 9.
11. *Ibid.,* p. 9.
12. It has been suggested that the acronyms COPE and COSE accurately reflect both the confident self-image and the couthy atmosphere of the CCC.
13. See, e.g., *CCC: Fourth Report,* p. 19.
14. For an account of the advisory service, see Chapter 6.
15. SED, *The Structure of the Curriculum in the Third and Fourth Years of the Scottish Secondary School,* HMSO, Edinburgh, 1977.
16. James Scotland, *The History of Scottish Education,* Vol. 2, University of London Press, London, 1969, p. 185.
17. Hunter, *op. cit.,* p. 38.
18. *CCC: Fourth Report,* p. 14.
19. *Ibid.,* p. 10.
20. SED, Consultative Paper, *Curriculum Development in Scotland: The Future of the Consultative Committee on the Curriculum and the Scottish Curriculum Development Service,* February 1980, p. 1. Hereafter referred to as Consultative Paper.
21. SED, *The Consultative Committee on the Curriculum: Statement by the Secretary of State for Scotland,* September 1980. Hereafter referred to as Statement by Secretary of State.
22. Consultative Paper, p. 6.
23. *Ibid.,* p. 3.
24. Statement by Secretary of State, p. 1.
25. SIO, *Factsheet 21: Consultative Committee on the Curriculum,* August 1982, p. 4.
26. Statement by Secretary of State, p. 3.
27. *Ibid.,* p. 3.
28. *Ibid.,* p. 2.
29. *CCC: Fourth Report,* pp. 80–81.

30. *CCC: Fifth Report,* Edinburgh, 1983, Annex 5. It should be noted that the Fifth Report, unlike the previous ones, was not published by HMSO but by the CCC itself.
31. Statement by Secretary of State, p. 4.
32. *CCC News,* No. 7, November 1980, p. 1.
33. *CCC: Fourth Report,* p. 77.
34. *Ibid.,* p. 77.
35. *Ibid.,* p. 76.
36. This is an updated version of the chart given in *CCC: Fifth Report,* p. 8. I am grateful to Mr D. R. McNicoll, Secretary, CCC, for supplying me with this information and for permission to reproduce it.
37. Statement by Secretary of State, p. 4.
38. *CCC: Fifth Report,* p. 11.
39. *Ibid.,* p. 11.
40. *Ibid.,* p. 29.
41. *Ibid.,* p. 23.
42. *Ibid.,* p. 23.
43. SCDS, *Annual Joint Newsletter,* No. 9, November 1983.
44. *CCC: Fifth Report,* p. 43.
45. *Ibid.,* p. 43.
46. *CCC: First Report,* p. 5.
47. *CCC News,* No. 16, November 1983, p. 3.
48. *CCC News,* No. 17, February 1984, p. 5.
49. CCC, *Primary Education in the Eighties: A COPE Position paper,* 1983.
50. *CCC News,* No. 17, p. 3.
51. *CCC: Fifth Report,* p. 12.
52. *CCC News,* No. 16, p. 2.
53. *Ibid.,* p. 1.
54. SIO, *Factsheet 21,* pp. 3–4.
55. *CCC News,* No. 16, p. 2.
56. *CCC News,* No. 7, p. 1.
57. Neil Munro, 'Consensus Man', *TESS,* February 10, 1984, p. 4.
58. *Ibid.,* p. 4.
59. *Ibid.,* p. 4.
60. At a staff seminar in the Education Department, Glasgow University, on February 20, 1984.
61. *CCC News,* No. 7, p. 1.
62. This was the title of Mr O'Hagan's article, and the phrase was subsequently repeated in a letter by Mr Kirk. The article appeared in the *TESS,* January 6, 1984, p. 56.
63. *Ibid.,* p. 56.
64. *TESS,* February 10, 1984, p. 5.
65. *CCC News,* No. 15, June 1983, p. 1.
66. Circular 1107, signed by Miss P. A. Cox and dated December 2, 1983.
67. Dated September 28, 1983. See also letter by Dan Marshall, *TESS,* April 4, 1984, p. 6.
68. These are listed in the *Annual Joint Newsletters* of SCDS.
69. *CCC News,* No. 16, p. 1.
70. *Ibid.,* p. 1.
71. *CCC News,* No. 1, May 1978, p. 3.
72. *CCC News,* No. 2, February 1979, p. 2.

73. For example, the Fourth Report refers to 'appropriate consultative procedures' (p. 10) regarding appointments, the desirability of having a Chairman with an 'appropriate background' (p. 71), and the requirement that COPE should 'report appropriately' (p. 27) to the CCC. This concern with matters of decorum is continued in the Fifth Report. It refers to the 'appropriate sub-structure' (p. 17) established by COPE, the devising of 'appropriate principles' (p. 12) to guide work at different levels of the education system, and the development of Foundation modules with 'an appropriate group of pupils' (p. 30).

74. Approved by COSE on October 27, 1983.

75. CCC, 'Guidelines on Confidentiality', para. 1.

76. Ibid., para. 2.

77. Ibid., para. 4.

78. Ibid., para. 5.

79. Ibid., para. 5.

80. Ibid., para. 6.

81. Ibid., para. 7.

82. Ibid., para. 9.

83. Ibid., para. 8.

84. Ibid., para. 10.

85. *CCC: Fourth Report,* p. 12.

86. *CCC News,* No. 10, November 1981, p. 1.

87. *CCC News,* No. 3, May 1979, p. 3.

88. *CCC News,* No. 19, October 1984, p. 3.

# 6
# *Local Democracy?*

## Introduction

It would be pleasant if, after surveying the authoritarian style of the SED in chapters 3 and 4, the local level of educational administration in Scotland could be portrayed as enlightened and liberal in comparison. Regrettably, that is far from being the case. Although conflicts between central and local government surface in education, as in other fields, it would be seriously misleading to present the education authorities as doughty defenders of important rights and liberties against the pernicious encroachments of the SED. What they object to is not the infringement of valued principles which they themselves uphold, but the perceived threat that almost any initiative from central government seems to pose to their own power base. Concepts such as 'local democracy' are regularly invoked but they are best understood as rhetorical pawns in a game of political chess rather than as evidence of a genuine commitment to the interests of local people. Moreover, despite the stridency of some of their political statements, locally elected representatives, in the shape of regional councillors, are fairly ineffective in counteracting the centralist tendencies of Scottish government — partly, it will be suggested, because of their poor quality. This leads to a familiar pattern of administration: power passes to unelected officials who are motivated more by bureaucratic concerns than by educational idealism. These officials, in pursuing their own interests, do not hesitate to treat their subordinates — not least classroom teachers — in a manner that frequently seems arrogant and contemptuous. The arrogance and contempt remain notwithstanding a level of performance by administrators that is often inadequate. In other words, the local government of Scottish education reveals similar features to those already identified at national level: political dereliction, alternating with wilful interventions based on limited knowledge; an obsession with hierarchies; a desire to suppress honest argument and criticism; a fear of those who fail to respond to the blandishments of power and patronage. These characteristics, it will be shown, are just as apparent in local authorities which claim to represent a radically different political philosophy from that of central government as in those which share the same outlook.

Dr William Gatherer has stated that 'The local authority is a political system, within which there is an educational system, which can be perceived as a political subsystem'.[1] In approaching this 'political subsystem' it will first of all be useful to explain the legal and administrative framework within which it operates. Thereafter, the workings of two bodies which represent the collective interests of groups with a direct responsibility for the provision of local educational services (the education committee of the Convention of Scottish Local Authorities and the Association of Directors of Education in Scotland) will be examined. This will prepare the ground for later sections which look in greater detail at the relationships between councillors and officials, and officials and teachers, and which comment critically on the ambiguous, intermediate role assumed by the advisory service. In illustrating these points, particular reference will be made to Strathclyde region, a bias which can be justified in terms of the scale of its operations and the number of Scottish people who are subject to its decisions. But other regions will not be neglected, and the importance of acknowledging variations between authorities will be stressed at several places.

## The Legal and Administrative Framework

The Local Government (Scotland) Act of 1973, which came into effect in 1975, established nine regional councils — Borders, Central, Dumfries and Galloway, Fife, Grampian, Highland, Lothian, Strathclyde and Tayside — and three islands councils — Orkney, Shetlands and the Western Isles. These councils constitute the education authorities in Scotland, and their principal obligations are set out in the Education (Scotland) Act of 1980, supplemented and amended by the Education (Scotland) Act of 1981. The 1980 Act stipulates that 'it shall be the duty of every education authority to secure that there is made for their area adequate and efficient provision of school education and further education'.[2] Associated facilities for social, cultural and recreational activities, and for physical education and training, must also be provided. Nursery provision is discretionary. Every education authority must, however, set up a careers service and a child guidance service, and offer special education for children with certain prescribed disabilities. They must also provide, free of charge, books, writing materials, stationery, etc., necessary for pupils to take advantage of educational facilities. Other important regulations relate to school meals, milk and transport, clothing and footwear grants, school attendance, the appointment and dismissal of teachers, and parental rights and duties. Education authorities are legally obliged to consult parents on a number of matters before taking action. These include proposals to close schools, provide new schools, change the sites of schools, alter guidelines on admissions policies, make single-sex schools coeducational or *vice versa*, and revise zoning arrangements.

The educational functions of the regional and islands authorities are normally delegated to education committees which the councils are, in any case, required to set up by law. In addition to the main education committee, there may be sub-committees dealing with specific stages — e.g., schools, FE, etc. The membership of the education committee must include, as well as elected councillors, at least two teachers from the authority's schools and three religious representatives.

It is stated in the Education (Scotland) Act of 1980 that councils must 'employ a director of education, who shall be the chief education officer of the authority'.[3] In all authorities directors of education have the support of a number of subordinate officials of varying rank and designation — depute and assistant directors of education, divisonal education officers, senior education officers, education officers, etc. These constitute the cadre of senior professional staff — the directorate — who are responsible for giving advice to elected members, implementing council decisions, acting as official correspondents for the authority, and controlling teaching and ancillary staff.

Offering a description of what the law demands is relatively straightforward. It is, however, quite another matter to give a satisfactory account of the way in which the pattern of administration that is established to meet those demands operates in practice. There are several major problems. First, it is difficult to generalise since there are significant variations in the size and character of the different regions. Strathclyde is very much larger than any of the other authorities: it provides educational services for approximately half the total population of Scotland, services which consumed a budget of over £600 million in 1983–84.[4] Administratively it is divided into six sub-regions — Argyll and Bute, Ayr, Dunbarton, Glasgow, Lanark, and Renfrew. This arrangement, which makes sense in respect of creating manageable administrative units, also makes for problems in respect of the consistency of policies and practices throughout the region. The authorities which come after Strathclyde in terms of size of population — Lothian, Grampian and Tayside — also make use of sub-regional units for educational and other purposes. Highland too, though much smaller in terms of population, is divided into sub-regions because of its geographical spread.

Other important differences between regions arise with regard to the degree of politicisation that enters into their operations. Some of the smaller authorities — for example Borders, and Dumfries and Galloway — still have a significant number of independent councillors, whereas in the larger ones strict divisions along party lines are the order of the day. In Strathclyde there has been a deliberate attempt to strengthen the party political input of elected members with the formation of policy review groups and member-officer groups.[5] The dominance of the Labour party in Strathclyde — in the 1982 elections it won 79 out of 103 seats — has made this easier, although, as will be shown later, the success of the exercise is open to debate. In other authorities, for example Lothian, the political scene is more evenly balanced, thereby making it less easy for the party in power to attempt to exert its will and ignore opposing arguments.

Questions of scale and political complexion combine to influence the kind of management structures that are set up. Of particular interest in this respect is the extent to which authorities have taken on board the recommendations of the Paterson Report[6] that they should develop a 'corporate' approach. The background to these recommendations is described by Keating and Midwinter:

> The 1960s and 1970s witnessed increasing discontent with the suitability of traditional management in local government for the needs of an increasingly complex, urbanised society, and the beginning of a movement towards corporate management. Traditional forms of management and organisation reflected the piecemeal development of local services. Local government was organised around

> specialised functions which in most cases had their own department, and, at elected member level, a committee. The management process was viewed as being dominated by technical and professional issues, at the expense of wider policy issues. 'Departmentalism', whereby people think in terms of self-contained policy problems, justify their actions by reference to professional values and attitudes, was described as the 'besetting sin' of local authorities. Traditional management was viewed as being fragmented and uncoordinated, with little long-term planning.[7]

Corporate management principles seek to remedy these defects by advocating structural changes designed to produce a unified approach to the formulation and implementation of policies. Such an approach calls for a reduction in the autonomy of individual departments, a recognition that elected members and officials have to work together if the integration of political and professional insights is to be effective, and the setting up of machinery to promote corporate attitudes. The principal developments under this last heading have been the establishment of Policy and Resources committees and the coordinating role assumed by Chief Executives and their staffs. Both of these developments tend to encourage centralisation but, once again, there is variety in the precise modes of operation adopted by different authorities.[8]

Keating and Midwinter observe that 'organisational reform, though often couched in the soothing language of management, is usually about the distribution of power'.[9] The effects of local government reform on the educational service, including arguments about the extent to which corporate management attitudes have been adopted, need to be understood in the light of this shrewd observation. The familiar features of rivalry within and between departments, of territorial sensitivity between officials and elected representatives, of unhealthy concern for marks of status and esteem, are to be found here as elsewhere. These preoccupations often serve to undermine the stated aims of education departments within the regions — aims which invariably stress service to the community — just as the preoccupations of SED officials often serve to undermine the claims made about the democratic character of Scottish education as a whole. In both cases, however, the reality of power confers upon members of the educational leadership class a remarkable capacity to ignore the gap that develops between what they say and what they do.

## The Education Committee of the Convention of Scottish Local Authorities (COSLA)

The objectives of COSLA are:

(a) to watch over, protect and promote the respective interests, rights, powers and duties of its member authorities as these may be affected by legislation or proposed legislation or otherwise.

(b) to provide a forum for the discussion of matters of concern to its member authorities and to obtain, consider and disseminate information on matters of importance and interest to member authorities.

(c) to provide (in conjunction, where appropriate, with other Local Authority Associations in the United Kingdom) such essential services for its member authorities as it may consider to be appropriate.[10]

Towards these ends, COSLA works through a series of committees — Policy, Arts and Recreation, Manpower, Planning, Environmental Health, Housing, Education, Roads and Transportation, Social Work, etc. — covering the various responsibilites of district and regional councils. The Education Committee has twenty-five members, under the chairmanship of Dr Malcolm Green of Strathclyde. In common with all COSLA committees, membership is confined to elected representatives. However, provision is made for the use of professional local government officers to act as advisers to the Convention or any of its committees. Matters of interest to COSLA committees can be referred to these officials for investigation and report. Officials asked to act as advisers may be invited to attend meetings and take part in the proceedings but are not entitled to vote.[11] The full-time secretariat of COSLA is small, and extensive use is made of the part-time specialist advisers, who, it should be noted, 'are nominated by their professional associations, not by the elected members'.[12]

It would seem, in fact, that the role of elected members, with the exception of the Chairman, is fairly minimal. Keating and Midwinter make the point that 'generally COSLA reacts to government requests for opinion/advice rather than initiates it'.[13] A common pattern of COSLA involvement in educational matters is that a senior civil servant in the SED writes to the Assistant Secretary of COSLA, asking for the views of the Education Committee on a particular topic — for example, a consultative paper or draft proposals for legislation. Often the timetable is tight, thereby limiting the opportunity for a full consideration of the implications. The Assistant Secretary will write to the twelve Scottish Directors of Education, enclosing the relevant papers (usually marked 'In Strict Confidence') and inviting their comments. On important or controversial matters, a small advisory group, consisting of perhaps three officials (usually Directors themselves though in the case of Strathclyde a Depute Director is more common), is set up to draft a response. These officials are expected to offer their own professional advice, not merely repeat the line approved by their own regional authority. The draft response prepared by the advisory group is then circulated to all Directors before submission to the COSLA Education Committee for approval. Sometimes the timetabling restrictions set by the SED make this impossible so that power to approve the officials' draft rests with the Chairman. It can be seen, therefore, that the opportunity for a policy input by elected representatives is not extensive. Responses may go forward in the name of COSLA but often they cannot be regarded as representing the views of members in anything other than the most superficial sense.

From time to time meetings are arranged between COSLA advisers and SED officials to discuss particular areas of concern. At these meetings — and this is also evident in the written responses of Directors to proposed educational changes — there tends to be a preoccupation with procedural matters rather than matters of substance. The focus is on how reforms are to be implemented rather than whether or not they are worthwhile. Questions of educational principle seem to be regarded as beyond the remit of those involved. This means that although there may be disagreement on points of detail, there is a high measure of continuity between COSLA advisers and SED officials in respect of role perception. Both inhabit the same kind of bureaucratic world and take its conventions for granted.

It would, however, be wrong to characterise the responses of Directors of Education to the COSLA secretariat's request for their views as entirely grey and uniform. In their individual written submissions, some Directors emerge as more reflective and forceful than others. However, even moderately robust individual submissions tend to be rendered harmless once they have gone through the COSLA machine. According to Keating and Midwinter, 'COSLA is not well geared up to influencing Parliamentary legislation',[14] and there is no evidence to suggest that the Education Committee is an exception.

It is, then, anything more than a talking shop, another arena for professionals and politicians to parade their sense of importance? Defenders of the contribution of COSLA's Education Committee might point to such things as its support of the call for an independent review of teachers' salaries in 1984 or its earlier commissioning of a working party to investigate alternatives to corporal punishment in schools. But COSLA's impact on both of these areas was poor. Its recommendation on teacher' salaries was ignored by the Secretary of State, and the working party report did not help to prevent the development of disciplinary problems in several regions following their decision to abolish the belt. The commissioning of working party reports is one thing: ensuring that their findings are adequately disseminated and intelligently acted upon is quite another. COSLA exemplifies a common fault found throughout Scottish education — the assumption that to make a bureaucratic response to a problem is to provide a practical solution.

## The Association of Directors of Education in Scotland (ADES)

ADES (not AIDS) has been in existence since 1920 and, according to a former President, Ian Flett, the Association has always had 'a close contact with the Scottish Education Department'.[15] At a formal level, regular standing liaison meetings involving SED and ADES' representatives take place to discuss items on an agreed joint agenda. The Association is invited, for example, to comment on proposed legislation, draft circulars, etc., which the Department plans to issue. In addition, there are frequent informal meetings between SED personnel and office bearers of the Association. The presence of the Association of Directors can be felt throughout the Scottish educational system, for it is invited to send representatives to many other bodies including the CCC, the GTC, the SEB, the National Committee on the In Service Training of Teachers, etc. In 1980 some sixty-nine organisations included representatives nominated by ADES.[16] Given this pervasiveness, it is rather surprising that the existence and functions of the

Association are not better known among teachers. Like HMIs, however, Directors of Education and their subordinates prefer to keep a low profile, and it is probably not an exaggeration to suggest that most teachers would be hard put to name a Director apart from the one in charge of the educational service in the authority in which they themselves are employed.

Membership of ADES is not confined to the twelve Directors of Education in the regional and islands authorities. Their senior support staff are also eligible: it 1980 there were 145 members,[17] almost all of them men. The Association is run by a Council, which consists of the twelve Directors, one extra nominated member from Lothian region, two extra nominated members from Strathclyde region, and six members elected at the annual business meeting. There is also a system of sector committees covering primary, secondary, further, community and special education. As well as an annual conference, which leading figures in Scottish education are regularly invited to address,[18] the Association arranges a training weekend for members and one-day conferences on particular topics. These various events can be regarded as a form of staff development, though it would seem that the amount of management training that directorate staff receive is limited. Some, but by no means all, will have acquired Master of Education degrees in which the study of educational administration may have played a part, but there remains a need for regular updating of knowledge. Some concern has been expressed by Mr J. Havard, Director of the Scottish Centre for Studies in School Administration at Moray House College of Education, at the low level of interest shown by the education authorities in management courses.[19] Particular mention was made of the very small representation from Strathclyde region at courses run by the Centre.

Despite their limited commitment to their own in-service training, members of ADES are not slow to pass judgement on the quality of the teaching force. Following the issue of an SED paper on this topic, the Association's Primary Committee, at its meeting on September 23, 1982, endorsed comments expressing a lack of satisfaction with the standard of teachers and called for a greater measure of 'professionalism'. Somewhat ironically, the Committee insisted that Directors of Education have a major role to play in efforts to improve the quality of the teaching profession but at the same time maintained that, where problems with unsatisfactory teachers arise, the principal responsibility lies with the Head Teacher. ADES' members evidently have little to learn about the advantages of using their subordinates to protect their own position.

The kinds of issues that concern ADES' members often reflect characteristic bureaucratic fears about the intrusion of outsiders into the workings of the administration. For example, at a meeting between Directors and SED representatives on January 28, 1982, the former voiced disquiet about the volume of interest from researchers on the implementation of the Education (Scotland) Act of 1981. Despite assurances from the SED representatives that researchers would be advised not to 'overburden' authorities, the Directors argued for a moratorium on research except for that sponsored by the SED or the Directors themselves. This stance demonstrates a desire to 'manage' research projects to ensure that any potential threat is minimised. Interestingly, SED-sponsored projects are regarded as acceptable, a view that again suggests a measure of continuity of outlook between SED officials and members of the directorate.

Ian Flett has stated that 'The Association's power is its capacity to influence'.[20] Although it has little or no *formal* power, the Association is very much part of the network of communication through which the educational leadership class in Scotland operates. ADES' members are among the principal beneficiaries of Scottish Office patronage. Moreover, the use of members of the Association as advisers to COSLA's Education Committee is clearly very acceptable to the SED. On at least one occasion, the SED has assumed that an SED/COSLA liaison group could be regarded as constituting a consultative group with the Directors, a perception that the Association did not object to.[21] This example serves as a further indication of the extent to which the politicians on the COSLA Education Committee are ineffective.

Finally, the Association, in common with other agencies in Scottish education, has a somewhat complacent self-image. A manual of information produced for members some years ago made the modest claim that it offered 'an excellent conspectus of the collective good sense and of the spectrum of distinguished talents and abilities which characterise the Association'.[22] Less extravagantly, Ian Flett, on the occasion of ADES' jubilee, stated that its history testified 'to a meritorious record of unobtrusive and unwavering dedication to the service'.[23] As has been noted in earlier chapters, a preference for unobtrusiveness need not be accompanied by a distaste for the exercise of power.

## The Democratic Process

The received wisdom insists that the administration of education at local level is properly democratic. It is argued that officials are directly accountable to elected members on the education committee and, through that committee, to the full council. Elected members, in turn, are responsible to the voting public who are regularly given the opportunity to make their views known through the ballot box. Councillors who do not act in the interests of their constituents — so the argument continues — will fail to be re-elected. It is also claimed that there are other safeguards in the form, for example, of consultative machinery to ensure that the opinions of teachers and parents are canvassed when policy changes are proposed. The setting up of school and college councils following regionalisation in 1975 is usually cited as evidence of a concern to ensure the involvement of local people in the running of the educational service. All of these arguments, it will now be suggested, are open to question.

With regard to the first defence of existing arrangements — that officials are accountable to councillors — it can be shown that councillors themselves are less than fully convinced that this is what happens in practice. An unpublished study of certain aspects of the administration of secondary education in Strathclyde region[24] reveals substantial levels of dissatisfaction among councillors, a particularly interesting finding in view of the fact that Strathclyde is the most heavily politicised of the Scottish regions. One senior councillor described the education department as a 'bastion of élitist bureaucratic control'[25] and remarked that the idea of bringing in a firm of management consultants 'to turn the department of education inside out'[26] was not unattractive. Another councillor, in more temperate vein, criticised the protective professionalism of officials who seek to keep councillors at arm's length: 'The accusation of interference by unqualified outsiders must be resisted'.[27] Overall there was a feeling that individual councillors on the education committee had relatively little influence on the formulation and implementation of educational policy.

This picture must, however, be qualified in two ways. First, a distinction must be made between the chairman and the other members of the education committee. Particularly where a councillor has acted as chairman for a long time, his power, if not necessarily the quality of his contribution to educational thinking, may be quite significant. Indeed, sometimes it can encourage an embarrassing degree of deference on the part of officials — at least in public. Such deference may, nevertheless, be the means whereby officials retain their own authority in relation to others. It is not uncommon, in fact, for a measure of collusion to develop between directors and committee chairmen.[28] They form an alliance which can be used not only against external critics, such as teachers or parents, but also against backbench councillors. This is not really surprising. After all, both the Director of Education and the chairman of the education committee have a direct personal interest in claiming that the service for which they are jointly responsible is being run efficiently: thus it is to the advantage of both to join forces against detractors. Interestingly, in the study of Strathclyde councillors referred to above, the chairman tended to take a more administration-oriented line than his colleagues.[29]

The second qualification derives from the fact that the work of the education committee does not exist in isolation. It is subject to pressures from other, more powerful groupings — the Policy and Resources Committee, the full Council, and, not least, the private caucuses of the party in power. As local government has developed more and more on party lines, the freedom of individual councillors has diminished. Increasingly they are required to toe an approved party line. This means that backbench members of a committee who belong to the party in power have to tread carefully even when they disagree profoundly with their chairman. If they push their disagreement too far, they may find themselves subject to party 'discipline'. In other words, in so far as councillors on the education committee feel themselves to be ineffective, they must accept a measure of responsibility for that position.

Just as the notion that officials are fully accountable to councillors cannot be accepted at face value, so the notion that councillors are fully accountable to the electorate must be questioned. In the first place, the turnout at regional elections is low — 43% in 1982.[30] Several possible reasons for the apparent apathy can be offered — a sense of alienation, particularly in the case of the larger regions, a feeling that the really important decisions are taken at national level, dissatisfaction with the quality of candidates. This last explanation is not normally given much consideration, especially by politicians themselves. Presumably it is rather uncomfortable to contemplate. It is, however, quite possible that the low levels of participation in local government elections are an expression of public distaste for some of the candidates who present themselves. Certainly anyone who takes the trouble to attend council meetings is unlikely to be impressed by many of those present. In the case of Strathclyde education committee, for example, the quality of contributions — with a small number of honourable exceptions — is often very poor indeed. It sometimes seems, in fact, that many councillors do not bother to read the papers relating to meetings. Unfortunately, however, that does not prevent them from participating in the debates — usually in the form of empty political jibes at their opponents which have very little to do with the subject under discussion. The combination of limited talent and unlimited self-importance does not make for good government.

Reactions to these criticisms are likely to take the form of conceding that local government in Scotland is far from perfect but asserting that alternatives which would represent an improvement are elusive. Furthermore, councillors would argue that they would welcome increased public involvement in the democratic process and, in the field of education, might point to the creation of school and college councils as evidence of a move towards a more participatory kind of democracy. The first argument — that it is not easy to think of viable alternative forms of local government — is both unduly complacent and unduly pessimistic. It indicates a failure to take seriously the issues raised by increasing public dissatisfaction (as yet not fully articulated) with the weaknesses of present forms of representative democracy and an unwillingness to explore alternative ways of running public services which rely more on direct community participation than on the combined efforts of councillors and officials. The second argument — that existing councillors would welcome more public involvement — is, in many cases, doubtful. Able councillors would have little to fear from such a development but their weaker colleagues would be exposed to a greater degree of critical scrutiny than hitherto, an experience that they might not enjoy. At party level, the shadowy process whereby men and women of distinctly modest abilities and achievements are selected as candidates — often, it seems, because of an unenviable record of many years of doing as they are told within their own constituency organisations — would be subjected to the public gaze in a way that might well prove embarrassing. In other words, a good measure of public apathy suits the book of many local politicians very well indeed.

The limited gestures that have been made towards devolution of authority in education do not give grounds for a more optimistic reading of the situation. In the case of school councils, for example, it is up to each authority to decide what powers to give its councils and, in many instances, they are little more than advisory bodies. Even where they have some executive power — for example, in relation to school placing requests or truancy or the letting of premises — it is very carefully circumscribed.[31] Many school councils feel extremely frustrated at the way they are treated by education authorities, and quite serious conflict has surfaced in different parts of Scotland. In 1981, for example, three school councils in Grampian region (Kincorth, Linksfield and Hazelhead) passed votes of no confidence in the education committee.[32] They were objecting to what they regarded as totally inadequate consultation procedures over school closures, amalgamations and re-zonings resulting from falling rolls. One school council chairman said, 'We are being used and we are being abused. There is a tremendous feeling of anger, hopelessness and frustration ... '[33] Again, a high level of dissatisfaction developed in Dumfries school council leading to the resignation of the chairman and a former chairman.[34] The education authority had been reviewing the future role of school councils and had asked for proposals. Dumfries school council made a number of fairly modest recommendations, all of which were rejected by the education committee, on the advice of a sub-committee, on the grounds that they could lead to a conflict of responsibility between the authority, head teachers and school councils.

Similar problems have arisen within Strathclyde. In a letter to *The Glasgow Herald* in 1983 John Cairney recounted his experiences as a teacher representative on a school council. The subject of the 16–18 Action Plan had arisen, and when it emerged that a number of parents were concerned about the implications of some of the proposals, particularly those concerning travelling and the availability of subjects at their neighbourhood school, it was agreed that the topic should be fully aired at the next meeting of the council. The head teachers of the three local secondary schools were invited, and the views of teaching staff were to be canvassed. A week before the meeting was due to take place Mr Cairney received notification that the meeting had been cancelled due to an alleged 'lack of business'. On checking with the clerk of the council, he discovered that all three head teachers had declined the invitation to attend and state their views. Mr Cairney concluded that parents would simply be told what would happen without any real consultation and would have no option but to comply with the proposed arrangements. He added: 'How can they be expected to do otherwise when mere lip service is paid to 'consultative' procedures and those who are supposed to have the professional concern for their pupils will meekly comply with all that is imposed from above — headteachers because they don't want to rock the boat, and teachers because they think the boat is already awash'.[35]

Much the same message can be heard from those with experience of college councils. Hugh Dougherty, a lecturer at Stow College in Glasgow, and a staff representative on his college council for five years, has written about their mode of operation:

> College councils, quite simply, have been a disaster. Set up to replace the old boards of governors ... they were regarded by college principals as nothing but a nuisance which had to be neutralized as soon as possible lest their benevolent despotism came into question.[36]

When they were first set up, college councils were viewed with optimism, as an opportunity to involve all sorts of interested parties in the decision-making process — industrialists, trade unionists and councillors, as well as professional educationists. But soon 'a diet of incredible trivia and endless verbal reports on that trivia made the outsiders realize that there were better things to do with their time and some councils had difficulty raising a quorum . . . '[37] The quality of those who remained and the strategies employed to prevent discussion of substantive issues gave rise to concern. The chairmen, says Dougherty, were

> usually placemen in the choosing of the principal [who] tended to be re-elected time after time, and pity help the promotion prospects of the staff rep who dared to even suggest a new candidate for the post. To a man these tycoons of industrial decline represented the partnership between further education and industry, and not a few were distinguished by their business experience which had seen off more than one company into the hands of the liquidators.
>
> Now and then the staff reps got a say. But they had been well warned at so-called consultation sessions that no dirty linen was to be washed before the eyes of the outsiders. Those who had the temerity to ask if there would be outsiders present were judged to be particularly bolshie. If they did succeed in speaking to the meeting there was a problem of the education department assessor to be got round. These gentlemen had a nasty habit of ruling the staff rep offside by quoting some secret circular that no one but the directorate had seen . . .
>
> The minutes of meetings were written and rewritten until you began to wonder if the meetings had taken place at all.[38]

Criticisms of the councils reached the point where it was necessary to hold discussions with councillors. The outcome has been a new constitution, but it seems premature to offer enthusiastic congratulations to all concerned:

> Now Strathclyde has come up with a new constitution and a nice new leaflet about college councils produced at the ratepayers' expense by the public relations people. From now on councils will be meaningful and have meaningful discussions. But the whole thing is made a little less meaningful by the last clause in the new constitution which reserves the right of the authority to change the rules at the drop of a hat.[39]

A more academic study of college councils, carried out by Kenneth Scott, confirms that they have very limited room for manoeuvre.

> All the governing instruments make clear, with varying degrees of bluntness, that the ultimate responsibility for the colleges lies with the authorities. Equally, they all state that the principal is responsible to the director of education for the internal organisation, management and discipline of the college. Somewhere in between the two, college councils are supposed to find viable functions to carry out effectively.[40]

Two official reports — those of the Council for Tertiary Education in Scotland,[41] and, ironically enough, the member/officer group on FE set up by Strathclyde regional council[42] — have confirmed the status of college councils as 'ineffective appendages to the Scottish further education system'.[43] The Strathclyde report boldly and uncharacteristically suggests that the injection of a little honesty would not be amiss: 'if real powers cannot be given to college councils then the authority should clearly state that they have simply an advisory role'.[44]

These examples cast further doubt on the theory of educational democracy to which most officials and councillors subscribe. That theory — that administrators are accountable to elected members, that elected members are accountable to the public, and that genuine public participation is catered for through such bodies as school and college councils — is best understood as a convenient fiction which serves the interests of both officials and councillors. From both their points of view it has a number of distinct advantages: in particular, it allows for a substantial amount of buck-passing when things go wrong and it obscures the way in which real political power is exercised. In short, councillors and officials have a good deal in common, not least a fear of real participatory democracy that would encourage grassroots decision-making — for that, of course, would inevitably be accompanied by a loss of authority for both directorate staff and elected members of education committees. Expressions of mutual hostility between the two groups (officials and politicians) may sometimes disguise the extent to which they share common goals but, in the final analysis, there seems little doubt that their commitment to their own interests is greater than their commitment to the ideals which are supposed to underlie public service. Both the mutual hostility and the shared values will be illustrated in the next section.

## A Director's View

It will be useful at this juncture to introduce the opinions of one of the leading directors of education in Scotland on some of the key issues raised above. Like inspectors, Scottish directors are not noted for their willingness to express clear and unambiguous views in public: they prefer the protection afforded by obliqueness and anonymity. Just occasionally, however, they do let themselves go, especially when they feel they have a sympathetic audience. The context of the example chosen — a speech by Mr Edward Miller, Director of Education for Strathclyde, given to a meeting of the Association of Directors held in Pitlochry in 1981[45] — is important to an understanding of the ideas expressed. ADES' meetings may be regarded by directors as offering a rare opportunity to share experiences in an atmosphere of mutual therapeutic support. To outsiders, however, Mr Miller's remarks may be regarded as either refreshingly frank or engagingly indiscreet.

He began with an intriguing characterisation of conflicting stances on education among Labour Party members:

> Within the Labour Party opinion is now sharply divided between the moderates who still afford the education service some respect and a residual loyalty and the radicals who feel strongly that the service and its directors are thirled to middle-class, bourgeois values, that we have failed to deliver the goods which we promised, that we are autocratic, oligarchical bureaucrats who cannot be trusted.[46]

It is not difficult to deduce which brand of socialism Mr Miller prefers — some respect and loyalty, however residual, is better than none. Part of the blame for the perceived loss of status is attributed to the drive for corporate management approaches and the reduction in departmental autonomy following regionalisation.

Mr Miller regrets these developments: he describes accountants and planners, who have extensive cross-departmental functions, as 'the new aristocrats of local government' and criticises the degree of trust that many politicians place in them: 'If I were a politician I would have no more confidence in them than in the former prima donnas in the service departments'.[47] He is also somewhat suspicious of the role assumed by 'inexperienced and junior officials from the chief executive's office'[48] in the preparation of policy options statements. This is an exercise conducted annually in Strathclyde and involves the finance department working out resource allocations, within which departmental heads have to produce a series of policy options. The staff of the chief executive's office 'have to be carefully handled since they are in very close touch with a few key elected members and can prejudice committee consideration of the options through their briefing of those members'.[49] Moreover, the policy options exercise 'is extremely complex and is fully understood by very few elected members . . . '[50] Behind these comments, it is possible to discern a feeling that things would be much better if the 'professionals' within the education department were given more independence. Mr Miller employs a less than elegant image to make the point:

> . . . we now face an army of local government colleagues who wish to assess, evaluate, monitor, indirectly control, inspect and generally act as watchdogs, leaving their visiting card with every administrative lamp-post they pass.[51]

Politicians too come in for attack. Mr Miller refers to the 'lack of understanding of the back bench members' on the council and wonders 'whether politicians really trust democracy'.[52] He is careful, however, to express some support for the received wisdom: 'Policy-making, of course, has always been the prerogative of elected members'.[53] At the same time, he is prepared to admit that 'we would be less than honest if we denied the extent to which officials have influenced or even diverted policies and have failed to monitor implementation'.[54] As has been noted, in Strathclyde the response to this problem has been the setting up of member-officer groups to look at various aspects of educational policy — S1-S2 provision, FE, etc.[55] Miller's position on this development might be described as defensive:

> The theory is both interesting and revealing; it is based on the perfectly understandable view that elected members have little or no opportunity of influencing important educational development or of monitoring the progress and outcome of any significant initiatives which have been taken. It also presupposes that other departments, particularly social work, have a contribution to make in this field: this, frankly and with all humility, I would question. Finally, it assumes that department heads will stifle fresh ideas from their subordinates who normally have better ideas anyway.[56]

And again:

> The officer/member group concept is dangerously vulnerable to exploitation. Just as political leaders can use it as a sop to keep discontented back benchers quiet and

hopefully out of any real mischief, so also can idealistic or ambitious back benchers use it to advance their political cause or their political future.[57]

Mr Miller also fears that member-officer reports are likely to be 'much more influenced by elected members than by officials'.[58] Elsewhere in his address he refers to the necessity for his fellow-administrators to do their job 'very much better than the surrogates who wish to do it for us'.[59] It is not entirely clear who he means when he uses the word 'surrogates', but once more a distinctly defensive note can be detected.

What is interesting in all this is the insight it gives into the thinking and priorities of one of the leading directors of education in Scotland. Clearly large amounts of time and energy are devoted to the internal politics of local government. Keeping tabs on would-be predatory colleagues from other departments, ensuring that politicians are made to feel important but preferably without allowing them too much scope for 'interference', generally protecting the interests of the true 'professionals' within the education department — these are the concerns that emerge as uppermost in Mr Miller's mind. They constitute classic bureaucratic symptoms: the result is that a kind of siege mentality develops which begins to divert attention from the ostensible purposes of the service.

It would, however, be unfair to dismiss Mr Miller's argument entirely as a rather unconvincing plea that directors of education should be regarded as unfortunate (if well-paid) victims of the territorial ambitions of fellow-administrators and politicians. He does have some bracing comments of an incidental nature to offer. For example, he describes — yet again displaying his penchant for the apt word — the theory and practice of the main political parties with regard to education as ' 'pathetic' ',[60] and asserts that 'it is only at local level that one can discern some genuine political movement in education'.[61] The SED is dismissed as 'never really the friend of the education service'[62] — a view with which many would concur but which really requires justification of a sort that Mr Miller does not attempt to offer. Finally, in a spirit of confession, albeit accompanied by a desire to spread the blame, Mr Miller admits that part of the explanation for the growing disenchantment with the education service from the late '60s onwards was that 'both we and our political masters were singularly inept in industrial relations'.[63] The next section, which looks at links between the directorate and the teaching profession, will offer evidence which lends support to this interpretation.

The 'political subsystem' of education, as it operates at regional level, demonstrates the extent to which the maintenance and, where possible, extension of power, rather than the provision of improved services, is a prime motivator. Private goals displace publicly stated objectives. Mr Miller's complaints about fellow-administrators and elected members are best understood as representative of the internal power struggles which characterise many large organisations. The common desire for power by officials and politicians is more significant than the specific occasions which provoke disputes. Both groups may find it disagreeable, but the fact remains that their similarities are greater than their differences.

## The Directorate and Teachers

The classic authoritarian personality is subserviant (if resentful) towards superiors and bullying towards subordinates. Judged by this standard, Scottish directors of education emerge as successful authoritarians. They pay lip service to the 'democratic' rights of councillors, while striving to circumvent the extension of political control over their own activities. At the same time, their treatment of teachers in schools is often crudely directive. These points will be illustrated with reference first to relations between directors and head teachers and then to relations between directors and less senior staff in schools.

Traditionally, head teachers in Scotland have enjoyed a fair amount of autonomy in such matters as the curriculum, disciplinary arrangements and internal management structures. Their independence has, however, never been total and, in particular, the appointment and dismissal of teachers has been a matter for the education authority, not individual head teachers. In recent years, partly arising out of general arguments about the need for greater accountability in education, a feeling has emerged that further reductions in the freedom of head teachers would be desirable. This notion has wide appeal — to the directorate, to parents and to classroom teachers. The value of any system of accountability depends, however, on the quality and fairness of those who enforce it, and there are grounds for thinking that directorate staff, who have become the principal agents of enforcement, fall well short of the ideal in this regard.

The issue has exercised the minds of members of the Headteachers' Association of Scotland and in 1983 they produced a document entitled 'The Headteacher and his [*sic*] Employer — Some Thoughts on the Relationship'. This document notes that 'disputes have occurred between individual Headteachers and their Authority concerning the responsibilities of the Headteacher, whether stated or implied'[64] and concludes that a thorough investigation of the whole topic is required. It is clear that head teachers feel themselves to be increasingly constrained by a range of external forces — national legislation, SED policy, inspectorate 'advice', administrative instructions, memoranda and guidelines issued by education authorities, staffing levels and qualifications, parental pressures, the policies of teachers' organisations, resource limitations, etc. They recognise the validity — or, at least, the reality — of these constraints but nonetheless maintain, with some justice, that it is the head teacher who, in practice, carries responsibility for what happens in the school. He 'must in the last resort make any necessary decisions and it is important . . . that his role as decision maker in this area must be recognised and agreed'.[65] On the specific subject of relations between head teachers and the directorate the Association has this to say:

> In theory the Headteacher is responsible to the Education Authority; in practice, the Authority delegates its supervisory powers to officers to whom the Headteacher becomes responsible.
>
> In order to clarify the situation and to avoid difficulties that arise when the principles of line management are applied to educational administration, it should be

incumbent on the Authority to work out, in collaboration with local Headteachers, a clear policy on management structure and responsibilities. This would remove doubts and misunderstandings on Headteachers' relationships with Education Officers with special responsibilities, e.g. Further education, or with Officers of limited experience. The arrangement would depend on local conditions, e.g. size of Region and type of administrative structure. In drawing up such an arrangement, it is essential to keep in mind the special position occupied by the Headteacher as Head of his school, his special responsibility for the safety of his pupils — and his responsibility to parents and the community. The unique position of the Headteacher suggests that the school should be regarded as an independent establishment over which the Head has authority.[66]

These are clearly difficult issues, to which there is no simple solution. Some authorities have, however, shown little sensitivity in handling them and have opted for the issuing of directives. Lothian and Grampian regions, for example, have sent circulars to head teachers regarding the mechanisms for dealing with complaints.[67] The prescriptions of the Grampian circular, issued by James Graham, senior depute director of education, on the instructions of the chief executive, Douglas McNaughton, were fairly comprehensive in their coverage:

As there have been one or two occasions recently where Head Teachers have written to outside persons or bodies in their capacity as employees of the Authority, I have been instructed by the Chief Executive to make quite clear the fact that all Head Teachers owe a direct responsibility to their employer and, if they are aggrieved by any decisions taken by that employer, their official recourse is to take the matter up with the Director of Education.

I wish to reiterate, therefore, that members of Regional staff should not contact bodies, organisations or individuals, including Members of Parliament, in order to ventilate grievances about their work.[68]

The fear of public criticism is quite explicit here and betrays a willingness to suppress legitimate debate on important matters of public policy in the interests of administrative convenience. Insistence on proceeding *via* 'proper channels' serves both to identify critics and to control the sort of investigation that takes place. There is no recognition of the possibility that, if head teachers do contact outside bodies, it may be because they have found that 'official recourse' is no recourse at all. Unquestioning acceptance of the circular by head teachers would no doubt make life more comfortable for members of the directorate and other council officials, but that comfort might well be purchased at the cost of failing to address real problems experienced in the schools. John Fraser, rector of Mackie Academy, Stonehaven, expressed his objections in these terms: 'I don't accept ... that headteachers are line managers. We are there to represent the interests of our school, which must mean allowing us a certain freedom of expression and action'.[69]

Another head teacher, Brian Boyd of Barrhead High School in the Renfrew division of Strathclyde, has advanced the very reasonable general principle that 'The relationship between headteacher and education officials needs careful examination if educational progress is not to be hindered'.[70] He refers to the 'management-teacher split' as 'the most divisive and unproductive dichotomy in education today'[71] and expresses concern about the ambivalent role of headteachers, caught in the middle. Boyd also notes that recent advertisements for head teachers' posts in Strathclyde have stressed 'skills in participatory management' and 'consultation',[72] a somewhat ironic requirement given the poor record of the Strathclyde directorate in precisely these areas. It is evident, for example, from the activities of the area planning groups set up by Strathclyde as part of its post-16 strategy that 'consultation' is to be interpreted by head teachers as an ability to get their staff to 'cooperate' with regional policy. As in so many other areas of Scottish education, the 'dialogue' is carefully stage-managed, in this case under the chairmanship of an education officer.[73] At a meeting of Strathclyde's education committee in April 1984, the chairman, Dr Malcolm Green, stated firmly that 'The days of the autonomy and autocracy of the individual headteacher are dead and will not be revived'.[74] It is apparent that, within Strathclyde at least, they are to be replaced by the autocracy of the directorate, acting with the backing of the chairman, if not with the unqualified support of the education committee as a whole.

What of relations between the directorate and classroom teachers? Until very recently, directors of education have had little difficulty in controlling the actions and public statements of teaching staff. The promotion structure was used as a means of encouraging 'constructive' responses to proposals emanating from the directorate and discouraging expressions of criticism from potential dissidents. These are familiar tactics in most large organisations and they can be used in ways that make it very difficult to establish that any impropriety has taken place. For example, assessments of candidates given over the telephone are not subject to the constraints of written references. Selection procedures vary from authority to authority but the most important person in the process is invariably a member of the directorate. One assistant head teacher in Strathclyde, for example, who has served on a number of promotion panels, has never encountered a situation in which the preferences of the divisional education officer have been opposed. In such circumstances, a widespread belief that promotion depends on flattering one's superiors and suppressing doubts about the wisdom of regional policies soon develops. It is, of course, a belief that serves as an easy refuge for the bitter and the cynical, but the fact that it gains currency ensures that most teachers tread carefully. Their caution is reinforced by another factor deriving from their own value system. Teachers tend, as a group, to be fairly conformist. Indeed, their school and university careers have been marked by success in conforming to the expectations of others. Furthermore, Scottish teachers are, in social terms, often upwardly mobile, being recruited from the working and lower-middle classes: thus they seek status and respectability and eagerly embrace the self-interested ethic of 'professionalism'. All this tends to promote compliance.

There are, however, some indications that the external and internal pressures to conform are no longer working to the same extent and that Scottish teachers are increasingly prepared to risk the disapproval of directorate staff. Three reasons for this change can be identified, all of which can be traced to developments at national level but which, in practice, have been worked out at local level, since it is the education authorities that are formally responsible for the running of schools and the employment of teachers. First, there is the vexed question of salaries. Discontent among teachers about the low level of their salaries mounted during 1983 and led to selective industrial action throughout Scotland during 1984–85, a pattern which may well continue in the 1985–86 session. Their anger was increased by the refusal of the Secretary of State to allow an independent review on the grounds that this would constitute a 'blank cheque' — a tacit admission that the teachers' claims that they had fallen badly behind in financial terms were justified. The sense of injustice felt by teachers was intensified by the extra demands placed upon them by the various reforms that had been introduced — notably the Munn/Dunning programme and the 16–18 Action Plan. These extra demands constitute the second reason for the growing militancy of teachers. The third reason derives from the consequences of falling school rolls and the inevitability of closures. In such a situation, promotion prospects decline rapidly. Indeed, when schools are closed there is the added problem of absorbing existing promoted staff into the remaining institutions. Whereas in the early '70s it was not uncommon for teachers to be promoted as soon as their probationary period was finished, in the mid-'80s the prospects for able and ambitious young teachers are bleak. Their motivation is often not helped by a feeling that their promoted colleagues, who enjoyed the benefits of the years of expansion, are sometimes not wholly deserving of the status they enjoy. The overall result is a decline in respect for authority and the growing ineffectiveness of the promotion system as a control mechanism.

This is a relatively new situation for the authorities to have to deal with and they have responded in a fashion that can only be described as 'crisis management'. The decision by Strathclyde region's education committee to abolish corporal punishment from session 1982–83 may be taken as an example. As the session proceeded it became apparent that serious disciplinary problems had arisen in many schools as a result of the removal of the belt as a sanction. Letters began appearing in the correspondence columns of *The Glasgow Herald* signed by large numbers of staff in various schools — for example Waverley, Albert and Victoria Drive secondaries in Glasgow[75] — drawing attention to the severe difficulties they faced. Some of the letters, it should be emphasised, expressed support for the general principle of abolition but questioned the authority's management of the exercise, particularly with regard to timing and the effectiveness of alternative sanctions. One indicator of this last problem was that the number of pupils suspended from schools within Strathclyde region trebled between February 1982 and February 1983.[76] Some politicians and administrators seemed to suggest that part of the explanation for the increase was over-reaction on the part of teachers, an interpretation that did nothing to calm the situation. Suspicions that private pressure would be put on teachers to restrict the number of suspensions arose.[77] On March 8, 1983 a 'very angry meeting' involving Glasgow head teachers, the chairman of the education committee, Dr Green, and senior officials took place. It was subsequently alleged that head teachers were urged by 'members of Glasgow's educational hierarchy' to 'stay silent on the subject of increasingly grave disciplinary problems in . . . schools' — a strategy described as 'a deplorable attack on fundamental democratic rights'.[78] On March 18, in a move suggestive of closing the stable door after the horse has bolted, the education committee of COSLA, also chaired by Dr Green, agreed to form an internal working group to draw up guidelines for schools on alternative methods of dealing with disruptive behaviour, to be made available for the following session.[79] These moves failed to silence the critics who continued to bombard the press with increasingly outspoken comments. The chairman of the Glasgow local association of the EIS, G. A. Warnock, wrote, for example, of 'the desperate attempts by our political masters to deflect blame on any group or sector other than themselves'.[80] In the face of the unprecedented militancy of teachers, and the failure of the usual containment strategies, Dr Green and the Strathclyde directorate adopted different tactics. It was announced that the region would conduct its own study of the problem and that senior education officials would visit all secondary schools in the region before drawing up a list of recommendations. This internal exercise was preferred to an alternative proposal which would have involved parents and teachers as well as councillors and officials.[81] In May, anticipating the findings of the report, Dr Green stated that the situation had improved and expressed confidence that it would continue to get better. Finally, in July — significantly at a time when most teachers would be on holiday — the directorate's 'findings' were presented to the education committee.[82] It was asserted that 'there is no breakdown of a disciplined learning environment in Strathclyde schools'[83] and that 'Measures taken by the authority have been appreciated by schools and have contributed to an improvement in teacher morale'.[84] Other revealing comments included 'The key to discipline is in the hands of the class teacher'[85] and 'the question of discipline in schools should be given less publicity'.[86] Taken as a whole, the report seemed more concerned with the public image of the authority than with offering sensible practical suggestions.

As an exercise in crisis management, the corporal punishment issue is interesting for several reasons. First, it illustrates what Edward Miller himself has referred to as the region's 'singularly inept' record in industrial relations: by any standards, the matter was handled badly. Secondly, it reveals the resentment of councillors towards teachers who dare to express criticism of the education committee. One councillor, for example, referred to an 'orchestrated campaign' being mounted and said that he knew of no cases of teachers approaching their councillors through normal channels.[87] The possibility of teachers having no confidence in their councillors did not seem to occur to him. Anti-teacher feeling among elected representatives is not a new phenomenon, and part of the explanation is almost certainly the fact that teachers tend, in the main, to be better educated than most councillors: they are, therefore, less likely to be impressed by the self-serving rhetoric that politicians frequently resort to. Usually, however, teachers keep their dissent to themselves, and this leads directly to the third interesting feature of this particular episode. For once, the familiar tactics of subtle and not-so-subtle arm-twisting, reassurance, promises of 'consultation', etc., failed to work — at least for a while. The issue of indiscipline was finally swept under the carpet only because of the region's decision to play for time and the convenient intervention of the school holidays. But the experience of forcing the directorate and the chairman of the education committee onto the defensive, subjecting them to public embarrassment, requiring from them a degree of accountability to which they are not normally subject, is unlikely to be forgotten by teachers. It is indicative of a changed situation in which the carrot of promotion and the stick of directorate disapproval are ceasing to be effective as control mechanisms.[88]

## The Advisory Service

Located between the directorate on the one hand and teachers on the other are members of the advisory service. In June 1984 there were some 263 full-time and 38 part-time advisers in Scotland,[89] so, numerically at least, they constitute a significant group. Almost all are former teachers of wide experience. Their principal functions are to offer advice to education authorities and teaching staff in schools on curriculum matters although, as will be shown, in recent years their work has diversified in ways that have led to a fair amount of role confusion. Before developing this point, however, it will be useful to expand a little on the mainstream work of advisers and to sketch the development of the service. These tasks are made easier by the publication, in June 1982, of a report by the Association of Educational Advisers in Scotland examining the work of the service.[90]

Once particular educational policies have been approved at national and local levels, advisers offer support to the schools in translating them into practice. This includes the provision of in-service courses, which may be based in schools or at teachers' centres, advice about the selection and use of resources, visits to schools to monitor progress, and the dissemination of knowledge about successful strategies. Frequent contact with schools to discuss curriculum, assessment, organisation and teaching methods is regarded as basic to the work of advisers. Their acceptance by teaching staff is dependent on a recognition of their expertise which, in turn, depends on an appreciation of the practical problems encountered in schools. Advisers also participate in the work of local study groups and working parties, and assist with the running of resource centres. Their advice is sought by administrators on the selection, placement and promotion of teaching staff. They are involved in liaison with colleges of education and HMIs, especially in relation to in-service provision, and they are frequently called upon to give talks to conferences. At national level, they contribue to the work of the CCC, the SEB and other bodies.

Although the work of advisers is wide-ranging in character, their formal powers are very limited, and this means that they must rely on persuasion and cooperation rather than direction. In some respects, diplomatic skills are more important than intellectual ones as frequently advisers have to remain patient in the face of indifference or obstruction on the part of some schools and teachers, and rigidity or lack of understanding on the part of some administrators. In short, they occupy a rather delicate position in the educational hierarchy, a position that is not made easier by the fact that the service has had a relatively short history. Prior to the 1960s, there were few advisers employed by education authorities in Scotland and, where they did exist, they usually had very specific remits associated with creative and aesthetic subjects. The number of advisers increased rapidly in the late '60s and early '70s, a growth that is usually explained in terms of 'the many developments taking place at that time in the school system'[91] — developments such as those signalled by the publication of the *Primary Memorandum,* the ending of selection for secondary education, and the raising of the school leaving age. There were differences between the primary and the secondary sectors when the first new appointments were made. Whereas primary advisers were usually expected to have a general expertise for the whole age and subject range, secondary advisers were very much subject specialists in, for example, English or Mathematics or Science. This pattern has gradually changed, with more primary advisers assuming, in addition to their general remit for a group of schools, responsibility for specific areas of the curriculum (for example, environmental studies, language arts, aesthetic subjects), and more secondary advisers adding general or cross-curricular responsibilities (for example, assessment, educational technology, multi-cultural education, school-industry liaison) to their particular subject remits. The 1982 report of the Assocation of Educational Advisers welcomes these developments but notes that they create some difficulties: in particular, an extended role brings with it increased involvement in extra activities, both local and national, and this eats into the time available for direct contact with schools, on which the credibility of the service ultimately depends. Questions of status are involved in this, although the report is hesitant about addressing them directly. Advisers undoubtedly want to contribute to policy-making — thus their keenness to be represented on SEB and CCC panels and committees — as this enhances their standing in the educational world. However, the more they are drawn into the bureaucratic machinery of regional committees and educational quangos, the more they are likely to be perceived by classroom teachers as part of an external hierarchy rather than as partners in a collaborative enterprise. It is, in any case, doubtful whether advisers are really committed to a partnership model, despite many statements to that effect. Some comments convey the impression that they are keen to distance themselves from classroom teachers in respect of status. For example: 'It is worth noting . . . that nearly all advisers had already held a promoted post (Head Teacher, Assistant Head Teacher or Principal Teacher) before appointment and consequently had an appreciation of a range of educational issues greater than one could reasonably expect of a class teacher'.[92] This can be linked to a later passage dealing with the 'prospects for job-satisfaction and career opportunities for advisers'[93] at a time of rapid educational change. An oblique approach is made to the possibility of a system of promoted posts. Reference is made to 'a concept of a spectrum of advisory styles'[94] ranging from 'those whose duties lie mainly in the field of forming policies and strategies from a centralised position, to those whose work is mainly conducted in the schools'.[95] Some authorities, it is noted, 'have responded to this spectrum of duties by introducing a hierarchical structure with up to six levels (*viz* Chief Adviser, Principal Adviser, Senior Adviser, Adviser, Assistant Adviser and Advisory Teacher)'.[96] It is acknowledged that 'a non-hierarchical structure' might be the best way of ensuring that credibility in the eyes of teachers which was earlier deemed so vital but, nevertheless, the report concludes by rejecting this on the grounds that 'every other branch of the education service has a clear hierarchy of posts allowing for career development'.[97]

It is easy to castigate advisers for their concern with status and their pursuit of a system of differentiated positions and rewards. Given the prevailing forms of local government, however, their aspiration is understandable, if not particularly commendable. In those authorities, such as Strathclyde, where all advisers are nominally of the same status, their position is weak. They have little scope for independent initiative and often feel themselves to be impeded by members of the directorate, to whom they are formally responsible. By contrast, the Chief Adviser in Lothian is himself a senior member of the directorate and this means that his staff have greater authority and greater access to the policy-making process. Viewed in this light, the Association of Advisers' preference for a clear career pattern is perhaps best regarded as a pragmatic response to the existing structures of local educational administration. It is a response that demonstrates the potency of those structures in shaping the perceptions of those who work within them, and that reinforces the necessity, observed in Chapter 2, of trying to explain the *interaction* of individual, professional and institutional forces.

The report also comments on the question of accountability — both the accountability of schools and of the advisory service itself. It is said that advisers have a part to play in assisting schools to formulate and present their aims and objectives, in helping them to establish criteria for internal evaluation, and in devising strategies for the monitoring of standards across a region or division. The need to assess the work of advisers is also accepted, but 'the nature of the process by which the assessment would be carried out is far from clear'.[98] An impression of considerable caution on this issue is conveyed. It is acknowledged that 'goals and objectives would have to be established',[99] against which the advisorate could be assessed, but the report makes no attempt to specify these goals. The only proposal, expressed in vague terms, is that 'The agents of assessment would probably have to include ... [the] directorate, schools, HM Inspectorate and advisers themselves'.[100]

The relation between advisors and inspectors is of particular interest because there is some overlap of function between the two groups. The Rendle Report on the inspectorate makes reference to this in its comments on the failure of education authorities to take sufficient responsibility for policy development. Instead of always looking to the centre, education authorities should, Rendle recommends, 'aim to be more self-sufficient'.[101] As part of this, it is urged that greater use should be made of the advisory service which, in manpower terms, is two and a half times stronger than the inspectorate: at present there is 'a lack of clarity . . . as to how the roles of the Inspectorate and of advisers relate to each other . . . '[102] Again:

> It is unfortunate . . . that . . . advisers seem not, in general, to have a credibility throughout the system which is in keeping with the role they play, or should play . . . [T]he tendency for the Inspectorate to regard advisorates as a whole in a somewhat patronising way seems to mark a slight unease at the possibility that effective advisorates might threaten their own role.[103]

In the light of this statement it is disappointing to note how timid the report of the Association of Educational Advisers is in its remarks about the future role of members. Certainly the possibility that advisers should take on a more inspectorial role than hitherto is not viewed with enthusiasm. Such a role would involve them in passing formal judgement on the competence of teachers and schools and would alter the nature of their relationship with teaching staff. Advisers undoubtedly do form opinions about the strengths and weaknesses of particular teachers, subject departments and schools — and these are generally taken into account when teaching staff are being considered for promotion — but they prefer to operate in an informal way, building up relationships and adopting a supportive rather than a judgemental stance when problems arise. A formal role might tend to undermine the existing pattern of informal links on which advisers feel the success of their work depends. At the same time, however, that very informality helps to explain their weak position in the system: they simply do not have the authority of inspectors or members of the directorate.

This leaves them open to manipulation, and it is likely that they will be pushed in the direction of an inspectorial role whether they like it or not, of a kind that they are likely to be unhappy with. The Secretary of State's decision to publish the results of inspections carried out by HMIs has had important repercussions at regional level. An adverse report on a school is perceived by directors of education as an adverse report on the authority. This can be publicly embarrassing, and some authorities are already using advisers as 'early warning' monitors who are expected to anticipate problems and ensure that schools are not subject to serious criticism. This practice might, of course, be defended on the grounds that it keeps schools up to the mark, but it will undoubtedly alter perceptions of the purpose of the advisory service. Furthermore, the motive behind it would appear to have as much to do with ensuring that the directorate do not become subject to direct public scrutiny as with maintaining good standards of teaching and learning.

It is, in fact, possible to detect the beginnings of a trend in which advisers are increasingly being used for political rather than educational purposes. This can be seen in the case of Mr Kenneth Fee, a teacher of English at Hillpark Secondary School, Glasgow, who was compulsorily transferred following disciplinary action. Mr Fee, a prominent SNP activist, was disciplined for absenting himself from school to attend a St. Andrew's Day rally. This provoked a storm of protest, especially as it was claimed that other teachers who later took part in a day of action in support of the miners' strike were not similarly punished.[104] Accusations of political double standards were made against the ruling Labour administration in

Strathclyde. The problem was further exacerbated by the fact that there had been a history of conflict at Hillpark between, on the one hand, the teaching staff and, on the other, the head teacher and members of the directorate. In an attempt to defuse the situation, a member of the advisory service *from another division in Strathclyde* was drafted in to offer 'support' to the English staff at Hillpark. It is hard to resist the conclusion that this move was an attempt to take the heat from education officers in Glasgow by using the unfortunate adviser as a barrier to protect them from direct criticism. In a sense, he was being placed in a 'no win' position. If he failed to resolve the situation, he would be regarded as unsuccessful in the eyes of his superiors: but, equally, if he succeeded, he would be looked upon by teaching staff as merely acting for the directorate.

The report of the Association of Educational Advisers does address itself briefly to the general question of relations with the directorate. Circumspect reference is made to a feeling among advisers that since the reorganisation of local government their relationship with educational administrators has deteriorated. It is not stated directly — and, in this respect, the submissive tone of the report could be said to reflect the problem which it seeks to identify — but it is hinted that advisers have become little more than functionaries, expected to carry out the directives of administrators. In order to remedy this

> A structure of communication including regular meetings with all members of the directorate is essential. One member of the directorate should have responsibility for general coordination of the advisory team; meetings with this officer should be frequent and he should represent the advisory service on the authority's senior management team. Goodwill and an emphasis on good personal relationships, together with a clear structure for consultation, should ensure that, on the one hand, administrators will appreciate the full implications of curricular policies and, on the other hand, advisers will appreciate the demands and constraints arising from other aspects of the local authority system.[105]

The extent to which this pattern of communication would actually improve the position of advisers is doubtful. It is much more likely that the member of the directorate responsible for the advisory service would 'represent' the directorate's views *to* the advisorate, rather than *vice versa.* Furthermore, the uncritical acceptance by advisers of a remit confined to 'curricular policies' is hardly likely to lead to them being taken more seriously. The truth of the matter is that advisers do not possess sufficient muscle to make much of an impact within the structure of local government. For this they are partly to blame themselves because of their supine attitude towards the directorate. In addition, the nature of their work means that they have few natural allies and limited opportunity to organise themselves as an effective pressure group.

Towards the end of the report, three questions are posed: 'If advisers are essentially a source of expertise, is this source being tapped as effectively as it might be? ... Are all head teachers sufficiently responsive to the needs of their staffs to encourage their participation in [in-service] work [provided by the advisory service]? ... Do directorate staff and elected members make adequate use of the advice available to them in the pursuit of their decision-making?'[106] The implied answer to all of these questions is 'No' but, symptomatically, the writers of the report do not have the courage to argue their case explicitly. In the absence of such courage, it seems likely that advisers will continue to be dissatisfied with their lot and remain open to exploitation by the directorate.

*Notes and References*

1. W. A. Gatherer, 'The boss's job', *TEES,* May 25, 1984, p. 16.
2. *Education (Scotland) Act 1980,* HMSO, London, para. 1(1).
3. *Ibid.,* para. 78.
4. See Strathclyde Regional Council, *Estimates of the Education Committee for the Year Ending 31st March 1984.* Detailed statistical information about the educational service in Strathclyde can be found in the *Annual Data Reviews* produced by the Department of Education.
5. See A. Worthington, Policy Review Groups, unpublished MEd thesis, University of Glasgow, 1979 and Gordon D. Jeyes, Political Administration of Secondary Education in the Strathclyde Region, unpublished MEd thesis, University of Stirling, 1984.
6. *The New Scottish Local Authorities: Organisation and Management Structures,* HMSO, Edinburgh, 1973.
7. Michael Keating and Arthur Midwinter, *The Government of Scotland,* Mainstream, Edinburgh, 1983, p. 117.
8. Limitations of space prevent a detailed consideration of these differences, but see *Ibid.,* chapter 6.
9. *Ibid.,* p. 123.
10. *COSLA Information Booklet,* Edinburgh, 1982, p. 22. See also Keating and Midwinter, *op.cit.,* pp. 102–107.
11. *COSLA Information Booklet,* p. 31.
12. Keating and Midwinter, *op.cit.,* p. 105.
13. *Ibid.,* p. 106.
14. *Ibid.,* p. 107.
15. Ian Flett, ' 'A spectrum of distinguished talents' ', *Education,* September 12, 1980, p. 254.
16. *Ibid.,* p. 254.
17. *Ibid.,* p. 254.
18. For example, in 1981 the principal speakers were J. Munn, Chairman, CCC and D. McNicoll, Secretary, CCC.
19. At a meeting of the Council of ADES in Edinburgh on June 11, 1982.
20. Flett., *op.cit.,* p. 254.
21. See ADES' Council *Minutes,* November 7, 1980, para. 3 (c).
22. Quoted in Flett, *op.cit.,* p. 254.
23. *Ibid.,* p. 254.
24. Gordon D. Jeyes, Political Administration of Secondary Education in the Strathclyde Region, University of Stirling, 1984.
25. *Ibid.,* p. 53.

26. *Ibid.,* p. 59.
27. *Ibid.,* p. 54.
28. See Ronald Young, 'Management of Political Innovation', *Local Government Studies,* Nov./Dec. 1981, p. 18.
29. See, e.g., Jeyes, *op.cit.,* p. 52.
30. See 'What's the Score in Scotland's Regions?', *Local Government Forum,* No. 2, Paisley College of Technology, 1982, pp. 4–5.
31. See A. M. Macbeth, M. L. Mackenzie and I. Breckenridge, *Scottish School Councils: Policy-Making, Participation or Irrelevence?,* HMSO, Edinburgh, 1980.
32. See report in *TESS,* May 23, 1981, p. 1.
33. *Ibid.,* p. 1.
34. See report in *TESS,* August 5, 1983, p. 1 and letter by Morris J. Service, *TESS,* August 12, 1983, p. 5.
35. John Cairney, *GH,* December 28, 1983, p. 8.
36. Hugh Dougherty, 'Viewpoint', *TESS,* November 18, 1983, p. 72.
37. *Ibid.,* p. 72.
38. *Ibid.,* p. 72.
39. *Ibid.,* p. 72.
40. Kenneth B. Scott, 'The Development of College Councils in Scottish Further Education Colleges', *Scottish Educational Review,* Vol. 15, No. 2, 1983, p. 130.
41. Council for Tertiary Education in Scotland, *Review of Structure and Management,* SED, Edinburgh, 1981.
42. Strathclyde Regional Council, *The Further Education College Service: The Basis for Future Provision,* Glasgow, 1981.
43. Scott, *op.cit.,* p. 131.
44. Quoted in *Ibid.,* p. 130.
45. Edward Miller, 'It's never too late', *Education,* May 8, 1981, pp. 419–420.
46. *Ibid.,* p. 419.
47. *Ibid.,* p. 420.
48. *Ibid.,* p. 420.
49. *Ibid.,* p. 420.
50. *Ibid.,* p. 420.
51. *Ibid.,* p. 419.
52. *Ibid.,* p. 420.
53. *Ibid.,* p. 420.
54. *Ibid.,* p. 420.
55. For a detailed discussion of the member-officer initiative, see Jeyes, *op.cit.*, Chapter 6.
56. Miller, *op.cit.,* p. 420.
57. *Ibid.,* p. 420.
58. *Ibid.,* p. 420.
59. *Ibid.,* p. 419.
60. *Ibid.,* p. 419.
61. *Ibid.,* p. 419.
62. *Ibid.,* p. 419.
63. *Ibid.,* p. 419.
64. Headteachers' Association of Scotland, 'The Headteacher and his Employer — Some Thoughts on the Relationship', 1983, 'Conclusion'.
65. Ibid., para. 6.1.
66. Ibid., paras. 4–4.2.

67. On Lothian, see letter by Mary Scolan in *The Scotsman,* January 20, 1984; on Grampian, see report in *TESS,* May 6, 1983, p. 3.

68. Grampian Regional Council — Education Department, Circular No. AEC/451/JGG/HP, April 29, 1983.

69. Quoted in *TESS* report, May 6, 1983, p. 3.

70. Brian Boyd, 'What price autonomy?', *TESS,* November 2, 1984, p. 2.

71. *Ibid.,* p. 2.

72. *Ibid.,* p. 2.

73. For a defence of Strathclyde's policy, see Neil Munro's interview with Frank Pignatelli, assistant director of education in Strathclyde, *TESS,* April 27, 1984, p. 5.

74. Reported in *TESS,* April 27, 1984.

75. See report on Waverley, *GH,* February 18, 1983, p. 5 and letters from the staff of Albert (March 3, 1983, p. 8) and Victoria Drive (March 17, 1983, p. 8).

76. See reports in *GH,* March 17, 1983, p. 5, and March 18, 1983, pp. 1–2.

77. See report in *GH,* March 17, 1983, p. 5.

78. Letter by D. Bowman, *et al, GH,* March 17, 1983, p. 8.

79. See report in *GH,* March 19, 1983, p. 3.

80. Letter by G. A. Warnock, *GH,* March 23, 1983, p. 10.

81. See report in *GH,* May 12, 1983, p. 5.

82. Strathclyde Regional Council, Department of Education, 'Discipline in Schools: Report by Director', June 30, 1983.

83. Ibid., para. 5.1.

84. Ibid., para. 5.2.

85. Ibid., para. 6.5.

86. Ibid., para. 5.8.

87. See report in *GH,* March 10, 1983, p. 5.

88. The management skills of the Strathclyde directorate have been particularly criticised, but similar difficulties have arisen in other authorities. In 1981, for example, relations between teachers and the Director of Education for Orkney reached what a meeting of the local EIS described as 'an intolerable level'. It was claimed that ten 'particularly bitter disputes' between teachers and the director had occurred since 1977 and that proper procedures in dealing with disciplinary and transfer matters had not been followed (see report in *TESS,* June 19, 1981, p. 1). Again, in 1984, Tayside regional council was found guilty of sexual discrimination by an industrial tribunal investigating the case of Miss Helen Budge, a blind music teacher at Kirkton High School, Dundee, who had been passed over for promotion. In the course of the evidence it emerged that the region's own statistics showed that three men to every one woman were chosen for promoted posts and that, at Kirkton, in the five years prior to 1984, all promoted posts for which equal numbers of males and females had applied had gone to men. Both the rector of the school and the convener of the education committee were severely criticised in the report of the tribunal (see reports in *The Scotsman,* May 12, 1984, p. 5 and *GH,* May 12, 1984, p. 3). Borders Regional Council has also been found guilty of sexual discrimination by an industrial tribunal which investigated its treatment of part-time teachers (see report in *The Scotsman,* March 9, 1984, p. 9).

Education authorities have also encountered problems arising from their dealings with parents, especially over interpretations of what is involved in 'consultation'. For example, parents of children at Ormiston Primary School in East Lothian complained in July 1983 about the absence of education officials at meetings held to protest about the proposed introduction of three composite classes. Notwithstanding the objections, the chairman of the regional education committee said he had every confidence in the Director of Education (see report in *TESS,* July 8, 1983, p. 1). Finally, in November 1984 Highland Region's education committee was criticised by Sheriff William Fulton for failing to provide transport for a six-year-old boy who had to walk along almost two miles of exposed coast road in order to get to school. The authority had taken the father to court on the grounds that the boy had not been attending school regularly (see reports in *GH,* November 28, 1984, p. 3 and *Scotsman,* November 28, 1984, p. 11). According to the Sheriff, the committee had acted 'with either an astonishing disinterest in informing themselves of the full facts and circumstances of [the boy's] case, or what can only be described as an inhuman and appalling indifference to the safety and welfare of a six-year-old child . . . '

These represent only a few cases in which disputes have arisen. It cannot be assumed, of course, that in every instance the protestors have a monopoly of right. What can be said, however, it that problems occur with sufficient frequency, in authorities throughout Scotland, to suggest that regional officials are not particularly skilful in matters of procedure and communication, and that they often fail to convince teachers and parents that they have been dealt with fairly.

89. National Committee for the In-Service Training of Teachers, *Arrangements for the Staff Development of Teachers,* Report to the Secretary of State for Scotland, June 1984, para. 6.3.

90. Association of Educational Advisers in Scotland, *The Scottish Educational Advisory Service in the Eighties,* June 1982.

91. *Ibid.,* p. 2.

92. *Ibid.,* p. 2.

93. *Ibid.,* p. 5.

94. *Ibid.,* p. 6.

95. *Ibid.,* p. 6.

96. *Ibid.,* p. 6.

97. *Ibid.,* p. 6.

98. *Ibid.,* p. 8.

99. *Ibid.,* p. 8.

100. *Ibid.,* p. 8.

101. *Rendle Report,* para. 11.3.

102. *Ibid.,* para. 11.4.

103. *Ibid.,* para. 11.5.

104. See reports in *GH,* December 12, 21 and 29, 1983, January 24, 1984, and July 7, 1984.

105. *The Scottish Educational Advisory Service in the Eighties,* p. 9.

106. *Ibid.,* p. 11.

# 7
# *The False God of Professionalism*

## Introduction

In Chapter 2 professionalism was introduced as one of the key analytic concepts of this study. It was pointed out that Scottish teachers have always been very much concerned with professional status and have been anxious to secure greater recognition for their particular skills and the important social function they serve. At the same time, it was suggested that there were a number of ambiguities inherent in the notion of professionalism — deriving, for example, from the decidedly cool attitude which most teachers have towards their professional training, the implied devaluation of classroom teaching brought about by a promotion structure in which reward takes the form of transfer into administration, and the tendency for the interests of the professionals to assume greater importance than those of the clients. The aim of the present chapter is to examine these issues in more detail with particular reference to three important bodies that have a stake in promoting the idea of professionalism — teachers' associations, colleges of education, and the General Teaching Council (GTC). In each case an attempt will be made to give some basic factual information about the functions of the body (or bodies) concerned as a preliminary to the development of an interpretative position.

As the title of this chapter indicates, the argument to be advanced will be strongly critical of some aspects of professionalism. Lest this be misunderstood, it should be stated clearly at the outset that what will be challenged is the way in which appeals to professionalism are often deployed for rather unworthy purposes, especially by members of the leadership class. The intention is certainly not to denigrate the work of classroom teachers. In so far as the term 'professionalism' is used to indicate the importance of teachers who are intelligent, well-qualified and committeed to the welfare of their pupils, few people would deny that these are indeed valuable qualities. It is when other connotations are introduced that problems arise. The nature of linguistic usage is such, however, that it is impossible to strip away the accretions which have overlaid the basic sense of competence and service to the client. In fact, it can be argued that the point has now been reached where it is questionable whether the invocation of professionalism serves any creditable purpose at all. To suggest this will be regarded as heresy in many sections of the Scottish educational world. So potent has the idea of professionalism become that for many people it seems impossible to conceptualise education in any other terms. This point was made by Tony Worthington in an article written in 1981:

> A profession can grow so powerful in the way it structures a society's perception of the service it controls that people lose the ability to imagine an alternative. A profession can colonise the mind.[1]

In the process of colonisation, the teachers' associations, the colleges of education and the GTC have all played their part, and it is to an analysis of their respective roles that attention must now be directed.

## Teachers' Organisations

Whatever else they do, teachers' organisations exist to look after the interests of their members. These interests related not only to salaries and conditions of service — though often these are of most immediate concern — but also to the esteem in which teachers are held by the community at large and the extent to which their expertise is recognised and valued. The various teachers' associations in Scotland give different emphasis to these elements, which can be regarded as lying on a continuum from'unionism' to 'professionalism'. At one end of the continuum there is the National Association of Schoolmasters/Union of Women Teachers (NAS/UWT) which describes itself unashamedly as a trade union and tends to take a fairly militant, if somewhat conservative, stance on most issues: it was the first teachers' organisation in Scotland to affiliate to the Scottish Trades Union Congress (STUC). At the other end there is the Professional Association of Teachers (PAT), which is pledged never to strike or take other disruptive action in pursuit of its objectives. Both NAS/UWT and PAT are part of much larger organisations which have their headquarters in England, and they seek to make a virtue of this British dimension. However, their membership in Scotland remains small. According to Jim O'Neill, Scottish Regional Official, the number of NAS/UWT members in Scotland in July 1984 was approximately 2,500. John Bell, who became the first full-time Scottish official of PAT in 1983, stated that his assocation's membership in July 1984 was about 2,250.

A third organisation, the Scottish Secondary Teachers' Association (SSTA) exists, as its name suggests, to further the interests of secondary teachers. Indeed it was formed in 1946 because of a feeling that insufficient recognition was given to the qualifications of secondary teachers, whose salaries, it was believed, would be depressed if they did not clearly separate themselves from staff in primary schools. The SSTA occupies a middle position between NAS/UWT and PAT on the issue of unionism v. professionalism. It is affiliated to the STUC and its members are prepared to take industrial action, but it still regards itself as representing traditional professional standards and values. An official stated in July 1984 that its membership stood at just under 7,000.

The oldest, and by far the largest, teachers' organisation, with a membership of some 45,500 in July 1984, is the Educational Institute of Scotland, founded in 1847. It was from the EIS that a group of secondary teachers broke away to form the SSTA. EIS members include not only primary and secondary teachers but also lecturers in further education.[2] Like the SSTA and the NAS/UWT, it is affiliated to the STUC. The present General Secretary is John Pollock, a prominent member of the Labour Party in Scotland, and a former Rector of Mainholm Academy, Ayr. He has been described as 'an inspiring general leading a very uninspiring army'.[3] Whatever the merits of this judgement, the size of the 'army' makes it difficult and dangerous to generalise about the EIS's position on the unionism/professionalism spectrum. The Rank and File sector of the association, which has operated as a ginger group, has adopted a radical stance, shared by a recent President of the EIS, Kenneth McLachlan.[4] At the same time, large sections of the membership could be classified as moderate or conservative, rather than militant. This is particularly true outside the West of Scotland.

The stated aims of the EIS are such that people of very different political persuasions can readily subscribe to them. There are doubtless some advantages in this but it does lead to a measure of conceptual fudging. The EIS is committed to 'both the advancement of sound learning and the promotion of the interests and welfare of the teaching profession'.[5] In an excellent study of the detailed workings of the Institute, Donald W. McKenzie has drawn attention to the fact that these twin aims 'are not always reconcilable in terms of practical policies'.[6] He argues that there is an underlying confusion in the assumption that the promotion of sound learning and the welfare of the teaching profession will always coincide and, furthermore, 'The expression 'welfare of the teaching profession' subsumes, in a simplistic manner, the competing, divergent interests of groups within the group given the unifying appellation of 'the teaching profession' '.[7]

McKenzie's study is now somewhat dated but it displays a degree of semantic rigour that is alien to the language of politicians, pressure groups and propagandists. In this it may be contrasted with a more recent statement by a former senior official within the EIS, in which the question of unionism v. professionalism is addressed directly. This statement, in the form of an article entitled 'The teacher as professional and trade unionist',[8] was written in 1980 by Keir Bloomer. In the course of his career Mr Bloomer has held the post of Depute General Secretary of the EIS and has acted as chairman of the teachers' side of the Scottish Teachers' Salaries Committee. He subsequently became an Education Officer in the Glasgow Division of Strathclyde Region, a move which prompted some wry observations about the unattractive sight of poachers becoming gamekeepers.

His article reflects the ambiguities, indeed inconsistencies, in the self-perception of teachers' organisations. Consider, for example, the following statements:

> The essence of professionalism is an acceptance of responsibility.[9]
> The task of teachers' unions is to improve the professionalism of teachers.[10]
> Teachers' unions exist in order to protect and advance the interests of their members as perceived by those members.[11]
> Professionalism is primarily an attitude of mind: the connection with money is indirect.[12]
> The activities of teachers' unions have frequently been restrained by professional considerations.[13]

The juxtaposition of these comments raises several intractable questions which Mr Bloomer does not tackle. If the task of teachers' unions is to enhance professionalism, and the connection with money is indirect, why do organisations such as the EIS devote so much attention to attempts to improve salaries? If members perceive their interests primarily in terms of increased salaries, are they in some sense being unprofessional? If professional considerations serve to restrain unions, why should they continue to invoke the concept of professionalism to justify their actions?

The issue is further complicated by a distinction that Bloomer makes elsewhere in his article. Referring to the formulation of policy by teachers' organisations, he separates 'professional matters', which he defines as relating to salaries and conditions of service, from 'educational matters', which relate to union responses to proposals for change in the system (for example, the raising of the school leaving age, the introduction of mixed-ability grouping).[14] He observes that teachers tend not to be very interested in the educational policies of their unions: their main concern is with salaries and conditions of service. As an illustration, he notes that the publication of the Munn and Dunning reports in 1977 'did not produce a demand for a general meeting in any single branch of the EIS, whereas each spring the salaries campaign leads to many such meetings'.[15] As far as practising teachers are concerned, therefore, money features more prominently in their conception of 'professional matters' than Bloomer's earlier references to 'an acceptance of responsibility' and 'an attitude of mind' would suggest. Given the relative failure of teachers' unions to improve the salaries of their members, this order of priorities is understandable but, once again, it highlights the confused nature of appeals to professionalism. Bloomer comes nearest to an admission of the problem when he concedes that the words 'professional' and 'professionalism' 'are weapons freely employed both by teachers' unions and education authorities in debates over teachers' salaries and conditions'.[16] In other words, teachers seek the status and rewards of other, better-paid occupations, while employers stress commitment and responsibility. Both assume that, by definition, professionalism is a good thing: neither shows any capacity or inclination to cut through the rhetoric and admit the extent to which the concept has become a rather shabby bargaining tactic used in the pursuit of different forms of self-interest.

Bloomer does have some interesting observations to make on matters related to professionalism. He refers, for example, to the role of activists within the union movement. Since ordinary members are fairly indifferent to issues of educational policy — as distinct from salaries policy — the views of the union tend to be shaped by activists who 'do not necessarily reflect the views of the membership as a whole and can claim no real mandate for their policies'.[17] Thus, for example, the response of the EIS to proposals for various 'progressive' reforms 'reflected the views of union leaders, who are generally articulate, to the left politically, rather than those of the typical teacher'.[18] (The possible inference that the 'typical teacher' is not 'generally articulate' was no doubt unintended.) In these circumstances, the role of the leadership has often been to render acceptable to the membership ideas which may not have been initially attractive. This role might be defended on the grounds that, left to themselves, classroom teachers would invariably take a conservative line and needed reforms would proceed even more slowly. On the other hand, by promoting officially supported changes, union leaders run the risk of identifying themselves too closely with other 'progressive' agencies, such as the inspectorate and colleges of education, and so alienating themselves from the classroom teachers they claim to represent. There is certainly a suspicion among some teachers that senior union officials come to enjoy the sensation of 'living on the inside' of the policy-making process to the detriment of their more mundane, but perhaps more fundamental, work of a representative nature.[19] Union leaders would certainly deny that they are prone to assimilationist tendencies. The favoured self-image is that of the radical activist fighting for ordinary members against central and local government. Nevertheless, the world they inhabit — a world of committees, reports and working parties, in the company of officials of various kinds — may cause them to be regarded as part of the educational establishment, despite their protestations to the contrary.

Bloomer also has some comments to make on the effects of the promotion structure in Scottish schools which bear on the issues under discussion. He notes that in the decade from 1970 to 1980 there was a substantial expansion in the number of promoted posts, especially after the introduction of the guidance system in secondary schools in 1971. This was an astute move on the part of the authorities in that it allowed them, at relatively little cost, to hold out the prospect of advancement and so avoid having to offer a substantial increase to the whole teaching force. Bloomer is severe in his judgement on the effects of this development:

> Most of the posts remain as irrelevant now as on the day they were created ... Many secondary teachers, including many holders of senior promoted posts, willingly admit that they would be hard put to identify any specific educational advance which can be linked to the explosion in promoted posts.[20]

Furthermore, rewarding staff who move into administration diminishes the prestige of teaching, and those who remain in the classroom throughout their career come to be regarded as failures. The result is that self-esteem is diminished and 'Competition for promotion encourages toadying ... [and] acts as a powerful deterrent to militancy'.[21] He goes on:

> An obsession with hierarchies replaces professionl judgement and eclipses any real demonstration of academic freedom. It encourages the adoption of attitudes likely to be approved by those 'higher up'. This is as true of the attitude of the head teacher to the director of education as of the attitude of the youngest probationer teacher to his head of department.[22]

These are fair observations which accurately reflect the realities of the situation. When it comes to proposals for reform, however, Bloomer retreats rapidly from the implications of his argument. Instead of advocating a vigorous campaign of structural reform, designed to simplify career patterns and reward successful classroom teachers, he hastily reassures senior staff — many of whom, of course, hold positions of responsibility within the EIS — that their interests will be looked after: 'a feeling that the existing promotion structure is inherently unprofessional and anti-educational does not absolve a union of its obligations to members in promoted posts'.[23] This refusal to follow through the logic of an argument is, regrettably, characteristic of teachers' organisations, and part of the explanation is their extreme defensiveness in the face of criticism, however legitimate. If they themselves were to adopt a position of strong advocacy for major structural reform they would, in effect, be admitting that the existing educational service is deficient. This they are reluctant to do because their own attitudes and those of their members might be identified as part of the explanation for the failure. Thus the unions prefer to adopt a responsive and reactive position in relation to developments originating elsewhere. In doing so, they exhibit a lack of nerve and, in some respects, a lack of honesty.

One final example will reinforce the point. Bloomer offers a brief comment on the attitude of teachers towards their pre-service training: 'The readily expressed contempt of so many teachers for their professional training does little to enhance their standing'.[24] This focuses, yet again, on status, and the suggestion seems to be that teachers should, in their own interests, refrain from making remarks that have the effect of undermining their own professionalism. The critical issue, however, is why teachers should have such a low opinion of the training they receive and whether or not their complaints are justified. In failing to address these questions, Bloomer is not alone. Staff in the colleges of education reveal a similar preoccupation with status, a similar attraction to the rhetoric of professionalism, and a similar capacity to evade the central problems.

## Colleges of Education

Arguments regarding professional standing and professional standards have always been closely tied to the nature and quality of the training required by aspiring teachers. Indeed, the history of teacher training in Scotland can be seen as a progressive attempt to improve standards of entry to the profession and establish the distinctiveness of the teacher's skills.[25] These aims seem worthy enough in themselves but, when viewed in the context of the recent development of those institutions charged with upholding them, they soon begin to look rather tarnished. In order to prepare the ground for this interpretation a fairly detailed preliminary description of the college of education system as a whole is required.

There are at present seven colleges of education in Scotland — Aberdeen, Craigie, Dundee, Dunfermline, Jordanhill, Moray House and St. Andrew's. All the colleges offer a range of pre-service, in-service, certificate, diploma and degree courses, though some are more specialised than others. Dunfermline college, for example, which is located in Edinburgh, is concerned principally with the training of female physical education teachers but it has recently been developing a number of courses in the field of leisure and recreation, open to both men and women. St. Andrew's (previously called Notre Dame), based at Bearsden, near Glasgow, is the only Roman Catholic college, having absorbed staff and students from the former Craiglockhart college. Moray House in Edinburgh is the largest of the colleges of education in the east of Scotland and includes the Scottish Centre for Education Overseas, which attracts students from many parts of the world. Jordanhill in Glasgow is the largest of the colleges in the west and includes both the Scottish School of Physical Education, which trains male PE teachers, and the Scottish School of Further Education, which is the national centre for the training of FE lecturers in Scotland.

The requirements for entry to courses, and the conditions for the award of teaching qualifications, derive from the Teachers (Education Training and Registration) (Scotland) Regulations, drawn up in 1967, and subsequently revised in 1971 and 1973. A Memorandum on Entry Requirements to Courses is published annually by the SED.

Each college is administered by a Board of Governors consisting of representatives of the college staff and students, education authorities, religious interests, teachers in schools and other educational establishments within the area served by the college, the universities, directors of education, and, not least, the Secretary of State for Scotland. Academic matters are the province of Boards of Studies which are composed of members of the teaching staff.

The colleges like to think of themselves as independent bodies and as guardians of professional standards, although the fact that their funding comes directly from the SED, and SED approval is required before any new initiatives can be launched, raises immediate doubts about the degree of autonomy they actually enjoy. Principals certainly have a considerable measure of power within their own colleges, but there are grounds for thinking that the authority they are able to exercise in relation to their subordinates, and their strong representation on other bodies (such as the GTC), are partly dependent on their willingness to adopt a passive stance in relation to the SED. This can be seen most clearly in the activities of the Committee of Principals, which is the agency through which the collective interests of the Scottish Principals are channelled.

The Committee of Principals is, in effect, the executive arm of the Joint Committee of Colleges of Education in Scotland. This latter body consists of the Chairman and Vice-Chairman (i.e., the Principal *ex officio*) of each Board of Governors. A former Vice-Principal of Aberdeen College of Education, Gerald Osborne, has remarked drily: 'The full Joint Committee of Colleges was intended to meet only infrequently and to do very little. That intention has been realised'.[26] Whereas the full Joint Committee meets only two or three times a year, the Committee of Principals meets once a month. Also in attendance are the GTC registrar and two SED officials (one HMCI and one administrator). The minutes of the Committee of Principals are not publicly available but Osborne, who would have had access to them, has offered these astringent judgements:

> It makes virtually no contribution to the formulation of educational policy: Munn and Dunning and Pack ... invited it to give evidence but either received no reply or nothing more than a summary of the views of the several colleges.
>
> [T]opics which have taken up the Principals' time ... suggest a pre-occupation with

> bureaucratic rule-making . . . which is perhaps symptomatic of the residual nature of this particular committee's functions.[27]

Osborne concludes that, while the meetings of the Committee of Principals provide an opportunity for polite discourse among important members of the educational leadership class, the prospect of lively and constructive engagement with substantive issues rarely arises. In these circumstances, it is hardly surprising that 'some college staff seem to suspect that the SED uses the Committee of Principals to impose departmental policies on the colleges'.[28] The picture that emerges, then, is one in which college Principals have almost 'unfettered authority'[29] inside their own institutions but very little authority in relation to the SED.

These observations help to explain the structural context in which the colleges operate. It is now necessary to examine, at a more concrete level, the precise claims about professionalism that are made in regard to the work they do and the courses they offer. Their recent history has been dominated by the problem of contraction and the threat of closure. As a direct result of falling school rolls the demand for new entrants declined rapidly in the late '70s. For example, Jordanhill's student population was reduced from a total of 3,720 in 1975–76 to around 1,900 in 1983–84.[30] Colleges at Callendar Park, Falkirk, and Hamilton were closed amid considerable controversy and some bitterness. Craigie, which is the smallest of the remaining colleges, seemed at one stage to be a stronger candidate for closure than Hamilton. Its reprieve has been attributed by some to the fact that it is located in Ayr, the constituency of the present Secretary of State for Scotland, George Younger.

Against this background, the introduction, from session 1984–85, of a new four-year degree for primary teachers came as a particularly welcome development in the colleges. The intention behind this BEd qualification was to make primary teaching an all-graduate occupation, thereby, it was hoped, enhancing its status and improving the quality of teaching. Teachers' organisations, the GTC and the colleges themselves had, for some years previously, advanced the case for such a degree and, although the SED was concerned about the cost of the proposal, and had originally argued for a three-year course,[31] it eventually found it expedient to grant approval. Fears about the financial implications were circumvented by adjusting the proportion of primary teachers qualifying by an alternative, cheaper route — that is, by taking a one-year course following a university degree. Although no absolute increase in numbers was involved, the *proportion* of one-year postgraduate trainees went up from 15% of the total to 45%. The significance of this deal, arrived at by a working party consisting of SED and college of education representatives, will be considered later. For the moment, however, it will be instructive to examine the claim that the new degree will, in some sense, be quintessentially a 'professional' qualification.

The keenest advocate of the four-year primary BEd has been Gordon Kirk, Principal of Moray House College of Education and formerly Head of the Education Department at Jordanhill College of Education. He has asserted that the degree should be 'unashamedly professional', should focus on studies that are 'professionally relevant' and should aim to produce 'competent professional performance'.[32] Mr Kirk's frequent repetition of the term 'professional' is somewhat reminiscent of the language of religious revivalism, in which the ritualistic invocation of a key phrase is used to carry the audience along on a tide of emotionalism that discourages close examination of the substance of what is being said. His fondness for assertion rather than argument is also evident in his reliance on dismissive linguistic forms such as 'surely', 'manifestly' and 'it must be perfectly obvious that . . . '[33] What is far from obvious is the precise meaning to be attached to Kirk's conception of professionalism. It involves 'a very extensive range of skills and understandings'[34] but these skills and understandings are not specified in other than the most general terms. Again it affirms the importance 'of the professional over the merely academic':[35] the latter runs the risk, according to Kirk, of giving too much weight to theoretical understanding of a kind that produces nothing more than 'cerebral virtuosity'[36] and 'urbane and lively conversation'.[37] It is tempting to observe that these maligned qualities are not especially noticeable in the colleges of education and that their cultivation would not be amiss. Such an observation would, however, probably prompt Kirk to launch into a complaint about those who 'demean the professional activities and expertise of college of education staff'.[38]

The relation between theory and practice in teacher training has always been a problem, and Kirk seeks to resolve it by devising a course of studies which focuses 'explicitly and continuously on teaching and the context in which it is carried out'.[39] This will require close collaboration between schools and colleges and the integration of previously fragmented work within the colleges themselves, so that the contributions of primary 'methods' staff, subject departments (such as English and Mathematics), and professional studies departments (Education and Psychology) will form a coherent programme. The whole course, in other words, is to be permeated by pedagogical analysis: conventional academic studies will cease to exist as separate entities but without, Kirk insists, 'any diminution in the intellectual demands imposed'.[40]

This last stipulation is important if the degree-worthiness of the new qualification is to be maintained. Not all observers are convinced that the formula proposed by Kirk is the right one. One sceptic, Thomas Jones, has criticised the pattern of the new course for its narrowly conceived focus on the classroom, its heavy concentration on practical skills at the expense of theory, and its lack of flexibility in not allowing students to transfer to careers other than teaching. He states:

> Of course we need competent teachers but above all educated people with a variety of interests and experience outside teaching capable of infecting their pupils and colleagues with their curiosity, vitality and enthusiasm.[41]

He goes on to complain of the 'isolated, intoverted and sheltered' nature of the colleges of education and poses the question:

> Which is preferable . . . an 'extended' professional in professional blinkers or an educated person with a variety of interests?[42]

Jones would prefer to see a two-tier degree, the first two years of which would consist of academic courses: thereafter, those who wished to teach would follow a two-year primary training course and those who did not could follow courses relevant to other occupations. This pattern would, of course, require a flexible credit transfer system and would call for cooperation between different institutions of higher education, which would serve to counteract the inward-looking tendencies of the colleges of education.

Kirk, in a subsequent rejoinder, argued that 'the attack on professionalism is rooted in a series of misconceptions'.[43] Jones 'fails to acknowledge that professional problems impose demands that are as absorbing, as intellectually challenging, and as educative as anything offered by conventional undergraduate programmes'.[44] Somewhat ironically, in view of Kirk's own desire to extend the range of degree-level work carried out by the colleges, Jones is accused of 'an immature hankering after university status' and of making 'a straight appeal to academic snobbery'.[45] Kirk concludes — or, more accurately, asserts — 'it is a matter for celebration that the Secretary of State has agreed guidelines that require the adoption of a professional orientation in the degree'.[46]

What is to be made of these claims and counter-claims about the nature and place of professionalism in teacher education? As with so many other 'debates' in Scottish education, it needs to be understood in a wider political context. The arguments for a four-year degree have as much to do with the declining position of the colleges as with the merits of different types of course. Between 1971 and 1981 the number of students in training in Scottish colleges of education dropped from 12,200 to 4,900.[47] In this general atmosphere of contraction, the colleges that have survived have naturally been concerned about their future. The prospect of a new degree-level course offered some hope of security, especially as it involved an extra year's study in comparison with the previous three-year diploma course. In other words, a good measure of self-interest underlay the case for the new qualification, not least because existing diploma-holders would want to upgrade their qualifications to degree-level on an in-service basis.

Self-interest, however, is not an attractive or persuasive motivation, and when approval for the new course was being sought, it was necessary to advance the cause in other terms. It was at this point that the rhetoric of professionalism, eagerly subscribed to by the GTC, the unions and the colleges themselves, came into its own. By claiming that the new BEd represented a significant departure from conventional courses and offered a more truly 'professional' preparation than anything hitherto, its advocates successfully confined the discussion to questions of structure and content. As has been noted, few people in Scottish education are prepared to challenge the concept of professionalism, especially when advocated so vigorously by someone of Mr Kirk's standing, and so the degree was approved without significant opposition.

Two further points will serve to reinforce the interpretation that the appeal to professionalism in advancing the cause of the four-year primary BEd was more of a tactical smokescreen than a convincingly argued position. If the case for the pattern proposed by Mr Kirk, and subsequently enshrined in national guidelines

— yet another example of newspeak, since the alleged 'guidelines' are to be mandatory — is as overwhelming as he suggests, why did the colleges agree to an increase in the proportion of students taking the alternative entry route, i.e., the one-year course following a non-vocational degree? These students cannot be offered the integrated, concurrent course, the benefits of which Kirk maintains are immeasurably superior to the traditional consecutive pattern (academic qualification followed by professional training). Will they therefore be regarded, by a curious process of inverted snobbery, as second-class citizens within the colleges? The truth of the matter is that the whole arrangement was determined, not by an objective analysis of the merits of alternative routes, but by a rather unedifying compromise between the SED's desire to keep costs down and the colleges' desire to secure their own future.

The second point relates to the 'professionalism' of college staff. Mr Kirk is touchy about any criticism that seems to demean 'the professional activities and expertise'[48] of lecturers in the colleges of education. There are, however, grounds for thinking that the college Principals themselves have not been especially assiduous in defending those qualities of academic rigour and intellectual freedom among their staff on which effective teaching and learning depends. In May 1984 it was announced that the SED would fund twenty-four academic posts in the colleges, including several in the primary field, on the lines of university 'new blood' appointments. The idea behind these appointments was that they would allow an influx of fresh ideas after the period of contraction when hardly any vacancies had occurred. On the face of it, this seemed a promising development. It emerged on closer inspection, however, that the posts had been released on condition that the college Principals allowed SED officials to see the names of shortlisted candidates, together with information about their ages, qualifications and experience. An SED official claimed that there was no cause for suspicion about the department's motives. It was necessary to know how much the new staff were going to cost — thus the requirement that applicants' ages should be submitted so that their position on the salary scales could be calculated. The same spokesman added: 'We have no intention of interfering in the colleges' choice, but we feel it's important from our planning point of view to know what kind of people are being seen and whether they meet our criteria'.[49]

It is clear from this statement that cost was not the only consideration. If it had been, it should not have been beyond the wit of the SED to draw up general guidelines relating to the total cost of appointments and perhaps setting limits to the point on the salary scales at which particular appointments might be made. The reference to 'what kind of people are being seen' and 'whether they meet our criteria' indicates that other considerations, to do with the acceptability of applicants, were also involved. In effect, it appeared that the SED wanted to ensure that those appointed would be supportive of favoured policies emanating from the Department itself.

It is hard to see how the college Principals' acceptance of these conditions could enhance the 'professionalism' of their staff, however defined. Despite the publication of an article challenging them to explain and justify their position, none saw fit to respond.[50] If professionalism requires the appointment of people on the basis of ability rather than acceptability, and the encouragement of free intellectual inquiry, the action of the Principals on this occasion could be regarded as hindering rather than promoting it.

This example is not unrelated to the general weakness in Kirk's conception of professionalism. By succumbing to the pressures of bureaucratic control, the Principals merely reinforce the tendency inherent in the new BEd degree to accept uncritically the prevailing pattern of schooling. Training people to be teachers certainly involves giving them a realistic sense of the way things are, but it should also involve encouraging them to reflect on the way things might be. Staff who have been appointed because they are willing to go along with approved policies are unlikely to have the capacity or the vision to take students beyond the prevailing orthodoxies. In this respect, what they can offer is not *education* in any meaningful sense: it is rather an initiation into unimaginative, conformist thinking, a preparation for a career as pliant functionaries, not as creative and stimulating teachers. If these are indeed the implications of Kirk's advocacy of professionalism, Scottish education is better off abandoning it as a guiding principle.

## General Teaching Council

One of the main underpinnings of the claim that Scottish teachers enjoy professional status is the existence of the General Teaching Council. All teachers employed by an education authority in primary or secondary schools must be registered with the Council as a condition of employment. Eligibility for registration depends on the successful completion of a training course at a Scottish college of education or of an equivalent course approved by the Council. These arrangements, it is claimed, give the GTC the role of a self-regulating professional body and ensure that the quality of the teaching force is satisfactory.

In order to examine the validity of this interpretation it is necessary to look at the functions and composition of the Council more closely. The GTC was constituted on February 1st, 1966, under the terms of the Teaching Council (Scotland) Act of 1965. In 1969 the Secretary of State for Scotland published a memorandum entitled 'Review of the Constitution and Functions of the General Teaching Council', which led to a revised constitution under the Teaching Council (Scotland) Act 1965 (Amendment of Constitution of Council) Order 1970. The Council has five principal functions:

(1) to keep under review standards of education, training and fitness to teach appropriate to persons entering the teaching profession and to make to the Secretary of State from time to time such recommendations with respect to these standards as it thinks fit; and to make recommendations on such other matters (in the same field) as it thinks fit or as may be referred to it by the Secretary of State;

(2) to consider and make recommendations to the Secretary of State on matters (other than remuneration and conditions of service) relating to the supply of teachers;
(3) to keep itself informed of the nature of the instruction given in colleges of education and to undertake such other functions in relation to them as may be assigned by the Secretary of State;
(4) to establish and keep a register containing the names, addresses and such qualifications and other particulars as may be prescribed of persons who are entitled to be registered and who apply in the prescribed manner; and
(5) to determine whether in any particular case under their Disciplinary powers registration is to be withdrawn or refused.[51]

There are four statutory meetings of the Council each year with provision under its standing orders for the calling of additional or special meetings should these be deemed necessary. Much of the detailed work of the Council is conducted through its committee structure. The Council is statutorily required to have an Investigating Committee and a Disciplinary Committee, to examine cases where the possibility of withdrawal of registration arises, and also a Committee on Exceptional Admission. There are, in addition, the following permanent committees: Supply; Probation; Finance and General Purposes; Education; Visitation. The conveners of the various committees together constitute a Chairman's Committee.

Discussions are currently taking place on the precise composition of the Council but, as things stand at present, there are 49 members, 30 of whom are *elected,* 15 *appointed* and 4 *nominated* directly by the Secretary of State. The elected members, who must themselves be registered teachers, represent primary schools (11), secondary schools (11), colleges of education (5), and FE centres (3). The appointed members represent a range of interests — COSLA (4), the Association of Directors of Education (3), the Scottish universities (4), Central Institutions (2), the Education Committee of the General Assembly of the Church of Scotland (1), and the Scottish Hierarchy of the Roman Catholic Church (1). As well as nominating 4 members of the Council, the Secretary of State normally has 3 or 4 assessors attending meetings, though only 2 of these are official.

Probably the main achievement of the Council to date has been the elimination of uncertificated teachers from primary and secondary schools. Problems still remain, however, with regard to the eligibility for registration of some staff in further education centres and colleges of education. The number of teachers on the register in March 1984 was as follows:

| | |
|---|---|
| Primary | 37,522 |
| Secondary | 40,184 |
| Further Education | 1,683 |
| Colleges of Education | 724 |
| Non-voters | 21 |
| TOTAL | 80,134[52] |

Of the total, 7,053 were provisionally registered; i.e., they had not yet completed the probationary period (normally two years) necessary before full registration can be granted.

Is the GTC anything more than a registration council? How successful has it been in gaining the interest and support of teachers, and in contributing to educational thinking and policy making in Scotland? A detailed study of the work of the Council concluded in 1981 that 'it has been seen by teachers as being over-cautious and lacking in real influence in Scottish education. As a result there is considerable apathy among teachers towards the Council'.[53] The author of this study, David Barrie, was himself subsequently elected to the GTC in the 1982 ballot, and so his comments are of particular interest. Elections are held every four years and the present Council, which is the Fifth, will serve until 1987. If the figures for the number of candidates standing and the percentage of teachers voting at successive elections are examined, there are certainly grounds for concluding that attitudes of disenchantment and apathy have come to prevail.

*Number of Candidates Standing for Election to the GTC*[54]

| | |
|---|---|
| First Council | 233 |
| Second Council | 80 |
| Third Council | 73 |
| Fourth Council | 64 |
| Fifth Council | 45 |

*Percentage of Teachers Voting in Elections for the GTC*[55]

| | |
|---|---|
| First Council | 85 |
| Second Council | 36 |
| Third Council | 32 |
| Fourth Council | 33 |
| Fifth Council | 32 |

The high figures for the First Council can be explained in terms of novelty value and a general hope that the Council would improve the standing of teachers. Why has this aspiration apparently not come to fruition? Barrie offers several explanations: the reputation of the Council 'as being completely subservient to the wishes of the Secretary of State';[56] the fact that 'issues which have been under discussion for many years seem to make no progress';[57] 'the rather undistinguished nature of the teacher representation on the Council';[58] the suspicion that 'in spite of the numerical strength of the elected teacher representation on the Council the GTC is substantially dominated by the College of Education Principals';[59] its inability, with regard to the question of teacher supply, to advance 'the profession's control over its own affairs';[60] the Council's 'inherent caution in interpreting its scope and powers';[61] its reluctance to take action against teachers who 'although fully registered, [are] clearly not competent'.[62] It is not possible to examine all of these criticisms but some observations will be offered on three broad areas which touch on many of the specific points Barrie raises and which provide further insights into the nature of 'professionalism' in Scottish education. The three areas are, first, the effectiveness of the Council in relation to the supply of teachers; secondly, the extent to which it can be regarded as a 'representative' body; and thirdly, its own record in exemplifying those professional standards which it exists to promote.

When the Council was being set up in the mid-'60s there was a serious problem of teacher shortage and, related to this, serious concern about the employment of unqualified staff in schools. More recently, the difficulty has been an excess of supply over demand, contraction in the colleges and teacher unemployment. The Council has, therefore, had to live through a time of considerable difficulty in which there has been little continuity. It is, nevertheless, the Secretary of State's principal adviser on matters of supply, and one index of its effectiveness is the degree to which he is prepared to accept its advice. An editorial in the *GTC News* of January 1974 contrasted the system prevailing before the creation of the GTC with that obtaining afterwards:

> There was no co-operation, no consultation ... regulations took effect immediately. What happens now? The Secretary of State must have regard to the Council's recommendations, and if he does not accept them he must explain his reasons.[63]

It is interesting to juxtapose this confident statement with the events following the receipt, in March 1976, of an SED circular detailing proposals for a severe cutback in the number of entrants to teacher-training courses.[64] At a special meeting of the Council in April of the same year concern was expressed that the Secretary of State had ignored its special position as statutory adviser on supply matters. A letter was sent to the SED conveying the Council's disapproval at the way the matter had been handled. The Secretary of State's response was merely to confirm the draft proposals, a move which caused the Council to protest once again that the process of consultation appeared to have had no effect. A subsequent issue of the *GTC News* contained a number of strongly worded but anonymous comments on the government's action.[65]

It is tempting to depict this episode as yet another example of SED authoritarianism, but the GTC's own role needs to be examined. Why did the Secretary of State, Mr Bruce Millan, feel able to act with little or no regard to the GTC's formal position? Was it because its past record suggested that any protest it might make would be ineffective? Again, why did the GTC not anticipate the possibility of severe cutbacks, especially as the college principals on the Council should have been fully aware of the decline in demand? And, related to this, why did the Council adopt a purely reactive stance instead of having an alternative policy position ready?

Underlying all of these questions is an even more fundamental issue to do with the alleged independence of the Council. From the beginning it has been claimed that 'The main role of the Council is to be seen as a completely independent body, able to express a meaningful opinion on all matters concerned with teaching'.[66] However, on the question of teacher supply, it is doubtful if the Council can be regarded as independent, if 'independent' is taken to mean detached and impartial. On the contrary, it consists of people with clear vested interests in any recommendations that it makes. This is especially true of the colleges Principals, but it applies to all the teacher representatives to some degree. The interests of different groups *within* the GTC do not always coincide, as will be apparent shortly, but the general point remains: the basis of the claim that the Council is 'independent' is weak. This suggests that one of the reasons the Secretary of State felt able to steamroller opposition to his proposals was that he realised that the GTC's position would be regarded outside educational circles as self-interested special pleading.

Subsequent events seem to indicate that some rudimentary awareness of this strategic weakness began to dawn on members of the Council but it manifested itself in a way that hardly redounded to their credit. The supply question became even worse towards the end of the decade when the possibility of college closures began to be considered.[67] Initially, the Council expressed its opposition to any closures but, in the face of statistical evidence that was difficult to counter, it eventually agreed with reluctance at its meeting on March 5, 1980 that there should be a reduction in the number of institutions engaged in teacher training. A reading of the Minutes of the GTC covering this period conveys the impression of strong undercurrents of hostility between various sectional interests.[68] While the Council refrained from recommending the closure of particular colleges, it drew up a list of criteria which it suggested the Secretary of State should have regard to in reaching his final decisions. Keir Bloomer, the Council's Vice-Chairman at the time, later admitted to Barrie: 'the names of the colleges for closure may not have been explicit, but the implications of the criteria listed by the Council were plainly understood by all present'.[69] By taking such action, the Council may have displayed a greater awareness of the harsh realities of the situation than it had done in 1976, but it also played into the hands of the Secretary of State, whose subsequent actions were seen to have GTC authorisation. Not surprisingly, the Council found itself subject to accusations of ineptitude, especially from staff in colleges scheduled for closure.[70] Some of these were certainly exaggerated and were themselves based on a desire to obtain special treatment.[71] Nevertheless, throughout the debates about supply, there was, within the GTC, a lack of vision about the future, an inability to see beyond short-term sectional interests and an almost total blindness to the limitations of largely monotechnic teacher-training institutions as guardians of professional standards. On this last point the GTC and the colleges of education merely reinforced each other's prejudices and, by doing so, rendered themselves incapable of conceiving of an alternative scenario to that envisaged by the Secretary of State.

These criticisms are also relevant to the whole question of the representativeness of the Council. Dr Bone has claimed:

> The Council brings together all the various interests in Scottish education ... and does so in a more representative way than any other body which exists.[72]

And with particular reference to the Supply Committee he has stated: 'It does not operate as an adjunct to the teachers' associations ... '[73] These statements rest uneasily with Barrie's conclusion, regarding the elected sector of the GTC, that 'membership of, and sponsorship by, the teachers' associations has been the *sine qua non* of membership of the GTC'.[74] At election times there is undoubtedly considerable competition between teachers' organisations to secure the strongest representation. This is particularly evident in the ballot for secondary teachers where the EIS and the SSTA are the principal rivals. The 1978 election had resulted in the SSTA winning 8 out of 11 secondary places and, in an attempt to prevent a repetition in the 1982 election, the *EIS Journal* urged that 'only the official EIS candidates can be relied upon to speak and act on behalf of the profession'.[75] When it emerged that the EIS had succeeded in gaining 7 out of the 11 secondary seats, Donald Miller, General Secretary of the SSTA, said that he was 'naturally disappointed at the result but fairly satisfied in view of the very intense campaign waged by the EIS which bordered on the scurrilous at times by suggesting that only the EIS was fit to represent the teaching profession'.[76] In such an atmosphere, the question of whether elected GTC members owe their first allegiance to the Council or to the union that sponsored them arises. Barrie concludes that it would be wrong to regard sponsored candidates as being mandated to vote on particular issues in particular ways, although since he completed his study the EIS has decided that members who are on the GTC should give a report of their contribution to Council debates and decisions. In any case, Barrie does suggest that, when it comes to the election of a Chairman, the EIS normally uses its dominating position to secure the post for one of its members.[77] He was told by an interviewee that, when James Scotland, then Principal of Aberdeen College of Education, was elected Chairman of the Third Council following the resignation of Mr Tom Sneddon, some EIS members had reservations about electing a college principal rather than a teacher. However, Mr Scotland was a distinguished member of the EIS, being a recipient of its fellowship, and 'Even a college principal was to be preferred to a member of the SSTA'.[78]

There are other rivalries — between primary and secondary teachers, between school representatives and those from the FE sector, between nominated and appointed members on the one hand and elected members on the other. Even among groups where a very high measure of solidarity might normally be expected, conflicts of interest sometimes surface. A recent example of this, reflecting continuing problems relating to student numbers, has occurred within the college of education sector, in which four of the five places are occupied by college principals — a situation which, quite rightly, is now under review.[79] Dr Bone of Jordanhill and Mr Kirk of Moray House became involved in a public disagreement about the Council's position on the distribution of student intake figures for session 1984–85.[80] Mr Kirk said he was suspicious of the advice of the Supply Committee which seemed to favour colleges in the west of Scotland at the expense of those in the east. Dr Bone denied that there had been any unfair bias. A former GTC Chairman, John Vallely, was prompted to remark that the clash between Mr Kirk and Dr Bone appeared to be the result of them 'allowing their private capacities to interefere with their public membership of the Council'.[81] In the event, Mr Kirk's attempt to have the Supply Committee's advice to the Secretary of State amended was heavily defeated.

This particular episode was fairly unusual in that the conflict came directly into public view. Normally the social niceties are carefully observed and the veneer of civilised discourse remains unblemished. The fact remains, however, that there are identifiable sectional interests within the GTC and, in so far as they influence the actions of members, they serve to undermine the Council's position in two ways. First, they lead to a dissipation of energies which ought to be directed towards a consideration of wider policy questions affecting the Scottish educational system as a whole. The pursuit of petty internal wrangles deflects attention from these wider issues and reflects no credit on those who engage in them. Secondly, and perhaps more fundamentally, the SED can play off the various group interests against each other, thereby making it easier for the Secretary of State to impose his will. Indeed, he can sometimes even achieve the near impossible, by presenting himself as an honest broker in the midst of a collection of special pleaders.

The GTC's failure to live up to its own publicity with regard to its independence and representativeness also applies to its record on professionalism. It emerges as no more coherent on this subject than the colleges of education and the teachers' organisations. In the same issue of the *GTC News* — indeed in the same article — which stated that 'The main role of the Council is to be seen as a completely independent body' reference is made to 'the true role of the Council — real professional status for the teacher'.[82] There is little awareness here, as elsewhere, of the inherent tension between service to the community and the self-regard of the profession. As with the colleges and the unions, different elements in the rhetoric are employed at different times. In 1975 the GTC drew up a statement of professional principles, a high-sounding document which seems somewhat ironic in the light of some of the examples discussed above. The statement — which, it should be noted, is written as if all teachers and pupils were male — asserts that the teacher owes responsibilities to pupils, colleagues, parents and the community. Among the specific obligations mentioned are the following:

> [The] teacher puts the pupil's well-being before all personal considerations;
> his whole professional effort is directed to assisting the pupil to develop those aptitudes and abilities that enable him to cope with life;
> he respects the professional standing and opinions of his colleagues and maintains in his relations with them the highest standards of professional courtesy;
> he accepts the authority of senior professional colleagues, while retaining the right to express professional opinion in a proper manner;
> he makes every effort to encourage parents to interest themselves actively in the education of their children;
> his teaching and behaviour encourage respect for the law of the land and the best traditions of the community.[83]

Most of these items place their emphasis on concern for the client. On other occasions, however, the stress is on 'the privilege and the protection that pertains to a profession'.[84] For example, when legislation was introduced to extend parental rights in education, the move was seen by one GTC member as 'a further erosion of the teacher's status and a further attempt to question his professional competence and dignity'.[85] In response, George Jackson, a nominated member of the GTC and Chairman of the Scottish Parent Teacher Council, accused teachers of adopting a 'collective defensive posture' towards the reforms and of failing 'to demonstrate the true standing and worth of the profession'.[86] Whatever the merits of these particular proposals for greater parental involvement in the educational process, by taking a protectionist stance GTC members laid themselves open to the charge of failing to live up to their own code of professional principles.

It is unlikely, however, that they are over-concerned with this kind of inconsistency. As is the case with the CCC, the predominant impression to be gained from a study of the GTC's activities is one of self-satisfaction. Its members would almost certainly argue that the hopes of the Wheatley committee, whose report led to the setting up of the GTC, have been fully realised. That report stated:

> We envisage the creation of a powerful Council, which we hope would develop into a body of great prestige and act as a main source of ideas and initiative over a wide field of matters of concern to the teaching profession.[87]

It is extremely doubtful whether anyone outside the ranks of past and present GTC members would claim that that vision had been translated into reality.

## Conclusion

The notion of professionalism in Scottish education has become fundamentally incoherent. It is used for propaganda purposes in different senses at different times. Colleges of education, teachers' organisations and the GTC are among the worst offenders in this respect. At the heart of the problem there is an irreconcilable conflict between the altruistic interpretation of professionalism, which stresses social service, and the self-interested interpretation, which seeks to advance the interests of members. As Tony Worthington remarks: 'Traditional defenders of the notion of a profession claim that enlightened practitioners will selflessly serve their clients' needs. From the teacher unions and the General Teaching Council we get the subtle altruism of a Chicago gang'.[88] Of the EIS in particular, he says that it has 'failed to separate a responsibility for selfless analysis of the educational needs of Scotland from the defence of the legitimate but narrow sectional interests of existing teachers. The latter dominates all'.[89]

It would, however, be quite wrong to characterise all classroom teachers as selfish pursuers of their own short-term advantages. Once again, a distinction has to be made between the leadership class and ordinary teachers. In an important sense, teachers themselves can be regarded as victims of over-professionalisation. They have been persuaded by their superiors that the god of professionalism must be worshipped, and anyone who shows a disinclination to pay homage runs the risk of social ostracism and limited career opportunities. In fact, in the prevailing climate, to challenge professionalism is, in the eyes of many, to demonstrate unfitness as a teacher. It thus serves an important ideological function — in Corbett's words, it helps 'to condition men intellectually to obedience'.[90]

*Notes and References*

1. Tony Worthington, 'A profession can colonise the mind', *TESS,* February 20, 1981, p. 16.
2. In addition to the associations referred to in the main text, mention should be made of the following professional bodies covering staff in post-school institutions: the Scottish Further and Higher Education Association (SFHEA); the Association of Lecturers in Scottish Central Institutions (ALSCI); the Association of Lecturers in Colleges of Education in Scotland (ALCES); and the Association of University Teachers (AUT). SFHEA, ALSCI and ALCES together form the Federation of Associations of College Lecturers in Scotland (FACLS).
3. Quoted in Iain Thorburn, 'The Ayr enigma', *TESS,* November 25, 1983, p. 4.
4. See Iain Thorburn, 'The likeable revolutionary', *TESS,* June 8, 1984, p. 4.
5. *EIS Handbook,* section 1.1, n.d.. This handbook is issued to EIS representatives and is regularly updated. See also A. J. Belford, *Centenary Handbook of the EIS,* EIS, Edinburgh, 1946.
6. Donald W. McKenzie, The Pressure Group Activities and Political Development of the Glasgow Association of the EIS in the Post-War Period, unpublished MEd thesis, Glasgow University, 1974, p. 50.
7. Ibid., p. 53.
8. Keir Bloomer, 'The teacher as professional and trade unionist', in E. Hoyle and J. Megarry (eds.), *World Yearbook of Education 1980: Professional Development of Teachers,* Kogan Page, London, 1980, pp. 361-373.
9. *Ibid.,* p. 362.
10. *Ibid.,* p. 361.
11. *Ibid.,* p. 361.
12. *Ibid.,* p. 362.
13. *Ibid.,* p. 363.
14. *Ibid.,* p. 365.
15. *Ibid.,* p. 365.
16. *Ibid.,* p. 362.
17. *Ibid.,* p. 365.
18. *Ibid.,* p. 366.
19. See, e. g., letter by Alan M. Laing, *Scotsman,* May 12, 1984, p. 8.
20. Bloomer, *op.ct.,* p. 371.
21. *Ibid.,* p. 372.
22. *Ibid.,* p. 372.
23. *Ibid.,* p. 372.
24. *Ibid.,* p. 363.
25. See Marjorie Cruickshank, *A History of the Training of Teachers in Scotland,* SCRE, Edinburgh, 1970.
26. Gerald Osborne, 'Information Paper 3: The Committee of Principals of Scottish Colleges of Education', *Scottish Educational Review,* Vol. 11, No. 1, 1979, p. 74.

27. *Ibid.,* p. 75.
28. *Ibid.,* p. 75.
29. *Ibid.,* p. 74.
30. Jordanhill College of Education, *Prospectus,* 1984, pp. 4–5.
31. See SED Consultative Paper, *All-Graduate Entry to Primary Teaching,* Edinburgh, 1980.
32. Gordon Kirk, 'The unashamed professional', *TESS,* February 18, 1983, p. 2.
33. *Ibid., passim.* See also 'The New BEd in Scotland: Towards a Professional Degree', *Scottish Educational Review,* Vol. 16, No. 1, 1984, pp. 19–26.
34. 'The unashamed professional', p. 2.
35. 'The New BEd in Scotland: Towards a Professional Degree', p. 22.
36. *Ibid.,* p. 21.
37. 'The unashamed professional', p. 2.
38. 'The New BEd in Scotland: Towards a Professional Degree', p. 22.
39. *Ibid.,* p. 23.
40. *Ibid.,* p. 23.
41. Thomas Jones, 'Who wants to be an unashamed professional?', *TESS,* June 3, 1983, p. 2.
42. *Ibid.,* p. 2.
43. Kirk, 'The New BEd in Scotland: Towards a Professional Degree', p. 22.
44. *Ibid.,* p. 22.
45. *Ibid.,* p. 22.
46. *Ibid.,* p. 22.
47. *Scottish Statistics,* Scottish Office, Edinburgh, 1982.
48. Kirk, 'The New BEd in Scotland: Towards a Professional Degree', p. 22.
49. Reported in *Times Higher Education Supplement,* May 18, 1984, p. 3.
50. Walter Humes, 'Principals and principles', *TESS,* June 1, 1984, p. 80.
51. GTC, *Handbook,* 4th edition, 1981, p. 3.
52. GTC, *Minutes,* March 7, 1984, para. 4(a).
53. David A. Barrie, The Nature and Impact of Teacher Representation on the General Teaching Council for Scotland, unpublished MEd thesis, Glasgow University, 1981, p. 3.
54. Figures for First to Fourth Councils taken from Barrie, *op.cit.,* p. 31. Figures for Fifth Council taken from report in *TESS,* October 15, 1982, p. 5.
55. Figures for First to Fourth Councils taken from Barrie, *op.cit.,* p. 31. Figures for Fifth Council taken from report in *TESS,* December 17, 1982, p. 3.
56. Barrie, *op.cit.,* p. 73.
57. *Ibid.,* p. 80.
58. *Ibid.,* p. 133.
59. *Ibid.,* p. 128.
60. *Ibid.,* p. 91.
61. *Ibid.,* p. 118.
62. *Ibid.,* p. 117.
63. *GTC News,* No. 3, February 1974, p. 1.
64. See Barrie, *op.cit.,* pp. 85–86.
65. *GTC News,* No. 9, October 1976.
66. *GTC News,* No. 3, February 1974, p. 1.
67. See Barrie, *op.cit.,* pp. 87–89.
68. See, e.g., GTC, *Minutes,* June 4, 1980, para. 4(f).
69. Barrie, *op.cit.,* p. 88.

70. See David Forbes, 'So much for setting standards', *TESS,* April 4, 1980, p. 2.

71. For a vigorous, but less than fully convincing, defence of the GTC's actions, see Keir Bloomer, 'The GTC and the colleges', *TESS,* April 18, 1980, pp. 2 and 4.

72. *GTC News,* No. 12, December 1980, p. 4.

73. *Ibid.,* p. 4.

74. Barrie, *op.cit.,* p. 130.

75. Reported in the *TESS,* October 1, 1982, p. 1.

76. Reported in the *TESS,* December 17, 1982, p. 3.

77. See Barrie, *op.cit.,* pp. 64–67.

78. *Ibid.,* p. 66.

79. See GTC, *Minutes,* March 7, 1984, para. 6 and Appendix II.

80. See GTC, *Minutes,* March 7, 1984, para. 5. Also *GH,* March 8, 1984, p. 6 and *Scotsman,* March 8, 1984, p. 8.

81. Quoted in the *Scotsman,* March 8, 1984, p. 8.

82. *GTC News,* No. 3, February 1974, p. 1.

83. *GTC News,* No. 6, May 1975, p. 3.

84. *GTC News,* No. 10, October 1978, p. 1.

85. *GTC News,* No. 13, December 1981, p. 2.

86. *GTC News,* No. 14, October 1982, p. 5.

87. Quoted in Barrie, *op.cit.,* p. 122.

88. Tony Worthington, 'Lifelong learning: its battle against the enemy within', *TESS,* February 13, 1981, p. 14.

89. *Ibid.,* p. 14.

90. Patrick Corbett, *Ideologies,* Hutchinson, London, 1965, p. 57.

# 8
# *The Management of Research*

## Introduction

It might be thought that the educational research community would act as a powerful counterweight to the centralising and conformist pressures that have been described in previous chapters. After all, there are research bodies, project teams and individual academics who are actively engaged in the study of the educational process and who claim to be committed to the advancement of knowledge and the disinterested pursuit of truth. Is it not to be expected that researchers, in addition to providing a data-base for policy makers, should turn an unbiased eye on any aspects of the educational system that seem to merit attention? In short, does not the work of researchers represent that *critical* perspective which, it has been suggested, is lacking elsewhere in Scottish education?

The argument of this chapter will maintain that such expectations of educational research are, with a few honourable exceptions, not borne out in practice. On the contrary, research has become another arm of control, a particularly effective one since its ostensible function is to promote rather than suppress legitimate enquiry and debate. By permitting and seeming to encourage educational research, educational administrators bolster their own pretensions as benign facilitators and seem to undermine charges of manipulation. There are, however, many features of the way in which research in Scotland is managed which give rise to scepticism about its value, and which provide grounds for constructing an alternative interpretation of the purposes it serves. Among the features that will be considered are the process by which research is funded, the kinds of research enquiries that are permitted, and the relation between research and professional advancement. As a first step towards the development of these points, it is necessary to offer a description of the main agencies involved in educational research in Scotland, and the way in which they are linked to each other.

Four bodies are of particular interest: the Research and Intelligence Unit (RIU) of the SED; the Scottish Council for Research in Education (SCRE); the Scottish Council for Educational Technology (SCET); and the National Inter-College Committee for Educational Research (NICCER). These will be discussed in turn.[1]

## The Research and Intelligence Unit

RIU has, without doubt, been the most powerful influence on the nature and direction of research in Scotland over the last ten years. The position of the unit is currently under review, and some probable changes will be considered later in the chapter. Initially, however, it is essential to understand how it came to achieve prominence across the whole field of research activity.

RIU was formally constituted in 1972 and is staffed by members of the inspectorate together with research officers from the Central Research Unit, a body servicing all Scottish Office departments. The Director of the unit from its beginning until his retirement in 1983 was HMCI J. G. Morris. Morris has contrasted the modest origins of RIU, when he devoted half of his time to other duties and did not have the benefit of support staff, to its strength at the time of his retiral, with a staff of seventeen and a budget of some £3 million.[2] During his reign five operational branches developed:

1. RESEARCH (This branch has general responsibility for advising and running research and development programmes on all aspects of education.)

2. EDUCATIONAL TECHNOLOGY (This branch offers advice on and seeks to promote effective teaching methods in schools, FE, HE and community education.)

3. INTELLIGENCE INFORMATION (This branch deals with the dissemination of information about current educational research and development in Scotland: it also has responsibility for running an internal computerised information retrieval system.)

4. ASSESSMENT (This branch offers advice on assessment policy and techniques.)

5. MICROELECTRONICS IN EDUCATION (This branch is concerned with promoting the effective use of microelectronics in education and, in particular, with monitoring the Scottish Microelectronics Development Programme.)[3]

This description indicates that RIU is concerned with more than educational research, a point recently reinforced by HMCI R. S. Johnston, the man carrying out the review of the unit.[4] Mr Johnston suggested, in fact, that the name Research and Intelligence Unit is now something of a misnomer, given its increasing interest in the technological side of staff development and in-service training. It is — and always has been — a misnomer in another sense, for RIU staff do not themselves carry out research. Their work takes the form of negotiating, commissioning and monitoring research projects carried out by others — principally, but not exclusively, in colleges of education and universities. In the 1983 research register issued by the SED, 116 projects are listed, of which 53 are based in colleges and 40 in universities.[5]

RIU can be considered as occupying the centre of a network which embraces all the agencies engaged in the active business of conducting research investigations. In theory, the process whereby proposed topics receive backing is an open one. Suggestions can derive from a number of sources. There will be initiatives from RIU itself in response to policy options being considered by administrators and politicians. Quasi-autonomous educational bodies, such as SCRE and SCET, may put forward research proposals requiring funding of a kind that cannot be met from their own budgets. And individuals and teams within universities and colleges may suggest projects to RIU which they think are important and worthwhile. On the face of it, then, there seems to be a reasonable balance between ideas deriving from within the SED itself and those coming from external sources.

Closer inspection, however, reveals a somewhat different picture and, indeed, the Rendle Report posed the key question of 'whether responsibility for guiding the direction of research funding, for selecting the lines to be followed, is too firmly in the hands of the R and I Division'. It went on:

> The research field in fact epitomises some of the general qualms voiced in this report about —
>
> a. the Inspectorate's apparent freedom to set significant lines of enquiry (in this case research) in train
>
> b. the degree of influence and even, in a sense, control which is exercised over the activities of bodies which, according to their generic acronym, should be at least quasi-autonomous.[6]

Part of the explanation for the degree of control which RIU has managed to acquire lies in the personality of J. G. Morris. He is a forceful character, with considerable drive and energy, and the expansion and development of RIU was very much a product of his determination.[7] Morris succeeded in establishing a degree of independence for the operation of RIU, both within the inspectorate and within the SED as a whole. In order to do so, however, he must have had a patron in high places. Not surprisingly, the rather special position of RIU caused a certain amount of resentment within the department, and accusations of empire-building were said to have been voiced. Indeed, the present review of RIU might be interpreted as a delayed settling of old scores by disenchanted factions within the SED.

Whatever the truth of the internal politics of the matter, Morris certainly managed to secure a strong position for himself and his unit *vis-à-vis* the research community. In dealing with research proposals, the implication of other groups within the SED wanting to move against RIU could even be turned to advantage: RIU staff could hint that, unless broad acceptance of their conception of appropriate research topics and methods was forthcoming, researchers might find themselves having to deal with officials who would be much less supportive in their view of research and who might even doubt its value altogether. The statement of a former Permanent Secretary at the DES, Sir William Pile, could be invoked to back up the suggestion of an anti-research lobby among career civil servants. Pile remarked in 1976 that

> the great thing about research is that a part of it is rubbish and another part (I will not be specific about the proportions) leads nowhere and is really indifferent; it is, I am afraid, exceptional to find a piece of research that really hits the nail on the head and tells you pretty clearly what is wrong or what is happening or what should be done . . . People say they have done some research when they really mean they have stopped to think for three minutes.[8]

Faced with the prospect of such an entrenched and unsympathetic position, it is hardly surprising that some members of the research community in Scotland came to regard RIU as benign and enlightened in comparison. Their gratitude was, of course, likely to be enhanced if they themselves became beneficiaries of RIU patronage. This leads directly into another critical feature which helps to explain the degree of control exercised by the unit.

The funding arrangements for educational research in Scotland give what can only be described as an excessive measure of power to the SED, through RIU. It is not unreasonable that central government should determine *part* of an overall research programme, but if research is to remain worthy of the name, it is important that some of those involved should not be dependent on centrally controlled patronage. In Scotland, however, RIU penetrates almost all aspects of the system. In 1982–83, for example, in addition to £536,000 set aside for general research projects (the principal source of funding for educational researchers working in the universities), RIU was the channel for £284,000 going to SCRE, £364,000 going to Munn/Dunning related projects, £300,000 going to SCET for the Scottish Microelectronics Development Programme, and £120,000 going to colleges of education.[9] One consequence of this pervasiveness is that research proposals tend to be tailored to meet the perceived predilections of RIU staff. RIU staff, in turn, develop a value system in which the *worth* of a project becomes less important than their ability to 'sell' it to one of operational divisions within the SED, for sponsorship by one of these divisions is required before final approval can be given. These pressures encourage a high degree of pragmatism of a kind that can easily produce undesirable effects. Research comes to be defined in narrow, immediate terms and fails to address fundamental questions of meaning and value: the amount of money spent on Munn/Dunning projects is one example of this. Another consequence is that the whole process can become quite highly personalised, given that the power to grant or withhold funding rests with a relatively small group of people. This means that researchers who are unsuccessful in their bids may come to feel that their rejection depends as much on the fact that they do not belong to some inner, charmed circle as on the merits of their proposals. Such interpretations are purely speculative, but the prevailing pattern of funding does not serve to discourage them.

RIU, then, has achieved a dominant position in Scottish educational research. Supporters of its role would argue that this has led to a significant increase in the amount of research activity that has taken place over the last decade. Quantity, however, does not guarantee quality, and RIU's dominance has been decidedly double-edged. The cost of expansion has been a progressive loss of freedom by the research community. An examination of the recent history of SCRE, supposedly an independent research council, will serve to support this view.

## The Scottish Council for Research in Education

SCRE was established in 1928 as a result of the joint initiatives of the Educational Institute of Scotland and the Association of Directors of Education.[10] For many years the Council's budget remained at a distinctly modest level, being entirely dependent on contributions from the education authorities and the EIS. However, significant developments in SCRE's scale of operation, its funding, and its relations with the SED have taken place in the last twenty-five years. Professor John Nisbet, Chairman of the Council from 1975–78, has remarked that originally SCRE was simply 'an amateur spare-time association of those interested in research' and it was not until 1972 that this pattern of activity was discarded and 'a cadre of professional full-time staff' was built up.[11] Elsewhere, he has contrasted the budget for 1957–58 (£6,851) with that for 1982–83 (over £555,000) as an indication of the 'substantial growth of educational research and development in Scotland'.[12]

SED involvement with the Council began in 1946–47 but it was not until 1963–64 that financial support from the SED, granted under the Educational Development, Research and Services Regulations of 1946, grew to the point where it exceeded the contributions from the local authorities and the EIS. From the mid-'60s there was increasing reliance on SED funding to finance the steady expansion of the Council's activities. This, in turn, led in 1972 to a major reconstruction and substantial changes in the articles of association and composition of the Council. These changes remain in force at the time of writing, though a recent review of the work of the Council (to be considered shortly) holds out the prospect of further significant reforms. At present there are 21 Council members — 5 nominated by the Secretary of State for Scotland, 2 by COSLA, 2 by the Association of Directors of Education, 3 by the Colleges of Education, 3 by the Scottish Universities, 1 by the SEB, 3 by the EIS, 2 by other teachers' associations. In addition, there are 4 assessors from the SED.[13] Since 1972 the Chairman has always been a nominee of the Secretary of State. Full-time staff listed in the Annual report for 1982–83 consisted of a Director, Depute Director and Assistant Director, together with 16 research staff of varying degrees of seniority and security of tenure. On the support side, 5 part-time and 15 full-time staff are classified as 'Technical', 'Information and Library', 'Finance and Administration' or 'Clerical and Secretarial'.

The increasing involvement of the SED in the work of SCRE raises important questions about the way in which research policy is formulated and implemented. Can SCRE be regarded as genuinely independent or is it merely another example of a supposedly autonomous body which, in fact, is tightly controlled? In 1981, the then Chairman, Hugh Fairlie, acknowledged that the question of SCRE's overall research policy was a sensitive issue, 'especially when the Council is subject to many constraints, not least of which is the financial one, and its degrees of freedom are limited'.[14] Nevertheless, certain broad principles, first enunciated in 1978, were reaffirmed:

1. The Council's work should be concerned primarily with applied research. Its main function is to provide information which will aid those involved in education in Scotland to reach enlightened and informed decisions at national, regional or local level, as the case may be.
2. The process of 'negotiated research' should operate in the development of

contract research. The aim should be to match the requirements of potential clients to the contributions possible from Council staff. In a sense the Council in this respect has a responsive role, but it has to decide whether to accept a particular commission and, if so, how it should be carried out.

3. The Council must maintain an internal research programme from its own funds, and even in times of financial stringency it is essential that this capacity be maintained. Past experience shows that the Council, by identifying and investigating a number of educational issues, has in fact made a great contribution to educational development.[15]

The first principle is very much in line with a major strand in the historical evolution of SCRE — its concern with concrete, practical issues. When SCRE was established, informed educational opinion of the time held that 'the quantitative methods of the exact sciences could be applied with profit to the investigation and solution of many educational problems'.[16] The present Director of SCRE, Bryan Dockrell, has confirmed that the 'hard-nosed empirical and, indeed, often pragmatic psychometric approach' is still well represented in Scottish educational research.[17] Clearly there is something to be said for devoting a proportion of research energies to practical topics which can be investigated in this way, but it is important that they should not squeeze out other types of enquiry. Too narrow a focus on issues that seem immediately relevant can easily encourage a blinkered view of what research is and what it might achieve. In this respect, content and method are closely linked. The applied view of research, if pursued exclusively, leads to a devaluation of historical, philosophical and theoretical insights of a kind that may be necessary to challenge the prevailing educational orthodoxies. As Sir J. J. Robertson, the architect of the 1947 Advisory Council Report on Secondary Education, once remarked, the really important decisions on educational development are matters of educational philosophy, not of educational research, narrowly conceived.[18]

The second principle does not in any sense serve to counter-balance the first. It attempts to mitigate the effects of the customer/contractor model of research, enunciated most clearly in the Rothschild Report,[19] by stressing negotiation. The Rothschild formula effectively gives the agency sponsoring research the right to identify problems, control the form of enquiry and determine priorities. A cynical view of this model is that it is designed to tell the sponsor what he or she wants to hear, regardless of the facts of the matter. SCRE's talk of matching the requirements of clients to the potential contribution of Council staff, and of deciding whether or not to accept a particular commission, is intended to forestall such an interpretation. However, when money for research is in short supply and reseach agencies are competing for work, 'negotiation' soon becomes little more than a piece of face-saving rhetoric. There is no doubt that he who pays the piper calls the tune. In the words of a disarmingly frank article by two members of staff in RIU, 'research responds to events, but does not create them ... far from having an impact on policy and practice, research is itself directed by them'.[20] It is no doubt convenient for those involved in commissioning and accepting research contracts to imagine that the exercise is one in which equal partners respect each other's contribution. In many cases, however, this is simply an elaborate ritual designed to disguise the degree of direction on one side and submission on the other.

The third principle of SCRE research policy — the importance of maintaining an internal research programme based on its own perception of priorities — is the most defensible, though it is also the most vulnerable. As Hugh Fairlie remarked in 1981: 'Most of our current anxiety lies in our efforts to maintain and support this last item of policy ... '[21] Even if resources were not a major problem, there would remain difficulties regarding the Council's capacity to discharge this function effectively. The justification for an independent dimension to SCRE's work depends on a number of things: the expertise of its staff; the potential value of studies that are not determined by the limited perceptions of educational administrators; the importance of developing new investigative styles. All of these conditions are problematical. SCRE certainly includes among its staff several able and experienced researchers, but in many cases they occupy relatively junior positions, and their ability to influence decisions is limited. Again, the more SCRE commits itself to work of a contractual nature, the less able it is to maintain that degree of detachment required for the identification of issues which may be important, but which are not perceived as such by those who regard research as a means of conferring respectability on political decisions. And finally, the progressive concentration on forms of enquiry designed to produce limited answers to limited questions reduces the Council's capacity to conceptualise and develop research methodologies that break new ground.[22]

This reading of the situation would, not surprisingly, be challenged by Council members. However, if the list of projects given in the Annual Report for 1982–83 is examined, the pattern that emerges bears out the account that has been advanced. Twenty projects are listed: it should be noted that only nineteen of these were actually 'in progress' during 1982–83, of which fifteen were externally funded. If all twenty are taken into account, they can be classified under four broad headings. Seven studies relate directly or indirectly to current national policy priorities (including the secondary school curriculum, the consequences of falling school rolls, and the impact of the Youth Training Scheme). Four studies take the form of longitudinal investigations of a largely quantitative kind (including the international mathematics survey and the Scottish standardisation of the Wechsler Intelligence Scale). There are five evaluation projects (including the Craigroyston Curriculum Project and the Pakistan Primary Education Project). And, finally, there are four survey or data collection projects (including changing patterns of provision in FE colleges and the progress and destination of secondary school pupils).

Some of these research studies are undoubtedly important and worthwhile, but they reveal a strong bias in favour of investigations of existing practice together with an acceptance of policy guidelines deriving from national or local government. Given this bias, the opportunity to develop genuinely *critical* approaches to problems is minimal — the framework of what is 'given' and must be accepted is too restricting. It is not surprising, therefore, that historical and philosophical questions, which might open up critical perspectives, are hardly addressed at all, even as subsidiary elements in the projects. But, even if it is accepted that the 'practical' emphasis is justified, there are many vital topics of current interest which are either not represented or are treated marginally: examples would include the leadership styles of headteachers in a period of educational 'reform', the changing pattern of higher education, the effectiveness of the inspectorate as agents of change, the contributions of the CCC, the SEB and the GTC to educational development, the impact of contraction on the colleges of education, the appointment and promotion of teachers by local authorities, and the respective influence of professional and political forces in the evolution of educational policy.[23] All of these topics are, of course, 'sensitive', but that is precisely why they are important. Worthwhile research needs to be courageous. By contrast, SCRE has tended to take an over-cautious view of what counts as valid research activity. Partly as a result of its financial vulnerability it has been afraid to offend political sensitivities, both within the SED and the local authorities. Whether this has been a conscious strategy or merely the cumulative effect of the pressures to which it has been subject over the years is difficult to say. But, whatever the explanation, the consequence has been that the Council's recent contribution to educational research has been less distinguished than it might have been.

The process whereby approval is gained for SCRE projects reflects these weaknesses. A Research Committee, consisting of senior staff and Council members (including an SED assessor) meets five or six times a year to consider proposals and review the results of negotiations with other organisations. Proposals are categorised as Stage 1 or Stage 2: those which pass the Stage 1 hurdle are revised in the light of criticisms and suggestions and submitted again in a more detailed form. A reading of the minutes for the period 1981–83 reveals three disturbing trends.

First, there is evidence of a lack of confidence by SCRE research staff in the members of the Research Committee. Internal memoranda indicate a feeling among staff that the committee adopts a regulatory rather than a facilitating role, that it displays a negative and reactive attitude to proposals when what is needed is a positive and constructive one. It is even suggested that sometimes decisions are effectively taken before researchers have had a chance to speak to their proposed projects. Furthermore, concern is expressed that the overall research programme of the Council is determined too much on an *ad hoc* basis, with researchers on short-term contracts rather desperately seeking to secure their continued employment by putting forward proposals that will appeal to a funding agency.[24] In a letter to the then Chairman of the Research Committee in 1982, the Executive Committee representing ASTMS members among SCRE staff called for a more active contribution from the Research Committee in expanding and developing an overall programme. At a subsequent meeting these criticisms were rejected.[25]

The second area of concern is the position of the SED assessor on the Research Committee. Until his retiral in 1984 this was HMI W. Nichol. It is evident from the minutes that Mr Nicoll assumed a very active role. Indeed, frequently his contributions appear to have been decisive in the decision-making process, especially where he indicated that SED funding would or would not be likely to be forthcoming in relation to particular proposals. His stance, it should be said, emerges as quite consistent. Where suggested projects tie in with the research priorities of the SED and seem likely to have a pay-off at the level of practice, he generally gives his blessing. However, in so far as other members of the Research Committee are encouraged to take a similar attitude, then the pretensions of SCRE to be an independent body are further diminished. One member of the Research Committee, W. R. Dunn of Glasgow University, has argued strongly for greater diversification of sources of funding to reduce reliance on SED 'goodwill' but, so far, his recommendations have not been translated into action.[26]

Finally, the Research Committee, in common with many other agencies in Scottish education, seems to accept a consensus model of development. In 1983 proposals were advanced to strengthen relationships with the SEB and the CCC on the grounds that 'three major forces in education — good research, good curriculum development and good assessment — should work together in concert'.[27] (The confident, but unsubstantiated, attributions of 'goodness' may be noted in passing.) Attendance by a CCC/SCDS representative at SCRE Research Committee meetings would, it was claimed, ensure that 'projects approved were likely to articulate well with current concerns in curriculum development'.[28] In this, there is little awareness of the dangers of 'articulation' (currently a much-favoured word in official circles) as far as research is concerned. The detached, critical perspective on which valuable research depends is progressively compromised by the consensus model, especially where it is reinforced by a network of people who assume that they have the ability and the credentials to set the nation's educational agenda. Instead of resisting absorption into this unhealthy atmosphere, SCRE has shown a naive willingness to succumb to its contaminating effects.

## The Scottish Council for Educational Technology

SCET was established in 1975. Its aims are 'to promote and encourage the understanding and application of educational technology in its widest sense throughout education, both formal and informal, and in commercial and industrial training'; and 'to promote and encourage the understanding and knowledge of film and related media in their artistic and cultural aspects at all levels of the community'.[29] In pursuit of these aims, which clearly take in more than educational research, SCET works through three operational divisions — Education and Training, the Scottish Film Council, and the Scottish Microelectronics Development Programme (SMDP). In the present context, it is the last of these divisions that is of most interest, though it should be noted that SCET's research activities also include projects on media education and open learning systems. SMDP was set up by the government in 1980 to develop the use of microcomputers and microelectronics in Scottish schools, and to explore their implications for teacher education and the management of educational institutions. These objectives have since been extended to cover the provision of a national information service and the development and maintenance of a national library of computer software.

A recurring question concerning the research work of SMDP has been the extent to which it has been under the direction of the SED. SCET describes itself as an 'autonomous body' but the composition of the Council indicates that, perhaps to a greater extent than any other educational quango, it is firmly controlled through Scottish Office patronage. Fifteen members out of a total of twenty-one are appointed directly by the Secretary of State and only six by COSLA. In addition, there are two SED assessors in attendance at Council meetings. The Chairman is Dr T. R. Bone.[30]

The financing of SCET also encourages scepticism about its autonomy. By far the largest part of its income comes from the SED — more than £1.5 million (including SMDP funding) out of a total income of £2.3 million in 1983. Much smaller contributions come from the Scottish regional authorities and the Department of Trade and Industry. SCET also generates a proportion of its own income from the letting of premises, the provision of film library services, sales of materials, etc. (£486,000 in 1983).[31]

Within such a framework, there must be an initial presumption that the capacity of SMDP staff to act independently is questionable. This doubt was amply confirmed by an evaluation of the SMDP project carried out in 1982 by two researchers from Edinburgh University.[32] The evaluators identified a number of major areas of concern: internal conflicts which led to the resignation of the Depute Director of SMDP in September 1981; the determination of the SED to retain overall control of the management of SMDP while requiring SCET to retain administrative responsibilities; the use of the project Steering Committee, chaired by HMCI J. M. Morris, as a mechanism to ensure that SED proposals were rubber stamped; the constantly changing direction and priorities of the programme; and the low rating by teachers of SMDP's performance in meeting their needs.

Taken together, these criticisms amounted to a savage indictment of the whole enterprise.[33] However, the response of the SED was to adopt a familiar 'damage limitation' strategy. Morris claimed that the criticisms 'had been taken on board',[34] and eight days before the evaluation report was published it was announced that SMDP's life would be extended indefinitely, thereby forestalling any suggestions that the project might be scaled down or discontinued. Some months later, in June 1983, it was announced by the Secretary of State that an 'independent' committee, 'widely representative of Scottish education', would be established to run SMDP.[35] The chairman of this committee is James Graham, Senior Depute Director of Education in Grampian. Mr Graham's credentials as a defender of independent, critical thought are rather uncertain, for, in 1983 he was responsible for sending a letter to Head Teachers, on the directions of his Chief

Executive, forbidding them to air grievances against the region in public.[36] In short, there are few grounds for thinking that the criticisms of SMDP have been 'taken on board' in any serious sense. The events following the publication of the evaluation report are best considered as an exercise in public relations rather than a genuine attempt to stimulate the kind of open, exploratory approach that such an important and innovative project undoubtedly needs.

## National Inter-College Committee for Educational Research

NICCER was set up in 1973 to promote research in the Scottish colleges of education. Part of the motivation was a hope that college courses at both pre-service and in-service stages would be improved if their content was informed by research work carried out by the lecturing staff themselves. More immediately expedient reasons have since emerged: with the contraction in the number of colleges and the consequent reduction in staff, the argument that college of education lecturers should devote a proportion of their time to educational research, thereby weakening any suggestion that they are underemployed, has become decidedly attractive — not least to college principals keen to prevent further staff losses. In 1982 the equivalent of eight per cent of professional staff costs was available for research and development in the colleges.[37] 'In addition money is made available through Research Grant Regulations, currently about £120,000 annually, and is directed into approved projects on the advice of NICCER.'[38] Membership of NICCER consists of a college principal as chairman, three assistant principals, three heads of college departments, one senior lecturer, the depute director of SCRE, a member of the Centre for Educational Sociology at Edinburgh University, and two members of RIU.

College staff are not restricted to applying to NICCER for funding. They can also bid directly to the SED, especially where the estimated costs of projects are likely to be high. Here, however, they are in competition with researchers in the universities and elsewhere, and the odds against success are about 4 to 1.[39] The NICCER *Bulletin of Research* classifies projects as major or minor and explains that 'the term major is applied to those projects which receive substantial direct financial support from the Scottish Education Department or other interested bodies'.[40] Recently completed or continuing investigations under this heading include reading strategies in the secondary school, computer programs in geography, assessment in physical education, the development of social education courses, criterion referencing, the needs of profoundly mentally handicapped children, and environmental studies in the primary school. It is probably not unfair to say that the majority of NICCER projects are modest in scope and conception, and are often designed to 'service' developments which are initiated elsewhere, especially in the areas of curriculum and assessment. This conservatism has been reinforced by NICCER's dependence on the goodwill of RIU staff, to which it is always careful to pay tribute.

## Steering and Advising

In the section on SCET reference was made to the evaluators' comments on the role of the steering committee for SMDP. Most research programmes funded directly or indirectly by the SED have committees associated with them whose function is to act as a sounding board for the ideas of the project team and to comment on the development of the research. The initiators of a project are usually invited to put forward names for membership of these steering or advisory committees, but SED approval has to be gained and a representative of the department is generally included in the composition. In recent years, there has been a preference for the term 'advisory' on the grounds that the word 'steering' suggests a degree of manipulation. The former Director of RIU has claimed that committees are always 'enabling' and not 'interfering',[41] and at the annual conference of the Scottish Educational Research Association in 1982 two members of the Unit (Mr W. Nicol and Mrs H. Johnston) insisted that advisory committees never took an authoritarian line on the direction of research programmes. The somewhat authoritarian tone in which they expressed this view left some observers less than fully convinced.

The critical issues with regard to the function of steering/advisory committees are, first, the quality of the people who serve on them and, secondly, the role of the SED representative. Committee members undoubtedly give up a good deal of their time to undertake this voluntary work, and many of them are highly conscientious in travelling long distances to attend meetings and in reading the substantial amounts of written material produced by most projects. However, given that they are, in effect, appointed by the patronage system, which places a higher value on 'safety' than on intellectual independence, there is a danger that they will adopt a relatively passive position and merely validate officially approved lines of enquiry. If this is the case, the SED representative on the committee will have an easy task in ensuring that research projects proceed along desired routes. It has already been noted that the preferred style of HMIs is one of low visibility wherever possible so that charges of interference can be discounted. If, however, a steering or advisory committee should show signs of moving in the 'wrong' direction, a more active intervention may prove necessary. This is likely to be a relatively rare occurrence since the committee stage comes after a whole series of earlier stages which are designed to guarantee the political acceptability of approved programmes of research — the funding arrangements, agreement about the remit, control of publications, and, not least, approval of the researchers themselves. These constraints mean that even where a member of a steering/advisory committee feels unhappy about certain things — and critical voices are occasionally raised — the opportunity to effect desired changes is limited.

These mechanism of control are largely successful for a number of reasons. In the academic world, career advancement is increasingly dependent on research output rather than on teaching or administrative skills. Research publications deriving from large funded projects in the sciences and social sciences tend to be accorded higher status than those which are the product of academics working on their own. Furthermore, in the present economic climate, university staff are encouraged to seek funding from external agencies to help alleviate the effects of reductions in UGC grants: external funding helps to make a contribution towards running costs, and there is often a bonus to the university at the end in the shape of equipment purchased for the research project. It thus emerges that the pressures to secure funding operate at both personal and institutional levels. Many members of steering/advisory committees are themselves in the market for funding and are not unaware of the wisdom of proceeding cautiously.

However, some of the pressures operating within steering and advisory committees almost certainly operate at unconscious levels. The research community is relatively small: most of those involved know each other personally and meet fairly regularly at conferences. In these circumstances, informal alliances develop which may have undesirable consequences. The present Director of SCRE, Bryan Dockrell, has commented on the possibility of 'unconscious collusion' between researchers and policy-makers: 'There is a risk that a quiet word from a policy-maker will persuade a researcher that a particular direction to his research or a particular emphasis in his report should be played down'.[42] Such collusion is more likely to occur in an enclosed context, such as that of the Scottish research community, than in a larger, more open atmosphere in which substantive issues are less clouded by personal relationships. One advantage of a fully independent research council — sadly, SCRE, in its present form, does not qualify as such — might be that it would introduce a public and formal dimension to the whole process, which would, to some extent at least, counteract the less attractive aspects of the existing pattern of informal networks.

## Views From the Inside

The analysis that has been presented so far has been offered from the perspective of someone who has not been involved in large-scale funded research and it may, therefore, seem open to the criticism that it is speculative and lacking in inside evidence of a convincing kind. To what extent do the experiences of researchers who have sought and received SED funding bear out the interpretation that has been advanced? It is, of course, hardly likely that the principal beneficiaries of research patronage will be over-zealous in biting the hand that feeds them, but a nascent literature on the subject does exist and it is to be hoped that other researchers will be encouraged to contribute to the debate, notwithstanding the risks involved. First, however, it will be instructive, in the interests of balance, to look at the views of a defender of the existing arrangements for the sponsoring and funding of research.

Dr Alastair Macbeth of the Department of Education at Glasgow University has been associated with two major SED-sponsored studies, the Scottish School Councils Project (1976–80) and the Parental Choice Project (1982–84). In an article entitled 'Bureaucratic Funding of Independent Research' he has argued that it is highly desirable that bureaucracies should seek insights from sources other than their own ranks;[43] there is, in other words, a sound justification for 'a sensitive and sympathetic intelligence network',[44] drawing on the expertise of a range of outside specialists. The financing of external research does raise 'problems of selection of both topics and personnel'[45] for the sponsoring bureaucracy, 'and loyalty to the interests of the administration cannot, of course, be assured',[46] but the advantages, in terms of increasing the amount of research that can take place and the opportunity offered to outsiders to influence the thinking of the government machine, outweigh the dangers. There is, however, a crucial proviso: 'independent researchers must be treated as just that, and not as tame technicians helping to solve bureaucratic problems'.[47] Dr Macbeth suggests that his experience of direct SED funding has been generally very satisfactory, that his advisory committees have 'never sought to steer',[48] and that, despite a problem of delay between the completion of the School Councils Project and the release of the HMSO publication setting out the findings, 'the Research and Intelligence Unit did their part with commendable dispatch'.[49]

Dr Macbeth is aware of a number of counter-arguments. He refers to the criticisms of those with a 'more conspiratorial turn of mind': that 'the commissioning of research is sometimes used as a stalling mechanism . . . a means to inaction while appearing to act'; that researchers are used to carry out 'dirty work which government staff find either too tedious or too politically sensitive'; that 'too much of research funding in Scotland is controlled by the SED'.[50] The reasons given by Dr Macbeth for rejecting these criticisms seem inadequate. Instead of addressing the substantive issue of the nature and effects of existing arrangements, he simply asserts that he has little sympathy with the various complaints 'since researchers need not either seek or accept the work'.[51]

Other researchers who have sought and accepted SED-sponsored work are less sanguine about some of the consequences. John Raven, who has worked for SCRE for several years, and who has a substantial list of publications to his name deriving from a series of funded projects, has written of the unfavourable response of government officials to some of his research proposals and conclusions.[52] He attributes their lack of enthusiasm to the fact that his research 'regularly, and unexpectedly, kept pointing to conclusions which had to do with the operation of the political system and the public services, and civic and social attitudes'.[53] For example, his investigation of the education of 'deprived' children led him beyond conventional explanatory accounts based on institutional provision and parental attitudes: he came to hold the view that 'if anyone's education was at fault, it was . . . that of the leaders and managers of our society, who were unable, or unwilling, to analyse the way our society worked and manage it effectively'.[54] Raven's problem was, in effect, that he began asking a series of very fundamental questions 'about widely-shared beliefs and assumptions about how society should work',[55] questions of a kind that could not be accommodated comfortably within the remit of an ordinary social science research project. He found himself, on the basis of his research, 'asserting the need to find new ways of holding public servants accountable for their actions, for new concepts of citizenship, for open government, for diversity and choice in the public sector, and for new mechanisms to replace the economic market-place and to replace representative democracy'.[56] It is not hard to see how such questions would be perceived as either naive or potentially subversive by the agents of government patronage. They simply do not accord with conventional notions of legitimate educational research. Raven seems to recognise this when he suggests that a desirable first step towards tackling the wider political issues which his enquiries point to would be for the educational system to begin 'analysing what is happening in its own back yard'.[57] In a sense, the present volume is dedicated to precisely that task.

The criticisms made by Raven, although based on extensive experience of experimental studies, are general in character. A much more specific account of political pressures on educational research has been offered by Andrew McPherson, Director of the Centre for Educational Sociology (CES) at Edinburgh University. CES has established a strong reputation for its research work, especially large-scale survey research on school leavers. Its funding has come from a variety of sources, including SSRC (now ESRC), SCRE and the SED. In fact, it seems likely that one of the reasons for the success of the unit has been that is has not been entirely dependent on funding from a single source. It has, moreover, managed to steer a skilful course between descriptive survey work, concerned to provide a factual data base for policy-makers, and work that is often critical of existing practice. A case could certainly be made for saying that its output, taken in total, represents the best in educational research in Scotland. The fact that the unit is based in a department of sociology, rather than education, may not be insignificant, though it can be read as a comment on the failure of the Scottish professors of education and their staffs to develop sociological approaches to the study of education sufficiently.

In 1973 a liaison committee was set up between the SED and CES 'to direct SED-supported research in the CES towards the interests of the Department's operational divisions'.[58] Following regionalisation in 1975, CES sought help from the SED and the new regional authorities 'in the construction of a nationally representative sample of Scottish school leavers'.[59] This was a logical extension of earlier work carried out in 1971 and 1973 with the assistance and financial support of the SED. In 1975, however, serious problems arose 'over the issue of control'.[60] Part of the difficulty was the commitment of CES staff to what they called a 'collaborative model' of research whereby the facilities open to professional researchers and government officials should be extended to a whole range of other interested groups and individuals. Survey questions could, for example, be tailored to provide information on points relating to particular areas or to specific problems identified by teachers. 'Such an approach held out possibilities for enhancing teacher professionalism, for some convergence of research into practice, for the mobilisation of local initiative and knowledge, and for economy'.[61] It also meant, however, that 'there would be a growing constituency for informed educational debate outside the SED, a growing public competence ... and this was where the problem of control had arisen'.[62]

There was another aspect of SED hostility to the 1975 proposals of CES. This was the impending publication of *The Scottish Sixth* by Andrew McPherson and Guy Neave, a study based on an earlier CES project which had been partly funded by the SED. As is usual in such circumstances, the draft of the book had been sent to the SED, but it was only when the prospect of publication was imminent that a response was forthcoming. What then happened is best described in McPherson's own words:

> A liaison committee meeting was hastily cancelled and, days later, we were invited to sit at a table in St. Andrew's House whilst four of the five inspectors present (there were no administrators there) in turn explained to us what they thought was wrong with our study. Much of the discussion was detailed and informative. It was also argued that our attempt to clarify and test the assumptions on which policy for sixth year had been based went far beyond the proper limits of educational research. We were given the opportunity to reply. The chairman, who was not a member of the RIU, concluded by saying that the 'tone' of the report was 'unhelpful' adding, 'need I say more?' Possibly he did not need to, for what may have been implied was then spelled out by one of his colleagues. Leading me by the elbow to one side as we were leaving the room he told me that I could 'write what I liked' but that I 'should not forget that Scotland was a small country'. I was left to ponder the several things this might mean.[63]

And on a later occasion:

> An official told me that I had a record of maintaining rigid views in the face of reasoned argument. I would not rigidly deny this. I was also told by an official that one opinion within the Department was that I was a communist bent on dismantling authority both through the collaborative model, and also through our proposal to evaluate the response of government and others to our attempts to establish the model.[64]

Two external developments helped to introduce a note of sanity into the prevailing paranoia within the SED. First, *The Scottish Sixth* was accepted for publication by the National Foundation for Educational Research, thereby weakening SED's position. And, secondly, the Educational Research Board of the SSRC decided to award a substantial grant to support the collaborative research programme for four years. Both of these events, it should be noted, originated outside Scotland. The SED, unwilling to appear obstructive in public, staged a tactical withdrawal, initially adopting a neutral stance towards CES's proposals, later deciding that a weak supportive stance would be more expedient.

Andrew McPherson's own conclusions about this episode are cautious and carefully circumscribed. He does, however, draw attention to the importance of 'plural institutional provison for the independence of research'[65] and notes that 'the expansion of the SED's research and development activities, and the extension of its network of personalised control, has been followed by a deterioration in the institutional counterbalance to the potential of such a system for harm'.[66] He also anticipates some of the points that will be made in the final section of this chapter by suggesting that even tighter forms of control are likely to emerge in the near future. It is to be hoped that, whatever happens, the sheer quality of the work produced by CES will ensure that its activities continue to be funded by research agencies.

Less experienced researchers may not be so fortunate. One of the saddest aspects of the control of educational research in Scotland is that it drives able people out of the country altogether to pursue their careers elsewhere. A recent example is the departure of Ian Stronach, formerly Senior Research Fellow at the Scottish Vocational Preparation Unit (SCOVO), based at Jordanhill College of Education, to take up a post at the Centre for Applied Research in Education at the University of East Anglia. Explaining his decision to move south, Stronach commented:

> It is almost impossible to be an independent and critical voice in Scottish education today if you rely on short term contracts issued by the SED. The way to silence criticism is to refuse to fund or refund it. Scottish Education needs a more open debate, better informed and better researched. Yet the moves are towards closing debates, and imposing arbitrary and ill-considered 'solutions' to educational problesm.[67]

He went on to give a specific illustration of these processes at work:

> Grade Related Criteria are an outstanding example of what happens under such circumstances — the silliness and divisiveness of the criteria are widely, if privately, acknowledged and yet the drive for consensus — and the career penalties for dissent — induce the majority to confirm that indeed the Emperor has a fine set of new clothes.[68]

A few months after the appearance of Stronach's article, the SED decided to discontinue its funding of SCOVO after March 1985.

## Current Developments

It has been argued that SED control of research, through its funding powers, its infiltration of quasi-autonomous bodies, and its use of informal personal networks, has led to a situation in which the potential contribution of the academic community to the study of educational problems has been seriously undermined. Once again, however, it would be simplistic to portray the SED, without qualification, as the villain of the piece. Members of the academic community themselves, not least staff in the universities, must accept a large measure of responsibility for the present state of affairs. They have progressively compromised their independence by being drawn into the race for funding, which may be regarded as another form of patronage. Some researchers, it must be said, appear to be untroubled by the consequences. Indeed, a few are openly cynical about their own mode of operation — they find out what the SED wants and tailor their 'research' accordingly. The more widespread this approach becomes, the more 'research' can be viewed as a laundering mechanism, designed to give respectability to policy decisions.

Are there any signs that the situation is likely to improve, that researchers will seek to assert the importance of freedom from bureaucratic constraints more vigorously than they have tended to hitherto? There have been one or two sporadic attempts to raise the issue of control but it would be an exaggeration to claim that they have influenced SED practice in any significant way, except to increase the Department's determination to keep a tight hand on the reins. For example, following some of the disagreements within SMDP, a letter signed by a group of academics and researchers, posing a series of questions about SED interference, appeared in *The Times Educational Supplement Scotland.*[69] Whatever embarrassment it may have caused within the Department, there is no evidence to suggest that it prompted SED staff to re-examine their attitude to research in any fundamental way. On the contrary, two recent developments indicate that there are moves to assert even greater control. One concerns RIU, the other SCRE.

It has been observed in passing that the retiral of HMCI J. G. Morris in 1983 and HMI W. Nicol in 1984 has led to a review of the future role of RIU — a review which is being undertaken by RIU's acting head, HMCI R. S. Johnston. There are clear indications that the power which RIU managed to acquire, and which depended to a significant extent on personality factors, is unlikely to continue in its present form. Control of research will, however, remain firmly located within the Department. Mr Johnston's remit requires him to pay particular attention to internal matters; that is, links between RIU and the inspectorate generally and between RIU and the administration. He has stated that nothing can be achieved without the cooperation of the administrative side of the Department,[70] an observation that lends support to the interpretation of the usual relationship between HMIs and career civil servants advanced in Chapters 3 and 4. The signs are that RIU activities will be scaled down — there will be a reduction in the number of staff involved on a full-time basis (both HMIs and research officers) and an increased research role for individual HMIs not formally attached to RIU, subject to the approval of administrators. This perhaps marks the beginning of a programme of 'in-house' research by the SED, a development which will destroy any remaining pretensions to independence. The decision to discontinue funding of SCOVO may be regarded as a precursor of a wider strategy of embarking upon centrally directed 'evaluations' of Departmental policies.

SED personnel, anxious to think well of themselves, have been keen to deny any suggestions that these likely changes indicated a degree of disengagement from the research community. At the 1984 conference of the Scottish Educational Research Association a contributor made reference to the contraction in dialogue between government and the research community about the future of educational research in Scotland, an observation that Mr J. Linn, Assistant Secretary with responsibility for research, subsequently sought to counter.[71] The convention whereby nothing as vulgar as plain statement surfaces in exchanges between members of the leadership class had clearly been breached. More importantly, however, the pattern that is now emerging is merely the logical extension of arrangements that had been developing for a number of years. Benign control is simply being replaced by a more overtly authoritarian kind. Those researchers who were happy to settle for the former are in a weak position in attempting to resist the latter.

Similar tendencies can be seen in relation to SCRE. In November 1983, Ian Freeman, a civil servant, was assigned to undertake an investigation into the work of the Council, as part of the Pliatzky review of quangos. He was asked to address the following questions: (a) Is the function that is being carried out by SCRE essential; or if not, is it valuable enough to justify the time and money spent on it? (b) If the function is either essential or sufficiently valuable, is it best carried out by the Council rather than by any other means? (c) Is is being carried out well and economically? (d) Conversely, would there be any substantial loss or disadvantage if the Council were wound up? The very fact that these questions were posed in this way presupposes a weak body, vulnerable to government pressure. It was no surprise, therefore, that the findings of the review, which were intended to be confidential but were widely leaked, turned out to be extremely critical.[72] Unfavourable comment was made about SCRE's poor use of internal resources, its inefficient management structure, its lack of centrality in educational research and its failure to disseminate the results of its work adequately. It was not suggested, however, that SCRE should be abolished. The national character of the Council and the support given to it by local authorities were acknowledged. Reference was also made to its 'neutrality' and its close involvement with schools and teachers. Nevertheless, the recommendations for reform were far-reaching. It was proposed that two senior posts — those of Depute Director and Assistant Director — should be discontinued, and that a number of structural reforms designed to improve internal efficiency should be implemented. In particular, the committee structure should be abolished and the full Council should take responsibility for policy matters. The report also recommended that the Secretary of State's nominees should cease to be drawn predominantly from the academic world. This can perhaps be linked to another suggestion — that more projects of interest to the industrial sector should be undertaken.

On the question of the relationship that should exist between SCRE and the SED, Mr Freeman made recommendations that would secure the Council's future but at the cost of a further loss of autonomy. Funding from the Department should continue, but the conditions of the grant should be renegotiated. A jointly agreed and financed management plan, with forward projections for four years, should be worked out so that research themes could be identified and budgeted for. COSLA and the EIS would be involved in discussions about these research themes, but since the Department would provide the bulk of SCRE's income, there is no doubt where the principal influence would come from. These arrangements would, the review concluded, encourage the SED to direct more research work to SCRE than hitherto, and the Council could look forward to being used as a consultative body for the totality of the Department's research programme. The warm embrace of the SED, it would seem, is soon to become a cool and clinical stranglehold.

At the time of writing responses to the review are still being considered. As in the case of RIU, members of the research community have sought to defend the

Council's — and their own — interests.[73] Once again, however, they are in a weak position. Although Freeman's proposed solutions reveal yet another manifestation of the extension of bureaucratic control, it is difficult to deny that his preceding analysis contains valid criticisms. Ironically, SCRE's deficiencies can be attributed, at least in part, to the Council's failure to develop a coherent research policy which was based on criteria other than a vague desire to conform to the expectations of its patrons. With the change of personnel inside RIU, the patrons have become a little less genial and a little more coercive. The route which the Council's members will now be required to follow was, however, mapped out several years ago — and it was one that they embarked on willingly. The message is plain: in future, properly independent research in Scotland will only be possible for those who are prepared to eschew SED funding, whether it comes directly or *via* the various agencies (SCRE, NICCER, SCET) that are used to create the illusion that the Department is committed to the advancement of knowledge and the disinterested pursuit of truth.

*Notes and References*

1. Limitations of space prevent considerations of the small part played by UK agencies — such as the Economic and Social Research Council (ESRC), formerly the Social Science Research Council (SSRC) — in the funding of educational research in Scotland. The reason for researchers' apparent preference for Scottish-based sources of funding is, however, an important issue which cannot be explained adequately in terms of worthy nationalistic impulses.
2. See Neil Munro, 'The acceptable face of intelligence', *TESS,* November 4, 1983, p. 4.
3. J. G. Morris, 'Information Paper 8: The Research and Intelligence Unit of the Scottish Education Department', *Scottish Educational Review,* Vol. 13, No. 2, 1981, pp. 162–166.
4. At a meeting of the Scottish Universities Council for Studies in Education (SUCSE) in Edinburgh on March 9, 1984.
5. SED, *Educational Research 1983,* Edinburgh, 1983.
6. *Rendle Report,* para. 5.30.
7. For a sympathetic profile of Morris, see Munro, *loc.cit.,* p. 4.
8. Quoted in John Nisbet and Patricia Broadfoot, *The Impact of Research on Policy and Practice in Education,* Aberdeen University Press, Aberdeen, 1980, pp. 1–2.
9. These figures were given by HMI W. Nicol, a member of RIU until his retiral in 1984, at a staff seminar in the University of Glasgow, December 12, 1983.
10. See James Craigie, *The Scottish Council for Research in Education 1928–1972,* SCRE, Edinburgh, 1972.
11. John Nisbet, 'The SCRE's Contribution to Research in Education', in *The Scottish Council for Research in Education: 50th Anniversary, 1928–1978,* SCRE, Edinburgh, 1978, p. 8.
12. John Nisbet, 'The Changing Scene', in W. B. Dockrell (ed.), *An Attitude of Mind: Twenty-Five Years of Educational Research in Scotland,* SCRE, Edinburgh, 1984.
13. These figures are taken from SCRE, *Fifty-Fifth Annual Report, 1982–83,* Edinburgh, 1983.
14. SCRE, *Fifty-Third Annual Report, 1980–81,* Edinburgh, 1981, p. 11.
15. *Ibid.,* pp. 11–12.

16. Craigie, *op.cit.,* p. 2.

17. W. Bryan Dockrell, 'Educational Research in Scotland', in SCRE, *Forty-Eighth Annual Report, 1975–76,* Edinburgh, 1976, p. 52.

18. Reported by David G. Robertson, 'The Council and the Local Authorities', in *The Scottish Council for Research in Education: 50th Anniversary, 1928–1978,* SCRE, Edinburgh, 1978, p. 18.

19. *A Framework for Government Research and Development,* HMSO, London, 1971.

20. J. G. Morris and F. Hope Johnston, 'The Impact of Policy and Practice on Research', *British Journal of Educational Studies,* Vol. XXIX, No. 3, 1981, p. 210. Some of the statements in this article seem to have been designed principally for consumption within the SED and perhaps reflect a period of political manoeuvring regarding the role of RIU *vis-à-vis* other factions in the Department.

21. SCRE, *Fifty-Third Annual Report,* 1981, p. 12.

22. Cf. Nisbet and Broadfoot, *op.cit.,* p. 52: 'The educational research community is a constraint on itself in not questioning more rigorously the taken-for-granted nature of problems. If dominant paradigms and methodologies of educational research are unquestioned, there is little hope of making impact on the assumptive worlds of other groups. The non-problematic ideology of educational research turns it into an instrument of social control.' For a more detailed discussion of these issues, see W. B. Dockrell and David Hamilton (eds.), *Rethinking Educational Research,* Hodder and Stoughton, London, 1980. Some of the contributors to this volume offer a contrasting perspective to the one offered in the present text.

23. See Walter M. Humes, 'Research Not in Progress', *Scottish Educational Review,* Vol. 11, No. 2, 1979, pp. 143–151.

24. On the vulnerability of SCRE staff, see report in *TESS,* October 29, 1982, p. 1; also letter by E. Spencer *et al, TESS,* November 12, 1982, p. 5.

25. SCRE, *Research Committee Minutes,* March 24, 1983.

26. In a letter dated May 6, 1982. See also SCRE, *Research Committee Minutes,* May 12, 1982.

27. SCRE, Agenda for meeting of the Research Committee, May 11, 1983, Appendix 8.

28. Ibid., Appendix 8.

29. These quotations are taken from SCET's own publicity material, n.d.

30. SCET, *Annual Review,* 1983, p. iii.

31. *Ibid.,* p. vii.

32. Phil Odor and Noel Entwistle, *The Introduction of Microelectronics into Scottish Education,* Scottish Academic Press, Edinburgh, 1982.

33. For a concise review of the evaluation study, see Jennifer Boswell in *Computer Weekly,* February 17, 1983, pp. 18–19.

34. *Ibid.,* p. 18.

35. See report in *TESS,* July 1, 1983, p. 1.

36. For a fuller discussion of this episode, see Chapter 6.

37. J. G. Morris, 'Research in Colleges of Education in Scotland', Scottish Colleges of Education Inter-College Research Committee, *Bulletin of Research,* No. 5, January 1982, p. 5.

38. *Ibid.,* p. 5.

39. *Ibid.,* p. 6.

40. *Bulletin of Research,* p. 9.

41. Morris, 'Information Paper 8: The Research and Intelligence Unit of the Scottish Education Department', p. 163.

42. W. B. Dockrell, 'Practical Research', in *An Attitude of Mind,* p. 47.

43. Alastair Macbeth, 'Bureaucratic Funding of Independent Research', in Dockrell (ed.), *An Attitude of Mind,* pp. 88–97.

44. *Ibid.,* p. 89.

45. *Ibid.,* p. 89.

46. *Ibid.,* p. 89.

47. *Ibid.,* p. 91.

48. *Ibid.,* p. 92.

49. *Ibid.,* p. 93.

50. *Ibid.,* p. 91.

51. *Ibid.,* p. 91.

52. John Raven, 'A Public Servant's Dilemma', in Dockrell (ed.), *An Attitude of Mind,* pp. 127–136.

53. *Ibid.,* p. 127.

54. *Ibid.,* p. 127.

55. *Ibid.,* p. 128.

56. *Ibid.,* p. 128.

57. *Ibid.,* p. 132.

58. Andrew McPherson, 'An Episode in the Control of Research', in Dockrell (ed.), *An Attitude of Mind,* p. 112.

59. *Ibid.,* p. 112.

60. *Ibid.,* p. 112.

61. *Ibid.,* p. 115.

62. *Ibid.,* p. 115.

63. *Ibid.,* p. 117.

64. *Ibid.,* p. 118.

65. *Ibid.,* p. 121.

66. *Ibid.,* p. 122.

67. 'And So We Say Farewell . . . ', SCOVO, *Contact,* April 1984, p. 7.

68. *Ibid.,* p. 7.

69. David Hamilton *et al, TESS,* November 13, 1981, p. 2.

70. At a meeting of SUCSE in Edinburgh on March 9, 1984.

71. In the course of correspondence with a group of researchers who had expressed concern about the future of research policy.

72. See report in *TESS,* June 15, 1984, pp. 1 and 3.

73. See report in *TESS,* October 26, 1984, p. 3.

# 9
# *Bureaucracy as 'Rationalisation'*

## Introduction

The pattern of professional aggrandisement and bureaucratic control that has been shown to characterise the activities of the SED, the CCC, the GTC and many other bodies in Scottish education shows no sign of abating. In fact, there are definite indications to suggest that present trends will continue, and that the ideology which sustains the professionals and the bureaucrats in their endless quest to extend their power will come to affect more and more areas of the educational system. An important element in this ideology is the concept of rationalisation, a concept which, it should be noted, is highly compatible with the drive for consensus through 'consultation'. Advocates of rationalisation project themselves as scientific, logical thinkers, anxious to arrive at the kind of clear-headed solution to perceived problems which will be accepted by all 'reasonable' people. Apparent anomalies and idiosyncrasies are regarded as irritants, as barriers to the achievement of economy and efficiency. These barriers must be swept away in the interests of consistency and order, and the result, it is claimed, will be a fully rational organisational model. Objections to such utopian visions — on the grounds, for example, that variety of provision may have certain advantages, even if it does involve a measure of administrative untidiness — are dismissed as old-fashioned and out of touch with the needs of a modern educational system. In short, to argue against rationalisation is to expose oneself as unscientific and anachronistic.

The aim of the present chapter is to illustrate the probable effects of 'rationalisation' on three important areas of Scottish education — the examination system, the provision of in-service training for teachers, and the structure and management of tertiary education. If the developments that are currently taking place in these fields work out the way the planners intend, Scotland can look forward to a future in which even greater uniformity is imposed from the centre and justified as the only logical response to existing complexities. The first two areas (the examination system and the provision of in-service training for teachers) reveal a determination to set up new, or larger, administrative structures: the third (the management of tertiary education) also demonstrates this tendency but, at the same time, shows that political expediency can set limits to the degree of rationalisation that is deemed desirable. All three exemplify the extent to which questions of power underlie arguments about efficiency.

## The Examination System

In order to appreciate the impetus that has been given to arguments for rationalisation of examination arrangements, it is first necessary to give an account of the agencies that are presently involved in this field. The best known of these is the Scottish Examination Board (SEB), which conducts examinations for the Scottish Certificate of Education (SCE) and the Certificate of Sixth Year Studies (CSYS), and a fairly full account of its role will be given.[1] The other bodies involved are in the process of amalgamation and restructuring, and a briefer description of their development and mode of operation will be offered.

The SEB is a statutory body and 'is constituted and conducts its business in accordance with the terms of the Scottish Examination Board Regulations, 1981',[2] It has the following duties:

(a) to make arrangements and to conduct examinations each year for the award of certificates relating to secondary education;
(b) to award such certificates on such conditions approved by the Secretary of State as the Board may impose;
(c) to advise the Secretary of State on such matters relating to examinations for pupils receiving secondary education as the Secretary of State refers to them, or as the Board considers necessary;
(d) to give effect to such direction as the Secretary of State may give to the Board under these regulations as to the discharge by them of their functions.[3]

The Board has the following powers:

(a) with the approval of the Secretary of State to enter into arrangements for the performance of functions or the provision of services for other examination bodies or authorities, provided that such bodies or authorities meet the whole of the expenditure incurred by the Board in carrying out such arrangements;
(b) with the approval of the Secretary of State to enter into arrangements with other persons to enable them to discharge on behalf of the Board any of the Board's functions;
(c) to conduct or assist the conduct of research into, and to undertake development in connection with, examinations.

The Regulations stipulate that the Board shall consist of a Chairman appointed by the Secretary of State and thirty-seven other members. The other members, who are also formally appointed by the Secretary of State, fall into two categories. First, there are thirty-two members 'from among persons nominated by bodies regarded as representing the following interests, according to the numbers specified':[5]

| | |
|---|---|
| The Universities of Scotland | 8 |
| Education Authorities | 6 |
| Institutions of Further Education | 1 |
| Central Institutions | 1 |
| Colleges of Education | 1 |
| Directors of Education | 2 |
| Educational Advisers | 1 |
| Teachers Employed in Educational Establishments | 11 |
| Grant-aided and Independent Schools | 1 |

Secondly, there are five members 'who have experience in industry or commerce or who otherwise have qualifications which, in the opinion of the Secretary of State, make them suitable for appointment by him to the Board'.[6]

In addition to the main Board, there are five committees through which the detailed work of the SEB is conducted: a Chairman's committee; a Finance and General Purposes committee; a Fees committee; a committee on Research and Development of Examination Techniques; and an Examinations committee.[7] The last of these is 'responsible for the conduct of examinations and considering and reporting on all matters relating to them'.[8] David Elliot, the Board's Research and Development Officer, has explained the usual mode of operation:

> There are currently 23 subject panels working to the Examinations Committee, each of which normally consists of six or seven members, three drawn from secondary schools and one each from the universities or central institutions, the colleges of education, further education (if appropriate) and HM Inspectorate. In response to the introduction of Standard-grade examinations, panels may have two additional members who have experience of teaching the less able. In recommending individuals for appointment, the panel takes account of the nominations it has received from teachers' organisations, the Scottish Universities' Council on Entrance and the suggestions of the HMI member.[9]

An indication of the scale of the work of the Examinations committee and the panels which are responsible to it can be gained from the basic statistics for 1984. In that year the Board offered examinations in 44 subjects on the Ordinary Grade, 37 subjects on the Higher Grade and 21 for the CSYS: the total numbers of candidates who were presented for these examinations were 460,000, 173,000 and 12,600 respectively.[10] The Board has a full-time staff of over 100 and 'employs the equivalent of 194 full-time temporary staff'.[11] In addition, 'Administration of the examinations requires the part-time services of about 200 members of Panels, 1,300 examiners, 4,000 markers and 3,700 invigilators'.[12] In 1983 the Board's expenditure was £3.98 million and its approved estimates for 1984 were £4.81 million.[13].

The Chairman of the SEB, recently appointed for a third term of office, is Dr Farquhar Macintosh, Rector of the Royal High School in Edinburgh. He has been described as an 'exceptionally able man' who has chosen 'to play safe, or at least to [his] strengths'.[14] The same observer remarks on Macintosh's capacity to 'move with ease in the educational establishment of Scotland, amass his committee chairmanships, pick up an honorary degree from Heriot-Watt University and a CBE from the Palace'.[15] The pattern is a familiar one. That someone possessing Dr Macintosh's particular qualities should have been appointed to the chairmanship of the SEB is not at all surprising. It is an organisation which works closely with the SED[16] and which, in its operations, manifests many of the traditional bureaucratic features — a keen concern for procedure, an emphasis on confidentiality, a somewhat authoritarian style. This last feature will be appreciated by the many teachers who take on the grossly underpaid work of markers for the SCE and the CSYS examinations. The 'Instructions to Markers' which are issued typify the assumptions of SEB officials. Imperative forms abound: there is extensive use of the terms 'must' and 'should': bold type and heavy underlining feature prominently. Clearly teachers are not to be trusted.

It is, of course, important that an examination board should conduct its business carefully, with a proper concern for precision and — above all — fairness to candidates. Unfortunately, however, the SEB's own record in this regard is not entirely spotless. In 1983, for example, a major controversy arose over the alternative Higher History paper. Two questions relating to the period immediately after World War II appeared, and the suspicion arose that one of them should actually have referred to World War I.[17] This suspicion was intensified for three reasons: the absence of a question mark after the doubtful question, raising the possibility that at some stage the interrogative had been transposed to a roman numeral; the chronological placing of the question; and the fact that a question on the end of World War I had regularly appeared in previous papers. Expert opinion supported the view that a mistake had been made: Dr David Gillard of Glasgow University stated that the two questions 'overlapped so much as to be close to identical'[18] and said that he found it almost impossible to believe that a compiler would do this deliberately. Nevertheless, the Board strenuously denied that any error had been made. This position was somewhat weakened by a statement to the effect that candidates who had answered the doubtful question as if it related to World War I would not be penalised.[19] Not surprisingly, this caused further offence, particularly to candidates who had prepared for World War I, had assumed that the suspect question did indeed refer to World War II, and had been forced to choose another question for which they were not especially well prepared. The dispute continued and the Board was required to issue a formal statement outlining special marking arrangements.[20] It continued to insist, however, that apart from the omission of a question mark — described as a printer's error — no mistake had been made. One critic commented that the Board had 'sacrificed its reputation and its credibility to the myth of bureaucratic infallibility'.[21] When the results were announced it was claimed, to the astonishment of nobody, that the pass rate for the offending paper was similar to that of previous years.[22]

The role of the SEB in Scottish education has assumed greater prominence following the series of changes in courses and qualifications for 14–18 year olds at present being introduced or planned for. The first Standard grade certificates will be awarded in 1986: this will have consequences for the Higher grade of the SCE and for the CSYS, both of which are being reviewed. It is intended that the first of the revised Higher grade examinations will take place in 1987 and the first of the revised examinations to replace the CSYS in 1988. In addition to all this there are the implications for schools of the 16–18 Action Plan which will introduce a single vocational certificate — the National Certificate — for students taking the new courses in the field of non-advanced further education. These new courses are based on modules or short units of study, some of which will be available in schools. The National Certificate will not, however, be awarded by the SEB but by the successor to the Scottish Business Education Council (SCOTBEC) and the Scottish Technical Education Council (SCOTEC) — the Scottish Vocational

Education Council (SCOTVEC), which will begin operations in 1985. It is against this rather complicated background that the pressures for 'rationalisation' have gained force. Before examining the form that these pressures are taking, however, it is necessary to say a little more about SCOTBEC, SCOTEC and SCOTVEC.

SCOTBEC was established in 1973 'as a national body responsible for devising courses, conducting examinations and awarding certificates and diplomas for the business and related sectors of employment'.[23] In April 1974 it was incorporated under the Companies Acts as a Company limited by guarantee and not having a share capital. In terms of its Memorandum and Articles of Association it has a Board of Directors with a membership of twenty-four drawn from education and industry. Half the members are directly or indirectly nominated by the Secretary of State. Several bodies, such as the STUC, the CBI (Scottish branch) and COSLA, are entitled to nominate directly a specified number of representatives. In addition, two SED assessors are appointed by the Secretary of State. Throughout SCOTBEC's rather cumbersome committee structure — which, in its latest form, dates from 1979[24] — the SED is comprehensively, if not well, represented. Each broad area of study (Professional Studies, Clerical and Secretarial Studies, Administrative Studies, Computer Studies, Distribution Studies) is administered through a series of subject panels and course committees.

SCOTEC was also established in 1973 and, like SCOTBEC, is a company limited by guarantee. It has a Board with a membership of twenty-two drawn from education and industry: the basis of representation is similar to that of SCOTBEC. SCOTEC'S main responsibility has been in 'devising, preparing, organising, developing and reviewing technician courses in Scotland ranging from those just below degree level to those just above craft level',[25] and in administering the examinations and awards relating to those courses. It has collaborated closely with SCOTBEC in certain subject areas — notably computer studies, agriculture and information processing.[26] The two organisations also collaborated in the introduction in 1982–83 of the Scottish Certificate in Vocational Studies in which work experience is combined with an approach to vocational education.

These cooperative ventures were taken a stage further when in 1983 a Joint Steering Group of SCOTBEC and SCOTEC submitted detailed proposals for their amalgamation to the Secretary of State and to COSLA. It was proposed that the new body (SCOTVEC) would have a membership of twenty-four, including industrial, commercial and educational representatives, and two direct nominees of the Secretary of State. The Secretary of State subsequently suggested that he should nominate four members directly rather than two. He also proposed that he should appoint the Chairman himself. The Joint SCOTBEC/SCOTEC Steering Group had recommended that the Chairman should be elected by the members of SCOTVEC. In rejecting this recommendation, the Secretary of State said that the new council would be operating in 'markedly different' circumstances from SCOTBEC and SCOTEC and that he had a general responsibility for the efficiency of non-governmental public bodies.[27] He denied that this would compromise the council's independence.

In September 1984, before SCOTVEC had even been formally constituted, the

Secretary of State issued a consultative paper entitled *A Single Examining Body?* This paper purports to initiate a consideration of 'the advantages and disadvantages of creating a single body responsible for the award of all school and further education qualifications (below degree level) in Scotland'.[28] In other words, the possibility of amalgamating SCOTVEC and the SEB is being canvassed. Seven 'advantages' of amalgamation are listed in the paper, including 'the opportunity to rationalise administrative procedures both for the new single body and for schools and colleges'.[29] The explicit appeal to the principle of rationalisation should be noted. No 'disadvantages' are listed. Instead, a question is posed in a manner that hardly seems calculated to encourage responses: 'Are there any disadvantages of setting up a single body which ought to be taken into account?'[30] Clues to the unanticipated disadvantages can, however, be spotted at several points in the paper. For example, it is expected that the new examining body

> ... would be accountable to the Secretary of State in relation to educational policy; the Secretary of State would appoint the Chairman, some members of the governing council or board, and assessors, and would have a statutory power of direction.[31]

In practice, this would mean that the inspectorate, as the Secretary of State's agents, would gain additional power, a prospect that cannot be viewed with enthusiasm.

Another unattractive possibility emerges when the relation between examinations and the curriculum is being considered. The creation of a single examining body, covering both the upper secondary school and non-advanced FE would place the CCC in an anomalous position since its remit covers the school sector only. There is no equivalent body to the CCC covering FE. The logic of 'rationalisation' cannot tolerate this inconsistency, and the case for parallel provision in the field of curriculum development is examined. In a spirit of open-mindedness, it is left undecided 'whether the remit of the CCC should be extended ... or whether a separate body should be set up with responsibility for curriculum advice and development in relation to further education'.[32] Given the record of the CCC (see Chapter 5), the first option would seem to be eminently resistable, and the second, in view of the SED's treatment of SCOVO,[33] cannot be regarded as a promising alternative.

Towards the end of the paper, a series of questions about the issues to be addressed is posed but the interrogative form fails to disguise the government's long-term aim. As a leader in *The Times Educational Supplement Scotland* put it: '... to the underlying question as to whether the Scottish Examination Board and the ... Scottish Vocational Education Council should merge, the Secretary of State is clearly expecting the answer yes'.[34] Once again, the process of 'consultation' will take the form of confirmation.

A few belated glimmerings of what extended central control of the curriculum and examination system might entail began to dawn on some of the principal parties involved in the exercise towards the end of 1984. Andrew Moore, the chief officer of SCOTBEC, expressed concern that a single examination body would be 'too unwieldy and too powerful'.[35] The EIS, in a characteristically ambivalent stance, feared that there would be 'a substantial increase' in the influence of central government over curricula and examinations resulting from one body, but at the same time said that it remained committed to a single body for all students at 16+. Both SCOTBEC and the EIS argued that time should be given for SCOTVEC to become established before amalgamation with the SEB was contemplated.[36] Lecturers in the Scottish Further and Higher Education Association adopted a more consistent and coherent view by coming out clearly against an SEB/SCOTVEC merger.[37]

However, although these reservations may cause a delay in the setting up of the brave new super-Board, they are unlikely to prevent it altogether, especially as other voices will support it. SCOTVEC, for example, backs the notion of a single body with responsibility for curriculum, assessment and certification from the third year of secondary school right through non-advanced further education.[38] The main advantage of a single body, it claims, is that it would lead to a 'unified and rational system over the range of courses, subjects and modules in question'.[39] Given the combination of confused and willing victims, it can safely be predicted that the government will not find it difficult to come up with sufficient justification to enable it to do what it wants. Another triumph of 'rationalisation' will follow. In the process, the declared aim of improving efficiency will be transmuted into an exercise in the pursuit of increased power and status.

## The In-Service Training of Teachers

It has long been recognised that the initial training which teachers receive before embarking on their careers is inadequate to prepare them for a lifetime of work in schools. All sorts of changes — in curriculum, assessment, technology, etc. — make it desirable that they should have regular opportunities to update their knowledge and develop new techniques as part of a wider strategy of staff development. Accordingly, in-service training is provided by a range of institutions — the colleges of education, the regional authorities, the universities (including the Open University) — and takes a variety of forms, ranging from half-day sessions in teachers' centres or colleges to courses lasting a year or more leading to formal qualifications. In recent years there has been a trend towards school-based in-service provision, partly for reasons of economy, but also because of a belief that training which focuses on problems and situations experienced by teachers in their daily work will be more credible and effective than more general courses offered by outside institutions. However, courses leading to formal qualifications generally require attendance, whether on a part-time or a full-time basis, at a college or university, and it is with these that this section is primarily concerned. Whatever the form of provision, a number of important questions arise. Who should identify in-service needs — the teachers themselves, the regions, the colleges, the SED? Should in-service training be concerned primarily with the acquisition of practical skills or should it also encourage personal development of a less tangible sort? Should teachers be required to participate or should all courses be offered on a voluntary basis? What steps should be taken to coordinate the efforts of the various agencies involved in order to avoid serious overlap?

The body that is most concerned with these questions is the National Committee for the In-Service Training of Teachers (NCITT) which was first established by the Secretary of State in 1967 and reconstituted in 1976 and again in 1981.[40] The NCITT is a standing advisory body with a membership said to be representative of Scottish education: it includes nominees of COSLA, the Association of Directors of Education in Scotland, teachers' organisations, the Association of Educational Advisors in Scotland, the GTC, the universities and the central institutions. The Chairman is appointed by the Secretary of State. In addition to the main committee there is a lower tier of four area coordinating committees covering the North, East, South-West and South-East areas.

In 1979 the NCITT produced a report — which came to be known as the Green Report — on the subject of in-service courses leading to qualifications of various kinds.[41] This document offered a model for a national system of award-bearing courses which, it was hoped, would impose order on the existing diversity of provision and would allow for credit transfer between institutions. Three levels of award were proposed corresponding to the length and rigour of the course: level 1 for short courses leading to a certificate; level 2 for longer courses leading to an advanced diploma; and level 3 for courses leading to a master's degree. Although the Green Report was primarily concerned with the *structure* of in-service provision, its recommendations also affected matters of *content*. In-service priorities would be determined at national level by the Secretary of State on the basis of advice given by the NCITT. This has led one observer, David Hartley, to conclude, in the light not only of the Green report but also of subsequent developments, that such an arrangement would emphasise skills at the expense of more fundamental questions of educational principle:

> There is no ... provision for teachers to discuss the ends of education because these have already been agreed by officialdom; it is simply a matter of having teachers accept and grasp the pedagogical means whereby the ends may be realised.[42]

In other words, the new structure proposed by the Green report might simply become a vehicle for imposing approved national policies on the teaching force, with little opportunity to reflect on the validity of the aims underlying them.

In 1981 the Secretary of State indicated his broad acceptance of the recommendations of the Green report, and a reconstituted NCITT was charged with encouraging the development of the three-tier structure and advising the relevant agencies on the provision of suitable courses. Its remit also required it to address the broader issue of staff development in primary and secondary schools. Two further publications dealing with these areas were produced and submitted to the Secretary of State in 1984. On the three-tier structure, the NCITT makes proposals that confirm its preference for a prescriptive approach. It sees an important role for itself in the preparation of 'guidelines' for award-bearing courses.[43] Furthermore:

> Guidelines ... should represent a broad national consensus on the nature and purpose of a particular award.[44]
>
> Once guidelines were drawn up, it would be necessary to ensure that course proposals did not deviate from them.[45]

The members of the NCITT clearly feel that they have a major contribution to make to the whole exercise, for in addition to drawing up guidelines and monitoring the extent of adherence to them, they recommend that

> ... the overall planning of a national structure of award-bearing courses be delegated to the National Committee in the following respects:
>
> a. in identifying national priorities;
> b. in advising on a national structure of award-bearing courses;
> c. in reviewing existing provision in the light of a. and b. above;
> d. in advising the SED and the providing agencies about future developments.[46]

The report on staff development is no more reassuring about the likely shape of future in-service provision in Scotland. While it acknowledges in passing that an important motivator for teachers is the desire for 'personal professional development',[47] it nonetheless concludes that 'priority should be given to school-based staff development, *provided that this is within the framework of national and regional policies*'.[48] It is recognised that there may sometimes be a conflict between what individual teachers value and the desires of educational planners at local and national level. This is viewed, not as evidence of a real and valid diversity of educational ideas, but as a problem to be managed:

> One of the main tasks of those managing staff development is to avoid that conflict as far as possible by working towards a genuine consensus on goals and harnessing the talents and energies of individuals to attaining them.[49]

Three contexts through which staff development operates are identified — the school, the education authority, and the national context. The members of the NCITT claim that they 'do not wish to see the creation of a complicated and bureaucratic system of reporting'[50] but, at the same time, recommend the establishment of 'clearly identified arrangements through which the various processes of staff development can be carried out'.[51] David Hartley points out that the effects of these arrangements will, in fact, be highly bureaucratic: 'consultation' will take place only between contiguous levels of the structure so that the opportunity for classroom teachers to influence what happens at national level will be minimal.[52] The national context will shape the regional context which, in turn, will shape the school context. This hierarchical model accords well with other aspects of the way Scottish education is run but it makes a mockery of the references to 'consultation' and 'participation' which recur in NCITT publications. In the light of the paper on the three-tier structure, it comes as no surprise that one of the main recommendations of the staff development document is that 'the role of the NCITT should be expanded'.[53] and that this should involve the establishment of two major sub-committees — a Policy Review and Priorities Sub-Committee and a Sub-Committee on Award-Bearing and National Courses.[54]

If these were the only outcomes of the Green report and later NCITT documents, the situation would be bad enough. There is, however, another dimension to the process of 'rationalisation'. Although the NCITT envisages a bright future for itself in the preparation of 'guidelines' for award-bearing courses, it does not itself have the authority to make the awards. Approval by a validating body is necessary before the qualifications can be conferred. Colleges offering courses under the three-tier structure are faced with two options in this regard. First, there is the Council for National Academic Awards (CNAA) which validates a vast range of courses at certificate, diploma and degree level. CNAA was established by Royal Charter in 1964 following the Robbins report, and its creation enabled polytechnics and other institutions throughout the United Kingdom to develop a variety of advanced courses independently of the universities. In fact, CNAA is now the largest degree-awarding body in the country. However, it is probably fair to say that attitudes towards it are somewhat ambivalent. While initially it was regarded as a liberating force in higher education, enabling a 'public' sector to develop alongside the 'private' universities, it is now regarded in many quarters as unduly bureaucratic. The processes of submitting courses for approval, having them vetted by CNAA panels, preparing for visitation committees, etc., are often slow and cumbersome, and the amount of paper work that is generated can be daunting. At the same time, it has to be acknowledged that CNAA has acquired considerable experience of validation procedures and that it provides access to a national network of expertise. Some of the Scottish colleges — particularly those with previous experience of the Council in connection with BEd degrees — have decided that the CNAA offers the best prospect for the validation of award-bearing in-service courses.

Since 1983 another, purely Scottish body, set up specifically for the purpose, has come into being to offer alternative validation procedures — the Scottish Council for the Validation of Courses for Teachers (SCOVACT). The background to the creation of SCOVACT has been explained by its chairman, Professor David Sharp of Glasgow University:

> From the publication of the Green report, all of the Scottish universities were anxious that those colleges wishing to work in close collaboration with them could continue to do so and be able to extend awards to courses of in-service training. This desire was supported by the colleges of education and a joint working party recommended establishment of the Council.[55]

The intentions behind this move were varied. When the colleges first began to offer pre-service BEd degrees in the 1960s, some — indeed a majority — of them had sought validation from their local universities instead of CNAA. The universities hoped that they would wish to continue this connection for in-service work, and the establishing of SCOVACT set up the national framework whereby this would be possible. There was also a desire on the part of the universities to prevent a validation monopoly by the London-based CNAA by providing an identifiably Scottish alternative. And finally, it was hoped that the contribution of the universities themselves to the in-service training of teachers could be expanded *via* SCOVACT.

Subsequent developments have suggested that the universities' position had not been thought through with sufficient clarity. When the Secretary of State announced that from 1984 a new primary BEd degree would be introduced to replace the existing Diploma course, SCOVACT's remit was rapidly extended to include pre-service as well as in-service qualifications. This caused considerable confusion, for it opened up the possibility of colleges having to submit their new BEd courses for double validation — first to the Senate of their local university (which is what had happened previously in the case of secondary BEds) and then to SCOVACT. The possibility of acceptance by one body and rejection by another seemed to arise. At Glasgow University a 'solution' was found. The university would award the degree but the process of validation would, by an act of Senate, albeit acting under some pressure from Jordanhill college, be delegated to SCOVACT.

This decision, which members of Glasgow University Senate were persuaded was the most rational course at the time, has merely succeeded in creating another anomaly, affecting the third level of the new national in-service structure — the master's degree level. Five of the Scottish universities (Glasgow, Edinburgh, Stirling, Dundee and Aberdeen) offer Master of Education (MEd) degrees, which they are empowered to award in the same way as other degrees. Approval of courses is entirely a matter for the Senates of individual universities. If, however, the MEd degrees are to be included as part of the three-tier structure of in-service awards, they would have to be submitted to and approved by SCOVACT. In other words, they would be subject to precisely the kind of double validation exercise which was regarded as unacceptable in the case of the pre-service primary BEds offered by the colleges. Not surprisingly, the university departments of education have been extremely cautious about submitting their MEd degrees to SCOVACT — though a less charitable view of their stance would be that they have demonstrated a considerable propensity for collecting dithering. Lengthy, and fairly unproductive, negotiations between the Professors of Education and SCOVACT officials about the precise meaning of 'validation' and related terms, such as 'recognition' and 'accreditation', have taken place, but so far no MEds have actually been submitted for approval.

The anomalous position of the university MEd degree is likely to be viewed with some enjoyment in certain quarters. Traditionally, courses leading to an MEd have introduced students to educational concepts and principles in a way that has often encouraged critical reflection on existing practice. They have not been concerned merely to 'service' national and regional policies by initiating students into a narrow and specific range of skills. However, the *critical* potential of MEd degrees is not always appreciated by administrators as it leads to teachers asking fundamental questions of a kind that often challenge prevailing orthodoxies. The Green report stressed that level three courses should be 'closely linked to the work of schools',[56] and one of the later NCITT reports interpreted this as meaning that new patterns of MEd degrees might be developed as an alternative to the existing

MEd degrees of the Scottish universities.[57] It is not unreasonable to predict, given the track record of the NCITT, in alliance with the SED, that these new patterns — to be devised by the colleges of education — will offer little scope for an analysis of basic educational principles. 'This exclusion,' says David Hartley, 'constitutes a 'hidden curriculum' for teachers which will render them uncritical of the bureaucratic framework in which they work, and which will reduce their role to that of highly trained technicians, devoid of any analysis of education itself.'[58] Perhaps the saddest aspect of the desire to make Scottish teachers unreflective functionaries is that the universities, supposedly the guardians of intellectual freedom, have collaborated in the processes which make the outcome feared by Hartley likely to happen. At the first meeting of SCOVACT the hope was expressed that 'the Council would work in close co-operation with the Scottish Education Department, the National Committee, the CNAA, and other bodies which had an interest in the field of in-service training of teachers'.[59] Once again, it would appear that the power of 'rationalisation' is such that it can persuade even its victims to accept its 'compelling' logic.

## The Structure and Management of Tertiary Education

In June 1984 the Scottish Tertiary Education Advisory Council (STEAC) was set up by the Secretary of State for Scotland with the following terms of reference:

> To consider and report on the future strategy for higher education in Scotland, including the arrangements for providing institutions with financial support and the general principles which should govern relationships between universities and other institutions; to advise the Secretary of State on such other matters as he may remit to the Council; and to collaborate as necessary with the University Grants Committee, the National Advisory Bodies for local authority higher education in England and Wales, the Manpower Services Commission and other appropriate bodies.[60]

The background to the setting up of STEAC is complex, involving as it does developments both within and outside Scotland, and the legacy of an earlier, unsuccessful attempt to rationalise Scottish higher education. It is, however, necessary to offer an account of the main elements in this background before an attempt can be made to assess the role and significance of STEAC.

Tertiary education in Scotland is offered in four distinct sectors. First, there are the eight universities (Aberdeen, Dundee, St. Andrews, Stirling, Edinburgh, Heriot-Watt, Glasgow, Strathclyde) which are autonomous bodies governed by their respective Courts under Acts of Parliament or Royal Charter. Universities receive most of their income *via* the University Grants Committee (UGC) which disburses funds provided by the DES in London. That is to say, the Scottish universities are part of a UK network and are not subject to direct SED control. Decisions about course provision and student numbers are, by convention, made on the basis of advice from the UGC. As will be seen shortly, the extent of the UGC's understanding of the Scottish dimension and its freedom to act independently of the DES have increasingly become critical issues.

Central Institutions (CIs) form the second sector of Scottish tertiary education. In 1984 there were fourteen of these, eleven funded by the SED (Robert Gordon's Institute of Technology, Aberdeen; Paisley College of Technology; Dundee College of Technology; Duncan of Jordanstone College of Art, Dundee; Edinburgh College of Art; Glasgow College of Art; Queen Margaret College, Edinburgh; Queen's College, Glasgow; the Royal Scottish Academy of Music and Drama, Glasgow; Leith Nautical College; the Scottish College of Textiles, Galashiels) and three by the Department of Agriculture and Fisheries for Scotland (the North, East and West of Scotland Agricultural Colleges located in Aberdeen, Edinburgh and Ayr respectively). Most of the courses provided by CIs lead to degrees awarded by CNAA or to diplomas or certificates awarded by SCOTBEC and SCOTEC (shortly to be superseded by SCOTVEC awards). A strong vocational element is a feature of many courses, and there are usually close links between CIs and local industry and commerce. The colleges are managed by boards of governors which include educational, professional, industrial and commercial interests. These boards of governors are invariably described as independent, but SED approval is required before new courses can be offered and before vacant teaching posts can be filled.

The seven colleges of education, described in some detail in Chapter 7, constitute the third sector of the tertiary education system in Scotland. Like most of the CIs, they are funded directly by the SED and managed by 'independent' boards of governors. The main activities of the colleges of education are in pre-service and in-service teacher training but some of them also offer courses in social work and in youth and community work.

Finally, there are the further education colleges run by the local authorities and funded through the rates and the Rate Support Grant. Here a distinction is usually made between advanced and non-advanced courses, and STEAC's remit concerns only the former: 'an advanced course is one in which the standard of instruction exceeds that required for the Scottish Certificate of Education Higher Grade, the General Certificate of Education Advanced Level, the Ordinary National Diploma or the Ordinary National Certificate, or equivalent'.[61] Most of the FE colleges — there are more than fifty throughout Scotland — are principally concerned with non-advanced work but a minority offer a significant proportion of advanced provision and two of these, Glasgow College of Technology and Napier College of Commerce and Technology in Edinburgh will be transferred to the CI sector, with direct funding from the SED, in 1985. A third institution, Bell College of Technology in Hamilton, was also to have been transferred but, following negotiations between the SED and Strathclyde region, it was agreed that it should remain in the local authority sector.

The overall picture, then, is fairly complicated. There are variations between the four sectors in respect of the range and type of courses offered, the validation of awards, the system of funding, management structures, and relations with the SED. Even within a single sector there are significant differences deriving, for example, from variations in the size and strength of individual institutions. Among the universities, for example, there is a big difference between Glasgow

University, with more than 9,000 students, and Stirling University, with less than 2,500. Again, a similarity in one dimension may not be accompanied by similarities in other dimensions. Both the CIs and the colleges of education are funded through the Scottish Office and managed by their own boards of governors, but whereas the former are, in the main, in a relatively healthy state with regard to student numbers, the latter, as has been shown, have been going through a period of serious decline.

All this makes the cases for 'rationalisation' attractive to many people, though for a variety of reasons which are not always compatible. From the point of view of the SED, the setting up of some kind of machinery which would allow for central planning and coordination of provision across the whole field of higher education makes sense, especially during a period of severe financial constraint. A greater measure of central planning would also reduce the possibility of duplication of effort in the different sectors and would make the task of controlling student numbers easier. As will be seen later, however, other considerations come into play in determining SED thinking.

Individual institutions see different advantages in reviewing the tertiary structure. Small colleges and universities which regard themselves as vulnerable view the possibility of mergers as one way of securing their future: some informal discussions have, in fact, taken place along these lines although, as yet, they have not received formal support from either the Secretary of State or STEAC.[62] From the standpoint of the education authorities, which are involved in the whole range of post-school provision, both advanced and non-advanced, the path to rationalisation is more tortuous. On the one hand, they recognise the anomaly whereby some of the colleges for which they are responsible are engaged in similar work to that of the CIs but are funded and managed on quite a different basis. At the same time, they are reluctant to give up control of institutions which often have well-developed links with the communities in which they are sited and they fear the consequences of 'academic drift' for the non-advanced part of FE work. However, notwithstanding these problems, all of the parties with a stake in tertiary education accept that the existing system could be improved.

An earlier attempt at rationalisation, undertaken by STEAC's predecessor, the Council for Tertiary Education in Scotland, was unsuccessful. In 1980, a nine-member committee of the Council for Tertiary Education undertook a review of the structure and management of the tertiary sector, and in its report, completed in 1981 and published in 1982,[63] it recommended the establishment of a national authority, appointed by the Secretary of State and accountable to him, to oversee the system, including the allocation of government funds. A clear distinction was made between advanced course provision, over which the national authority would exercise control, and non-advanced provision, on which it would simply offer general guidance to the regional and islands councils who would be responsible for detailed decisions.[64] Some members of the committee were unhappy with this proposed dual system of management and in a minority report recommended that, while there should be a national authority, responsibility for the management of all tertiary colleges should be vested in the regional and islands councils.[65] This disagreement to some extent reflected the composition of the committee which contained a mixture of educationists with national and local loyalties. It was chaired by Sir Norman Graham, a former Secretary of the SED, and two of the three assessors came from the SED.[66]

There was another major reason for the failure of STEAC's predecessor. The remit of the Council for Tertiary Education in Scotland — and inevitably, therefore, its recommendations — specifically excluded the Scottish universities from consideration. At that time the universities were not keen to be involved in the review process, and their link to the UK system of funding and planning, through the UGC, was used as a reason for remaining aloof. The importance of maintaining a strong connection with the national and international academic community was stressed, and fears about the dangers of parochialism if the universities became part of a purely Scottish set-up were voiced. Parochialism comes in a variety of forms, however, and some of the objections were expressed in a fashion which testified to the continuing potency of the London-Oxbridge version. Nevertheless, the general stance of the universities in 1980, when the Council for Tertiary Education began its review, can, not unfairly, be described as indifferent.

Since then a number of developments have taken place which have caused them to alter their position quite significantly. In 1981 their previously supportive attitude towards the UGC received a severe blow when an extensive programme of financial cuts was announced. This exercise, painful in itself, was made even less palatable by a feeling that many of the decisions taken revealed extensive ignorance on the part of the UGC about the nature of Scottish education. The Scottishness of the Scottish universities was vigorously asserted, a tactic that was doubly ironic in view of both their previous reluctance to acknowledge the force of nationalistic arguments and the non-Scottishness of half of the university principals. A measure of unprecedented unity of action surfaced with the Scottish principals agreeing to keep each other informed about their dealings with the UGC and pledging to defend the distinctive character of their institutions. This spirit of cooperation was somewhat weakened, however, when it emerged that the cuts were not to be evenly spread. The large universities, Glasgow and Edinburgh, suffered much less severely than the smaller ones: Aberdeen and Stirling were particularly badly hit. But, regardless of their size, during the next eighteen months the Scottish universities were busily occupied with the task of future planning in the context of reduced student intakes and sharp financial cutbacks.

Two further developments caused a resurgence of their solidarity. In England a National Advisory Body (NAB) was established for the non-university sector of higher education to act as a central funding agency. In effect, NAB was being given extensive powers which had no parallel in Scotland. This, in itself, may not have particularly bothered the Scottish university principals, but when the DES indicated that consultation and collaboration between the UGC and NAB was expected, their anger quickly showed. Since the UGC is a UK body and since there is no Scottish equivalent of NAB, the proposal for UGC-NAB contacts over the whole field of higher education seemed to indicate either a serious lack of awareness of the situation in Scotland on the part of the DES or a willingness to take decisions which would affect Scotland on the basis of inadequate knowledge.

The second development reinforced the growing disenchantment. In November 1983 all universities received a questionnaire, supposedly aimed at helping the UGC in its forward planning. An accompanying letter from Sir Peter Swinnerton-Dyer, UGC chairman, contained the unfortunate statement:

> Parts of this letter refer primarily to the situation in England and Wales. We would ask readers concerned with the different systems in Scotland and Northern Ireland to make the appropriate adjustments.[67]

Quite apart from the offence the casual reference to 'appropriate adjustments' caused to Scottish sentiment, the survey itself proved a fiasco. Vast amounts of time and energy, which could have been better spent on teaching and research, were devoted to an extended exercise in pointlessness, for the mountain of paper that was produced was much greater than could be effectively processed and absorbed by the UGC. The Scottish universities reacted first by forming, early in 1984, a standing committee of principals and court nominees, a move which was designed to stress their national identity, and secondly by calling for the setting up of a Scottish sub-committee of the UGC.[68] This request was rejected but in the same month in which it was made STEAC was finally established — with an extension of its expected remit to include the Scottish universities.[69]

It is against this complicated background that the significance of STEAC and the prospects it holds out must be assessed.[70] Immediately after it was set up it identified seven areas, some of which clearly overlap, on which it was concerned to receive comments from interested parties: future demand for student places; the roles of the different sectors of higher education in Scotland in meeting demand for places; the funding arrangements for Scottish higher education; the way in which higher education in Scotland is organised; arrangements for academic planning and coordination; educational priorities, taking into account the aspirations of students, the requirements of employers and the interests of the taxpayer; the effect of new technology on the requirements of employers and the professions and, by extension, on the content of higher education courses. The most critical issue underlying these topics concerns the respective roles of the SED and the UGC, especially with regard to finance. In the past the SED has undoubtedly kept a very tight rein on both the CIs and the colleges of education. The former have not resented this too deeply, principally because the strong vocational dimension to their work has ensured that they have received government support for many new ventures. By contrast, the colleges of education have suffered badly under SED control and, at the same time, have shown little capacity, or even inclination, to shape an alternative future for themselves. They remain weak and vulnerable institutions. That part of the local authority sector which engages in a substantial proportion of advanced work has tended to feel that its claim to be regarded as belonging to the mainstream of higher education in Scotland would be enhanced if it were released from local authority control and handed over to the SED — a view that may be regarded as displaying a naive degree of trust in the SED but that also indicates a measure of dissatisfaction with 'local democracy'. Questions of perceived status are involved too.

Where do the universities stand in all of this? So far the line they have adopted has indicated a deep ambivalence. As has been shown, they are in the right mood psychologically, following their bruising experiences with the UGC, to regard closer accommodation with the SED as one way of drawing attention to the fact that Scottish universities are not the same as English. At the same time, however, in their individual submissions to STEAC they stop well short of recommending complete severence of the UGC link. They still see themselves as belonging to part of a UK network and fear the loss of prestige which assimilation into a common pattern of funding and planning, on an equal basis with other sectors within Scotland, might entail. One commentator has referred to the ambivalence of the universities' stance as a failure of courage: the result will be that 'the SED will concentrate on building up the CIs as the most dynamic sector at the expense of colleges of education, local authority colleges — and, indirectly, the universities themselves'.[71]

The official SED line is that it cannot pre-empt the deliberations of STEAC, but it is possible to draw some tentative conclusions on the basis of the membership of STEAC and some recent comments by the Secretary of the SED, James Scott. Unlike its predecessor, the Council for Tertiary Education in Scotland, STEAC is a small body and does not have a majority of educationists as members. There are nine people on the Council. The chairman is Donald McCallum, an industrialist with extensive experience of public service under the patronage system.[72] Four other members have an industrial, legal or accountancy background. The remaining four represent the world of education, with the ubiquitous Dr Thomas Bone, principal of Jordanhill College, acting as vice-chairman. Only one member, Sir Alwyn Williams, principal of Glasgow University, has a record of persistent public criticism of government policy on higher education.[73]

Judging from the composition of the Council, then, it seems probable that 'rationalisation' will, to a considerable extent, be viewed in terms of management efficiency and meeting the needs of the economy.[74] Arguments about the importance of academic freedom are unlikely to cut much ice. This suggests that the CIs will emerge reasonably well from the review process. The outcome for the other sectors is less certain, and much will depend on the preferred arrangements for the disbursing of funds. On this, the position of the SED is likely to be less straightfoward than may at first appear. On initial inspection, it may seem that the SED would automatically favour a single national body which would have responsibility for all sectors, including the universities: that would appear to be the simplest route to central control. No doubt there are people within the SED who would favour such a model, but its acceptability is likely to be constrained by wider political considerations. From the government's point of view, a single body might serve to heighten nationalist aspirations and provide an arena for political arguments of a potentially sensitive type. It has already been argued, in Chapter 4, that the SED owes its first loyalty, not to education, nor even to Scotland, but to the machinery of the British State. Anything that might serve to undermine that machinery is to be resisted.

There is a further important reason why a single national body covering all sectors may have limited appeal for the SED. At present the Department can exercise very direct control over the CIs and the colleges of education. There is no Scottish equivalent of the NAB in England with extensive financial and planning functions. If, however, the restructuring of Scottish higher education took the form of setting up such a body with a remit that extended to include the universities, the SED might have to relax some of its control. The price of including the universities could well be that the new national body might have to be presented as a kind of buffer between the Scottish Office and individual institutions; its credibility would depend on its not being seen as an agent of government but as an independent body. Even allowing for the SED's considerable experience in using supposedly autonomous bodies to further policies favoured by the Department, the result might be that CIs and colleges of education could start to break free of the detailed control to which they have been subject hitherto. Significantly, the Secretary of the SED, James Scott, has stated that he does not think a buffer between the government and Scottish tertiary institutions is needed.[75] Although he is keen to improve the planning relationship between universities and other institutions, he does not think that necessarily means funding all sectors *via* the SED. Scott's preferred model (and the economic values that inform it) is perhaps indicated when he says:

> What we can do is to try and exercise influence through the UGC and the Department of Education and Science by a circuitous route, to try and get a shift of emphasis that relates output to what we see as industrial needs.[76]

The 'circuitous route' has a twin attraction for the Scottish Office: it maintains that connection with London which is an important part of the strategy whereby devolutionary impulses within Scotland are contained; and it ensures that the SED's authority over those sectors which it has traditionally controlled — the CIs and the colleges of education — will not be weakened. 'Rationalisation' will be tempered by political expediency.

*Notes and References*

1. For detailed information about the work of the SEB, including statistical data about examination presentations and results, membership of the Board and its subject panels, income and expenditure, etc., see *Scottish Examination Board: Report for 1983,* SEB, Dalkeith, 1984.
2. *Ibid.,* p. 3.
3. *Ibid.,* p. 3.
4. *Ibid.,* p. 3.
5. *Ibid.,* p. 3.
6. *Ibid.,* p. 4.
7. See David Elliot, 'Information Paper 13: The Scottish Examination Board', *Scottish Educational Review,* Vol. 16, No. 1, 1984, p. 51.
8. *Ibid.,* p. 51.

9. *Ibid.,* p. 51.

10. SED, *School and Further Education in Scotland: A Single Examining Body?,* September 1984, Annex, SEB, para. 11. Hereafter this consultative paper issued by the Secretary of State for Scotland will be referred to as *A Single Examining Body?*

11. *Ibid.,* para. 10.

12. *Ibid.,* para. 10.

13. *Ibid.,* para. 10.

14. Willis Pickard, 'The growing interests of a 'peasant' ', *TESS,* January 20, 1984, p. 6.

15. *Ibid.,* p. 6.

16. It sometimes seems, in fact, that the SEB is simply used as a tool of the SED. This impression was conveyed, for example, when the Standard grade arrangements were being devised. Although the details were planned by joint CCC/SEB working parties for individual subjects, SED 'guidance' was involved at every stage. Indeed, Dr Macintosh admitted that the Board was under pressure from the Department to hurry things along (see report in *TESS,* February 17, 1984, p. 1). Some of the consequences of this relationship must be regarded as undesirable. For example, a member of SEB's English panel, Andrew Bruce, found that his critical views on grade-related criteria, set out in a note of dissent, were neither published nor acknowledged by the joint working party or the Board (see report in *TESS,* February 17, 1984, p. 1 and letters by Andrew Bruce, *TESS,* March 2, 1984, p. 2 and Marion Mills, March 9, 1984, p. 4). Mr Bruce claimed that the Board's own research cast doubt on the viability of grade-related criteria, a judgement shared by many other educationists. Nevertheless, efforts to open up the issue for serious discussion were resisted. Dr Macintosh took the line that a fundamental debate about grade-related criteria might lead to postponenment of the Standard grade programme, a prospect that could not be contemplated. He also stated that there were research projects to monitor the operation of the criteria. The fact that these projects would come only after the criteria had been introduced was not seen as a cause for concern. It seems more than likely that the SED will take a particular interest in the research: the 'monitoring' will itself be 'monitored'.

17. See report in *GH,* May 12, 1983, p. 1.

18. See report in *GH,* May 18, 1983, p. 3.

19. See report in *GH,* May 13, 1983, p. 5.

20. See report in *GH,* May 20, 1983, p. 6.

21. Letter by John McLellan, *GH,* May 25, 1983, p. 8.

22. See report in *GH,* July 29, 1983, p. 3.

23. SCOTBEC, *Structure of Committees 1982/83,* p. 3.

24. *Ibid.,* p. 3.

25. SED, *Further Education in Scotland: Directory of Day Courses for 1982–83,* Edinburgh, 1982, p. 5.

26. *A Single Examining Body?,* Annex, SCOTEC, para. 4.

27. See report in *TESS,* August 24. 1984, p. 3.

28. *A Single Examining Body?,* para. 1.1.

29. *Ibid.,* para. 4.1.g.

30. *Ibid.,* para. 4.2.

31. *Ibid.,* para. 3.1. iv.

32. *Ibid.,* para. 11.3.

33. See Chapter 8.

34. 'The 'super-merger' ', *TESS,* September 21, 1984, p.2.

35. Quoted in *TESS,* December 14, 1984, p. 3.

36. See report in *TESS,* December 21, 1984, p. 3.

37. See report in *TESS,* January 4, 1985, p. 3.

38. *Ibid.,* p. 3.

39. *Ibid.,* p. 3.

40. See W. B. Marker, 'Information Paper 2: Inservice Education in Scotland', *Scottish Educational Review,* Vol. 10, No. 2, 1978, pp. 62–64 and 'The Future of Inservice Training in Scotland: Some Alternative Models', *Scottish Educational Review,* Vol. 14, No. 1, 1982, pp. 5–14.

41. NCITT, *The Future of In-Service Training in Scotland,* 1979. Hereafter this paper will be referred to as the Green report.

42. David Hartley, 'Bureaucracy and Professionalism: the New 'Hidden Curriculum' for Teachers in Scotland', *Journal of Education for Teaching,* Vol. 11, No. 2, 1985, pp. 107–119.

43. NCITT, *The Development of the Three Tier Structure of Award Bearing Courses,* A Report Submitted to the Secretary of State for Scotland, 1984, para. 8. 6.

44. *Ibid.,* para. 8.7.

45. *Ibid.,* para. 8.12.

46. *Ibid.,* para. 8.3.xii.

47. NCITT, *Arrangements for the Staff Development of Teachers,* A Report Submitted to the Secretary of State for Scotland, 1984, para. 3.11.a.

48. *Ibid.,* para.3.16. Italics added.

49. *Ibid.,* para. 4.5.

50. *Ibid.* , para. 5.4.

51. *Ibid.,* para. 5.4.

52. See note 42 above.

53. *Arrangements for the Staff Development of Teachers,* p. 32.

54. *Ibid.,* para. 5.7.2.

55. David Sharp, 'Three levels, one system', *TESS,* September 2, 1983, p. 12.

56. Green report, para. 3.6.

57. *The Development of the Three Tier Structure of Award Bearing Courses,* para. 1.7.

58. See note 42 above. Also letter by R. Robertson, *TESS,* February 17, 1984, p. 2.

59. SCOVACT, *Minutes,* May 11, 1983, para. 1.1.

60. Letter from N. Macleod, Secretary, STEAC, to institutions invited to submit evidence to the Council, August 20, 1984, para. 2.

61. STEAC, *Review of Higher Education in Scotland by Scottish Tertiary Education Advisory Council.* 'Background Note', 1984, para. 2.

62. In Aberdeen, the possibility of amalgamating the university, the college of education and Robert Gordon's college has been mooted. Similar discussions have taken place between Stirling University and Paisley College of Technology.

63. Council for Tertiary Education in Scotland, *Review of Structure and Management,* September 1981.

64. *Ibid.,* Appendix A.

65. *Ibid.,* Appendix F.

66. Full details of membership can be found in *Ibid.,* Appendix E.

67. See report on the Scottish AUT's response to this letter in *Scotsman,* March 5, 1984, p. 5. Dr John Burnet, Principal of Edinburgh University, later described the whole exercise as 'totally misguided': see *Scotsman,* March 23, 1984, p. 11.

68. For an account of the attitudes of individual principals in mid-1984, see John Linklater, 'Academic devolution: where the universities stand', *GH,* June 20, 1984, p. 11. See also report in *GH,* June 14, 1984, p. 5.

69. See report in *GH,* June 19, 1984, p. 1.

70. An excellent survey of the issues can be found in Olga Wojtas, 'Scotland's Great Debate', *THES,* December 14, 1984, pp. i–iv. See also the editorial in the same issue, p. 28.

71. *Ibid.,* p. 28.

72. For a profile of Donald McCallum, see Neil Munro, 'Captain of Industry', *TESS,* June 15, 1984, p. 4.

73. For a profile of Sir Alwyn Williams, see *GH,* January 23, 1984, p. 7.

74. The composition of the Council has been widely criticised: see, e.g., *Scotsman,* July 31, 1984, p. 5. Also *Scotsman,* August 2, 1984, p. 7. In this later report James Milne, General Secretary of the STUC, is quoted as saying that the membership represented 'the newest thread in a pattern of political appointments ... in education ... and elsewhere, which are clearly designed to produce mouthpieces of Government departments'.

75. See Sarah Nelson, 'Education's new master lays down the law', *Scotsman,* January 9, 1985, p. 9.

76. *Ibid.,* p. 9.

# 10
## *From Demolition to Reconstruction*

The picture of the leadership class in Scottish education that has been presented in the preceding chapters has not been marked by unbridled adulation. Those qualities with which members of that class have been associated — bureaucratic expansionism, professional protectionism and ideological deception — hardly amount to a vote of confidence in their collective achievements. Moreover, when the recent history of their actions is assessed, it emerges that those aspects of the received wisdom which stress the democratic and egalitarian character of Scottish education and which appeal to notions of partnership and consensus, rest very uneasily with the extremely hierarchical way in which the system is organised, the endless pursuit of marks of status by individuals and organisations, and the concentration of power in the hands of a relatively small group of mutually admiring people. Taken together, these features lead relentlessly to the conclusion that much of Scottish education is now run, not for the benefit of pupils, their parents and the community at large, but to serve the interests of those who occupy senior positions in the hierarchy.

What is surprising is not so much that these charges are now being made, for the body of evidence to justify them is substantial, but that nobody has made them before — at least in a developed form. This, in itself, is indicative of the intellectual evasion of much educational debate in Scotland. Privately, many teachers and others working in education would express agreement with the criticisms that have been advanced, but getting them to voice their support in public is another matter. The vulnerability of young classroom teachers, especially those who have families to support, and who are keen to gain the modest financial benefits that accompany the first stages of promotion, has been noted as one explanation. It has also been pointed out, however, that this mechanism of control is beginning to break down, especially as far as those who have managed to make a little progress up the promotion ladder (say to Principal Teacher level) are concerned, since falling school rolls have drastically reduced the prospects of further advancement. Where some dissent *has* been voiced, it has tended to be limited to specific issues (such as corporal punishment or the effects of changes in the curriculum) and has often derived from a fairly conservative value position. Nevertheless, any development which holds out the possibility of the leadership class being challenged in a more sustained and systematic way must be welcomed, for such a challenge is a necessary prerequisite to the process of reconstruction. There are, however, other necessary prerequisites extending beyond the field of education, and these will be considered shortly.

It is also probable that some more senior people, including a number of those on the fringes of the leadership class, would give qualified support to the analysis that has been presented. To date, however, they have, for the most part, remained silent. Their unwillingness to speak out must be judged more culpable than that of classroom teachers, for two reasons. First, they are likely to be better informed about the detailed workings of the Scottish educational bureaucracy and would, therefore, be able to cast additional light on what happens. And secondly, their positions are more secure and they would be better able to withstand the pressures that might be brought to bear on them if they began to question some of the orthodoxies. What holds them back, of course, is their very proximity to the leadership class: the prospect of elevation — for example, from the advisorate to the directorate, or from a position of responsibility on a CCC committee to the inspectorate — serves to intensify that 'professional' caution which teachers, as a group, exemplify. Before any inroads can be made into the existing power structure, a significant number of people will have to be prepared to risk the disapproval which accompanies any attempt to open up genuine debate about the decision-making process within the Scottish educational system.

To make these points does, however, presuppose a general — if, as yet, unarticulated — acceptance of the case that has been outlined. Members of the leadership class and their apologists are unlikely to plead guilty without mounting some sort of defence; or, rather, without attempting a counter-attack, since the prospect of addresssing the particular issues that have been raised is likely to prove unattractive to them. More than one form of counter-attack can be anticipated. First, it might be claimed that the criticisms that have been advanced are cynical and destructive. Instead of looking outwards at the aims and purposes of education, the present volume has focused on the internal workings of the system and has sought to expose its failings. This, it might be argued, is a negative and unhelpful exercise, which fails to give credit for real achievements and which does nothing to advance the cause of Scottish education. How is this charge to be answered?

The accusation of cynicism invites rejoinders on two levels — one stylistic and one substantive. It will not have escaped the attentive reader that it has been a deliberate tactic to employ deflating irony at many points, often relating to statements written or uttered by members of the leadership class. Allowing them to condemn themselves out of their own mouths is much more telling than reliance on purple passages of self-righteous moral indignation. This technique, which might on occasion appear somewhat cynical to those brought up on a diet of Scottish educational writings marked by hard-faced piety and grim humourlessness is, however, not merely a kind of literary self-indulgence. The *style* in which arguments about Scottish education are conducted needs to change if the pretensions of those who currently control it are to be destroyed. Dull earnestness must be replaced by the urbane and the ironic. Irreverence is not, however, an end in itself, nor must it be allowed to degenerate into mere frivolity: underlying the shift of style is a serious purpose — the long-term regeneration of Scottish education.

At the level of substance, the charge of cynicism can be discounted on the grounds that it is misplaced. Who are the real cynics? Are they those who are concerned to confront the serious deficiencies of Scottish education — its paternalism, its obsession with hierarchies, its rewarding of the mediocre and the compliant — or those who, having secured their own membership of the leadership class, seek to defend the wisdom of existing arrangements by relying on spurious arguments about democracy and consultation and partnership, and who assert with monotonous regularity that everything is for the best in this best of all possible worlds? The latter may sometimes persuade themselves that their optimism is justified — a process made easier by the Pavlovian reinforcement supplied by the patronage system — but at the level of educational reality, as distinct from that of public relations rhetoric, the optimism is unlikely to convince. What is truly remarkable — and this is where credit for real achievement is due — is that many classroom teachers, despite their awareness of who the real cynics are, continue to work with enthusiasm and dedication. It is perhaps some small consolation to them that intelligence employed with integrity carries a measure of intrinsic worth, even if, in terms of extrinsic reward, the mixture may be regarded by their superiors as a tiresome liability.

The account offered in preceding chapters is also likely to be attacked on the grounds that it is unduly conspiratorial. It may seem to suggest the existence of some kind of coordinated plot, with a puppet-master (possibly located somewhere in the SED) pulling the strings. That, however, seriously misrepresents the case that has been advanced. What has been outlined is not a conspiracy theory, but the profoundly damaging consequences of certain forms of bureaucratic and professional socialisation, backed by a misleading and self-serving ideology. The members of Scotland's educational leadership class have progressively allowed themselves to be locked into a system of bureaucratic constraints of a kind that subvert the real purposes of education. Often they are not fully conscious of the processes at work and happily succumb to the conventions into which they have been initiated in the mistaken belief that they serve the public, not just their own, interest. This limited consciousness provides a further reason for not relying on a conspiracy theory to explain what happens. In a sense, the habitual or instinctive response, the conditioned reflex induced by a largely unquestioned socialisation process, is much more insidious than would be a planned operation to mislead or distort. A plot, once exposed, loses much of its power to cause harm: the habits of a lifetime are much harder to break.

It would, however, be wrong to suggest that leading figures in Scottish education are best regarded as unconscious victims of their environment, for that would allow them to plead diminished responsibility for their actions. Although they may not always be fully aware of the anti-educational character of much of what goes on, they are not totally lacking in awareness either. When, for instance, a public relations programme is mounted by the SED or one of the regions, senior staff know very well that it may serve a number of purposes, some of which are less than creditable — for example, pre-empting a 'consultative' process or preparing the ground for a later exercise in 'damage limitation'. In such cases, what will probably happen is that the individual will separate his or her personal knowledge and responsibility from a sense of institutional responsibility. The denial of the former will be justified with reference to the latter. This reaction, which may be regarded as a mild form of schizoid behaviour, has two advantages. First, it makes any conflict that might be experienced more bearable: the individual reassures himself that any personal qualms he might have about a particular course of action stand no chance against the forces of the organisation as a whole. But secondly, and more importantly, the act of acquiescence can be transformed into something that almost seems to invite moral approbation. The suppression of personal doubt can be looked upon as a kind of self-denial undertaken for the greater good of the organisation. Thus, it is the person who silences his or her personal reservations about approved policies, not the one who insists on speaking out, who becomes the paradigm of the good administrator.

This brief excursion into the psychology of bureaucratic evasion is not irrelevant to the task in hand. It has important parallels at political and cultural levels. The reluctance to face the truth about Scottish education is symptomatic of much deeper problems concerning Scottish politics and culture. Fear of what critical analysis may bring to the surface is not just a feature of the individual consciousness, hemmed in by institutional constraints. It is also a feature of the Scottish national consciousness, unable to come to terms with the many conflicting political and cultural pressures to which it is subject. These pressures provide the context within which Scotland's educational dilemmas must be worked out, and it is to them that the serious reformer must ultimately turn his or her attention. Such a move will, of course, be resisted by those who have lived by the myth that Scottish education is autonomous and who argue that it ought not to embroil itself in the contaminating world of politics. They will demand to know what specifically educational changes are being proposed as alternatives to the present system, a strategy that might enable them to set limits to any debate that would ensue. It is, in fact, very tempting to advocate a series of structural changes that could help to counteract the centralising and authoritarian tendencies in Scottish education. Examples might include the abolition of a number of quangos (with the CCC and the GTC at the top of the list), which, it has been argued, contribute little or nothing to the advancement of Scottish education (as distinct from the advancement of those who hold office in them); a radical reform of the promotion structure in schools, designed to reduce dependence on hierarchies and reward successful classroom teachers; the introduction of fixed-term contracts for senior officials in the SED and the regions; the discontinuance of monotechnic institutions for the training of teachers — despite previous attempts at reform, the colleges of education in Scotland remain in an unhealthy state;[1] improved mechanisms for the public accountability of local and national politicians who carry responsibility for the provision of educational services. These changes would aim to reassert the primacy of the contact between teacher and learner in the educational process, improve teacher morale, ensure that power was accompanied by responsibility, and offer scope for the kind of ability and imagination that are at present discouraged by the consensus model of development.

But while it is tempting to elaborate on these possible reforms, it would be premature to do so. Any programme of reconstruction, if it is to be effective, must be based on a thorough analysis and understanding of the underlying political and cultural causes of Scotland's educational malaise. A rudimentary framework for such an analysis and understanding was set out in Chapters 1 and 2, but it needs to be developed further before the merits of any detailed proposals for structural change can be properly assessed. For example, a fuller study of the nature of the relationship between Scottish society as a whole and the precise form which the educational system has assumed is necessary. That relationship would appear to be a mutually supporting and inter-dependent one, but the specific connections — and, in particular, the extent to which ideological confusion is a common element — invite further investigation. In the remaining paragraphs, some indication of the difficult questions that still need to be tackled will be offered.

It was stated above that the psychological evasions of professionals and bureaucrats have parallels in Scottish politics and culture. At the political level, the clearest example can be found in the continuing refusal of the Scottish people to come to any kind of coherent decision about their constitutional future. This is symbolised most obviously in the results of the 1979 referendum on devolution. Of those Scots eligible to vote, more than a third did not bother to go to the polls and, among those who did, opinion was fairly evenly divided between those who wanted the provisions of the Scotland Act 1978 to be put into effect and those who did not. This collective indecision is indicative of a deep uncertainty among Scots about their identity, their nationhood and their ability to shape their own destiny. To nationalists, the result of the referendum was a severe blow: it seemed to express a failure of nerve, a lack of will, among the Scottish people, and an unwillingness to take on the responsibility that would go with major political change. To unionists, the result was a relief, a welcome recognition by Scots of the realities of political power in the modern world and an acceptance of the hard facts of economic life. The national ambivalence was embodied most fully in the Labour Party — the party that most Scots voters traditionally support — which managed to contain both views at the same time.

However, although a substantial vote in favour of devolution would have been a significant decision for Scotland, it would be a serious mistake to imagine that it would have represented an easy solution to the many problems the country faces. Indeed, some interpretations of what greater independence for Scotland would mean must be regarded as another manifestation of the national fondness for romantic retreat. Take the question of anglicisation, for example. A more independent Scotland might well reduce its effects, both direct and indirect, but to imagine that that, in itself, would mark a major advance is naive in the extreme. An expatriate Scot, Daniel G. Clark, has made the point forcefully:

> Even if Scots instead of Englishmen were appointed to certain key positions, the social fabric which is Scottish character would not change perceptibly. A united effort by every citizen is needed for that. Two things continue to work against such a possibility.
>
> Individual worth is crushed out of effective existence by the weight of the archaic and highly authoritarian socio-economic fabric. Real individual enthusiasm, energy and competence have nowhere much to go. They would rock the boat. Second, the educational system is geared to produce pass men to fill the archaic pyramid. The system is not concerned whether these pass men have individual qualities.

> Whether Scotland is in fact a democracy or is a book-based bureaucracy is a good question. Outward form and formality have displaced human worth. When very ordinary people who were merely at the right place at the right time or had the right passes are shoved into vacancies in the pyramid, they acquire absolutely unreal notions about themselves and their abilities. They never have to question themselves. If they did, assuming they were able to, they might find only the anatomy of parochialism. It is a surreal situation.[2]

These comments draw attention to two extremely intractable problems which a more independent Scotland would have to face. One of these is directly educational: the fact that those who currently succeed and gain positions of some importance are often not particularly well-equipped for the tasks that they face. Unless political change were accompanied by some kind of revolution in manpower deployment — and this seems unlikely, since what usually happens in such cases is that existing service classes become more, rather than less important — then many of the present defects might be intensified, not reduced. Indeed, the self-image of the present educational leadership class could well receive a further boost, for they would undoubtedly project themselves as the inheritors and guardians of Scotland's great educational tradition and would seek further scope to exercise those claimed talents of guardinaship. Their 'credibility' — with which, as has been shown, they are much exercised — would, by a particularly bitter twist of irony, be enhanced rather than destroyed. Their 'parochialism' would become the norm and would be largely immune from countervailing influences.

The second problem is more obviously political. Clark refers to the 'highly authoritarian socio-economic fabric' of Scotland, and its concern with 'form and formality'. There is no guarantee that a new political arena, whether an assembly or parliament or anything else, would oppose those tendencies. On the contrary, if existing patterns of administration are taken as a guideline, the most likely aspiration of such a body would be to establish and, if possible, extend its authority using the recognised forms of coercion. David Donnison has spelled out the dangers very clearly:

> If devolution only shifts power to a Scottish Kremlin which reinforces the authority of every petty official and professional throughout the land it will not be worth having.[3]

The use of the phrase 'a Scottish Kremlin' is almost certainly not accidental and it may be taken as an oblique reference to the political complexion and bureaucratic tendencies of Strathclyde region. If the present pattern of Scottish politics were to be reflected in an assembly, then the Labour Party would undoubtedly dominate. It also seems probable that many of those who have gained political prominence at local level — and particularly, given its size, in Strathclyde — would move to the national arena. Once again the quality of representation becomes a critical issue and there are very limited grounds for optimism in this regard. The Labour Party, in common with the other political parties in Scotland, certainly contains people of talent but, sadly, too few of them are appointed to positions which would enable them to exert a beneficial influence. Here, as elsewhere, the preference for dull, grey, consensus men and women, who are ideologically 'sound' but bereft of imagination and vision, has cast a dead hand over Scottish society. It should be added than even if, contrary to expectation, the Labour Party did not dominate an assembly, there would still be a major problem, for the present generation of councillors and MPs, regardless of their party affiliation, have not shown themselves strongly inclined to move away from traditional foms of political paternalism.

Greater political independence for Scotland, then, would not, by itself, diminish the centralising and conformist pressures that have been described in previous chapters. In fact, unless it was accompanied by much more fundamental systemic and cultural changes, it might even make things worse. At the same time, it must be recognised that any attempt to initiate significant political reform involves risks, and the mere existence of risks does not provide an adequate justification for accepting the *status quo,* however unsatisfactory it may be. Many people in Scotland, of very different political persuasions, agree that the existing machinery of the Scottish Office is unsatisfactory: it is too centralised, too secretive and insufficiently accountable to the people of Scotland. How, then, can these defects be overcome without producing the unattractive consequences outlined above? David Donnison offers this thought:

> If Scottish talents are to flower and this country is to develop as creatively as it might, then the devolution of powers from London and the demystification of central authority must be followed right through to ground level. We must open up government, make authority accountable, and give people greater responsibilities wherever we can — in the cities and in the streets.[4]

These desirable developments will not occur by accident. They will only come about if the legislative framework permits them and if there is a sufficient upsurge of popular opinion to support them. On the legislative front, it is possible to point to those areas which need attention: the necessity of a Freedom of Information Act; the desirability of reforming the present two-tier structure of local government and, in particular, of dismembering Strathclyde region; the case for strengthening the powers of the Parliamentary Commissioner for Administration and the Commissioner for Local Administration to investigate cases of maladministration in central and local government.[5]

Legislation on its own, however, will not be enough, for the enforcement of legislation, even where it is ostensibly designed to devolve power, will continue to depend on those groups, politicians and officials, who have been found wanting. The dislodging of the existing political and administrative élites is not likely to happen quickly or easily. It is here that the importance of popular opinion, as well as the very considerable obstacles to its being effectively mobilised, becomes apparent. Daniel Clark refers to the immense difficulties of transforming 'the social fabric which is Scottish character' and says that 'a united effort by every citizen is needed for that'. The cultural barriers to such a united effort are very substantial indeed. Modern Scotland is marked by what can only be called profound cultural confusion, with deep historical, economic and religious roots, which militates against united efforts of any kind. Tom Nairn, in his brilliant study of nationalism, refers variously to the 'lacerating *contradictions*'[6] of Scottish culture, its 'Jekyll-and-Hyde fragmentation',[7] its 'remarkable assemblage of heterogeneous elements, neurotic double-binds, falsely honoured shades, and brainless vulgarity'.[8] The pressures which cause Scots to go south or abroad, which promote religious ignorance and bigotry, and which encourage retreat from the painful realities of Scottish civil society into Kailyard sentimentality, combine to prevent that coordinated effort which might hold out the possibility of significant reform. It is a deprressing thought but it may, in fact, be the case that these problems will prove to be culturally insoluble and that Scotland will be condemned to an indefinite future of social and political alienation.

However, to the observer who is sufficiently interested to embark on the task of analysis and criticism, acceptance of failure in advance is not a serious option. The hope must remain — tenuous though it may be — that Scotland, despite the substantial obstacles that exist, will be able to evolve a cultural idiom that is distinctive without relying on nostalgic or anti-English stereotypes, that is confident without being defensively arrogant, and that embodies, not just proclaims, the principles of democracy and equality.

The potential contribution of education to the regenerative process introduces further ambiguities: as R. F. Mackenzie has observed, 'Scotland's schools are at the centre of Scotland's perplexity'.[9] Education, paradoxically, is both an instrument of containment and a possible source of liberation. It is capable of being used not only as a means of promoting unreflective conformity, of churning out 'pass men to fill the archaic pyramid', but also of releasing creative intelligence, of giving scope to 'individual enthusiasm, energy and competence'. At present, the first set of 'capabilities' is much more pronounced than the second — but that need not continue indefinitely. Given the right injection of individual and collective will, education — along with other cultural agencies — can contribute to the work that needs to be done. Indeed, the process of extending analytic and critical understanding of Scotland's political and cultural dilemmas will depend crucially on a strong educational input. Whether that understanding will ever be sufficient to induce action, and whether that action will be successful, remains to be seen.

Scottish education, as it exists at present, might be portrayed in many ways: as a vast comic pageant in which SED officials and directors of education play the part of chief clowns; as a elaborate protection racket in which the 'protectors' demand regular payments of flattery and subservience and, in return, graciously bestow patronage on those with a particularly well-developed capacity for self-abasement; as a decidedly down-market Henry James novel in which the public rhetoric of the leading characters is much less significant than what remains unspoken; as a second-rate game of chess in which the pawns are pupils and teachers, and the players are representatives of the leadership class who, despite occasional skirmishes, always end up realising the wisdom of settling for a draw, however undistinguished. Each of these descriptions contains an element of truth, and it might be diverting to elaborate them further. But argument by analogy is always, in the final analysis, misleading: it simplifies and distorts and trivialises. The importance of education requires that it should be addressed in literal, not metaphorical, terms. Ultimately, it cannot be compared to a dramatic performance, a criminal sub-culture, a work of fiction or a game. Ironic comparison is a strategy, not an end in itself. The value of education resides in the fact that it contains the potential, given the right political and cultural context, to transform the lives of individuals in innumerable beneficial ways, thereby enhancing their contribution to society as a whole. In Scotland, it has been argued, the political and cultural context is at present hostile to the liberating powers which education, properly conceived, can bring. That is the issue that needs to be addressed, and it is only by tackling it honestly and directly — however painful the process might be — that a start can be made of the arduous task of reconstruction.

*Notes and References*

1. Almost fifteen years ago the GTC set up a committee to review the training of secondary teachers. This resulted in a report, *The Training of Graduates for Secondary Education,* HMSO, Edinburgh, 1972, which came to be known as the Brunton Report. After more than three years of fairly unproductive discussion of its recommendations, a joint GTC/SED committee was set up in 1976 to explore the issues further. In 1976 this committee produced the Sneddon Report, *Learning to Teach,* HMSO, Edinburgh, 1978. Seven years later, post-Sneddon research studies are still proceeding.

2. Daniel G. Clark, letter in *Scotsman,* August 10, 1982.

3. David Donnison, 'Personal Column', *Sunday Standard,* April 24, 1983, p. 14.

4. *Ibid.,* p. 14.

5. The present Commissioner for Local Administration in Scotland, Mr Eric Gillett, has recently complained about the restrictions which prevent him from examining vast areas of local authority activity and his powerlessness when local authorities refuse to take action on his recommendations. He feels that he can no longer offer complainants against local authorities a reasonable guarantee that they will be given remedies even if his findings are in their favour. See *Report of the Commissioner (Ombudsman) for Local Administration in Scotland for the year ended 31 March 1984,* HMSO, Edinburgh, 1984, paras. 6–9.

6. Tom Nairn, *The Break-Up of Britain,* 2nd edition, Verso, London, 1981, p. 172. Nairn's italics.

7. *Ibid.,* p. 167.

8. *Ibid.,* p. 168.

9. R. F. Mackenzie, *The Unbowed Head,* EUSPB, Edinburgh, 1977, p. 6.

# *Postscript*

All writers who deal with contemporary events face the constant difficulty that their descriptions and interpretations may soon become dated. At a simple level, for example, named individuals may move to other jobs between the time a book goes to press and its actual publication. In the case of the present volume, the general expectation among political commentators that there will be ministerial changes at the Scottish Office before the end of 1985 could well affect references to George Younger and Allan Stewart. Less speculatively, a number of developments have already occurred since the completion of the main text which call for brief comment. Some of these are comparatively minor and simply require to be recorded: the decision of the Association of Lecturers in Scottish Central Institutions to amalgamate with the EIS, and of the Association of Lecturers in Colleges of Education in Scotland to consider following ALSCI's example (see Chapter 7); the strong probability that Leith Nautical College will lose its status as a central institution and be transferred to the control of Lothian Region (see Chapter 9). Other developments mark the implementation of plans outlined in the preceding chapters, or the continuation of arguments about proposed plans. The first meeting of SCOTVEC, which has taken over from SCOTEC and SCOTBEC, was held in April 1985 (see Chapter 9). On the research front, the debates about the future of SCRE and on the role to be assumed by the RIU unit within the SED are not yet fully resolved, but current indications do not give any grounds for a more optimistic reading of the situation than that advanced in Chapter 8. And with regard to the much broader question of the efficiency of the SED's management strategies, one event is worth noting. In June 1985 a report by the Comptroller and Auditor General expressed criticism of some aspects of the department's role in the running of colleges in the higher education sector: in particular, SED estimates of the capacity of colleges of education were described as unreliable, and adverse comment was passed on the failure to carry out a comprehensive survey of the relative costs of colleges of education and central institutions, to the detriment of the latter (see Chapters 3, 7 and 9).

There remain two topics which call for slightly fuller treatment, as developments here suggest a possible need for revision of the interpretative line advanced in the main text. First, there is the question of the likely recommendations of STEAC. The council's remit has been complicated by the appearance, in May 1985, of a government green paper, *The Development of Higher Education into the 1990s.* This relates to the UK as a whole and enunciates certain general principles reflecting government priorities: the need to plan for the amalgamation or closure of some institutions in anticipation of a fall in student numbers during the 1990s; the concentration of resources on science and technology; commitment to maintaining high standards and achieving value for money; emphasis on vocational training, including the updating of professional skills in mid-career. Although the green paper has been widely criticised in many quarters — a leader in *The Times Higher Education Supplement* of May 24, 1985 described it as 'negative and philistine' — the members of STEAC are bound to take account of it. One possibility is that it will provide a basis for a stronger version of 'rationalisation' than that predicted in Chapter 9. For example, James Scott, Secretary of the SED, while answering questions put to him by the House of Commons Public Accounts Committee on the critical report by the Comptroller and Auditor General referred to above, speculated about STEAC's likely recommendations on the colleges of education. He said that the council might propose that the present monotechnic function of the colleges could be broadened, or that they could be merged with university departments of education. Either of these possible developments would constitute a more radical form of 'rationalisation' than that considered likely in Chapter 9. When linked with the proposal in the green paper to commission a review of the role of the UGC, the possibilities of substantial structural reform in Scottish tertiary education are further increased.

Finally, there is the dispute about teachers' salaries, which received a brief mention in Chapter 6. This has assumed major importance in Scottish education and has provoked considerable bitterness among the various parties involved — unions, local authorities, central government and parents. The Scottish Joint Negotiating Committee, the body responsible for making recommendations on salaries and conditions of service, has been caught between a recognition of the justice of the teachers' claims and the financial constraints imposed by the government on local authorities. At the same time, the industrial action taken by teachers — which has included the targeting for strikes of secondary schools in constituencies represented by Scottish Office ministers, withdrawal from curriculum development work, and a refusal to carry out clerical tasks associated with the presentation of candidates for national exams — has led to concern among parents and a hardening of attitude by the SED (evident, for example, in the attempt to introduce a prescriptive lists of teachers' contractual duties). One consequence of all this is that the timetable for the introduction of the Standard Grade programme, as described in Chapter 9, will take longer than originally intended.

The significance of the dispute resides not only in the particular form it has taken, but also in what it might reveal in the longer term about the changing pattern of power politics within the world of Scottish education. For once, teachers throughout Scotland (not just in Strathclyde) have abandoned their traditionally passive attitudes in favour of industrial action: indeed, in the early stages of the dispute it seemed that the ordinary membership of the EIS was more militant than the leadership. Even if they do not 'win' at the end of the day, teachers will have learned a great deal about their strengths and limitations in a situation of conflict. Moreover, their campaign, whether one approves of it or not, has been conducted with a fair measure of skill and consistency. In this, it contrasts with the actions of both central and local government. In an article in *The Scotsman* of April 12, 1985, Sarah Nelson described the SED's conduct as 'a puzzling mixture of carrot and stick, with headline leaks one day, wooing words the next, and a string of letters that seem different or contradictory'. The local authorities have been rather more constructive in seeking solutions (through COSLA as well as the Scottish Joint Negotiating Committee), but they too have behaved erratically, alternating between support for the teachers' call for an independent review and the use of coercion in an attempt to limit the effects of industrial action on examination and development work. As it is the local authorities that carry statutory responsibility for educational provision, a fear of possible litigation by parental groups has no doubt played a part in their uncertainty. When a settlement is finally reached, there will be a need to reassess the relations between teachers, parents, local councillors, members of the directorate, civil servants and Scottish Office ministers. At this stage it is not possible to predict whether the episode will mark a watershed, leading to an acknowledgement of the damaging consequences that can result from the pursuit of professional ideology and bureaucratic power, or will simply serve as a stimulus for the leadership class to devise more sophisticated and effective strategies of containment.

One further consequence of the teachers' dispute needs to be mentioned. It concerns the proposed merger of the SEB and SCOTVEC, discussed in Chapter 9. In October 1985 it was announced that this would not go ahead — at least in the foreseeable future. SCOTVEC, it was felt, needed time to establish itself. More importantly, however, the government recognised that, in a climate of industrial unrest, the chances of an easy amalgamation would be slim. The long-term intention probably remains unaltered, but political expediency has caused a change of short-term tactics. As a leader in *The Times Educational Supplement Scotland* of October 11, 1985 put it, 'the SED wisely decided not to take on more foes for the time being'.

# *Select Bibliography*

Detailed references to sources are given at the end of each chapter. The following select list covers books, reports and articles in two broad categories: (a) those which are referred to extensively in the main text; (b) those which, though not quoted at length (or, in a few cases, at all), were nonetheless influential in the formulation of the argument. With regard to (b), it should be emphasised that, in some instances, the influence took the form of provoking disagreement.


M. Albrow, *Bureaucracy,* Macmillan, London, 1970.

R. D. Anderson, *Education and Opportunity in Victorian Scotland,* Clarendon Press, Oxford, 1983.

Association of Educational Advisers in Scotland, *The Scottish Educational Advisory Service in the Eighties,* June 1982.

D. A. Barrie, The Nature and Impact of Teacher Representation on the General Teaching Council for Scotland, unpublished MEd thesis, Glasgow University, 1981.

P.M. Blau and M. W. Meyer, *Bureaucracy in Modern Society,* 2nd ed., Random House, New York, 1971.

K. Bloomer, 'The teacher as professional and trade unionist', in F. Hoyle and J. Meggary (eds.), *World Yearbook of Education 1980: Professional Development of Teachers,* Kogan Page, London, 1980.

T. R. Bone, *School Inspection in Scotland, 1840–1966,* SCRE, Edinburgh, 1968.

G. Brown and R. Cook (eds.), *Scotland: The Real Divide,* Mainstream, Edinburgh, 1983.

T. Bush and M. Kogan, *Directors of Education,* Allen and Unwin, London, 1982.

Committee of Public Accounts, Ninth Report, Session 1983–84, *Hamilton College of Education: Disposal of Land and Buildings,* HMSO, London, 1984.

Consultative Committee on the Curriculum, *CCC: First Report 1965–68,* HMSO, Edinburgh, 1969.

Consultative Committee on the Curriculum, *CCC: Second Report 1968–71,* HMSO, Edinburgh, 1972.

Consultative Committee on the Curriculum, *CCC: Third Report 1971–74,* HMSO, Edinburgh, 1975.

Consultative Committee on the Curriculum, *CCC: Fourth Report 1974–80,* HMSO, Edinburgh, 1980.

Consultative Committee on the Curriculum, *CCC: Fifth Report 1980–83,* CCC, Edinburgh, 1983.

P. Corbett, *Ideologies,* Hutchinson, London, 1965.

Council for Tertiary Education in Scotland, *Review of Structure and Management,* SED, Edinburgh, 1981.

J. Craigie, *The Scottish Council for Research in Education 1928–1972,* SCRE, Edinburgh, 1972.

M. Cruickshank, *A History of the Training of Teachers in Scotland,* SCRE, Edinburgh, 1970.

D. Daiches (ed.), *A Companion to Scottish Culture,* Edward Arnold, London, 1981.

G. E. Davie, *The Democratic Intellect: Scotland and her Universities in the Nineteenth Century,* 2nd ed., Edinburgh University Press, Edinburgh, 1964.

W. B. Dockrell (ed.), *An Attitude of Mind: Twenty-Five Years of Educational Research in Scotland,* SCRE, Edinburgh, 1984.

W. B. Dockrell and D. Hamilton (eds.), *Rethinking Educational Research,* Hodder and Stoughton, London, 1980.

H. Drucker (ed.), *John P. Mackintosh on Scotland,* Longmans, London, 1982.

*Education (Scotland) Act 1980,* HMSO, London, 1980.

*Education (Scotland) Act 1981,* HMSO, London, 1981.

D. Elliott, 'Information Paper 13: The Scottish Examination Board', *Scottish Educational Review,* Vol. 16, No. 1, 1984, pp. 51–53.

K. Fenwick and P. McBride, *The Government of Education,* Martin Robertson, Oxford, 1981.

W. A. Gatherer, 'The boss's job', *TESS,* May 25, 1984, pp. 16–17.

M. Gethins *et al, The Welsh Office, the Scottish Education Department and the Northern Ireland Office: Central or Devolved Control of Education?,* Unit 3, Course E222, Open University, Milton Keynes, 1979.

P. Gordon (ed.), *Is Teaching a Profession?,* Bedford Way Papers 15, Institute of Education, University of London, 1983.

N. Grant, *The Crisis of Scottish Education,* Saltire Society, Edinburgh, 1982.

J. Gray, A. F. McPherson and D. Raffe, *Reconstructions of Secondary Education: Theory, Myth and Practice since the War,* Routledge and Kegan Paul, London, 1983.

A. H. Halsey, *Change in British Society,* 2nd ed., OUP, Oxford, 1981.

D. Hartley, 'Bureaucracy and Professionalism: the New 'Hidden Curriculum' for Teachers in Scotland', to be published in the *Journal of Education for Teaching;* Vol. 11, No. 2, 1985, pp. 107–119.

C. Harvie, *No Gods and Precious Few Heroes: Scotland 1914–1980,* Edward Arnold, London, 1981.

C. Harvie, *Scotland and Nationalism: Scottish Society and Politics 1707–1977,* Allen and Unwin, London, 1977.

W. M. Humes and H. M. Paterson (eds.), *Scottish Culture and Scottish Education 1800–1980,* John Donald, Edinburgh, 1983.

S. L. Hunter, *The Scottish Educational System,* 2nd ed., Pergamon Press, Oxford, 1972.

G. D. Jeyes, Political Administration of Secondary Education in the Strathclyde Region, unpublished MEd thesis, Stirling University, 1984.

M. Keating and A. Midwinter, *The Government of Scotland,* Mainstream, Edinburgh, 1983.

J. G. Kellas, *Modern Scotland,* 2nd ed., Allen and Unwin, London, 1980.

J. G. Kellas, *The Scottish Political System,* 2nd ed., CUP, Cambridge, 1975.

G. Kirk, *Curriculum and Assessment in the Scottish Secondary School: A Study of the Munn and Dunning Reports,* Ward Lock, London, 1982.

G. Kirk, 'The New BEd in Scotland: Towards a Professional Degree', *Scottish Educational Review,* Vol. 16, No. 1, 1984, pp. 19–26.

G. Kirk, 'The unashamed professional', *TESS,* February 18, 1983, p. 2.

D. Lawton, *The Politics of the School Curriculum,* Routledge and Kegan Paul, London, 1980.

J. Lello (ed.), *Accountability in Education,* Ward Lock, London, 1979.

W. B. Littrell *et al* (eds.), *Bureaucracy as a Social Problem,* Jai Press, Greenwich, Connecticut and London, 1983.

A. M. Macbeth, M. L. Mackenzie and I. Breckenridge, *Scottish School Councils: Policy-Making, Participation or Irrelevance?,* HMSO, Edinburgh, 1980.

D. McCrone (ed.), *The Scottish Government Yearbook 1984,* Unit for the Study of Government in Scotland, Edinburgh, 1983.

D. W. McKenzie, The Pressure Group Activities and Political Development of the Glasgow Association of the EIS in the Post-War Period, unpublished MEd thesis, Glasgow University, 1974.

W. B. Marker, 'The Future of Inservice Training in Scotland: Some Alternative Models', *Scottish Educational Review,* Vol. 14, No. 1, 1982, pp. 5–14.

W. B. Marker, 'Information Paper 2: Inservice Education in Scotland', *Scottish Educational Review,* Vol. 10, No. 2, 1978, pp. 62–64.

E. Miller, 'It's never too late', *Education,* May 8, 1981, pp. 419–420.

J. G. Morris, 'Information Paper 8: The Research and Intelligence Unit of the Scottish Education Department', *Scottish Educational Review,* Vol. 13, No. 2, 1981, pp. 162–166.

J. G. Morris and F. H. Johnston, 'The Impact of Policy and Practice on Research', *British Journal of Educational Studies,* Vol. XXIX, No. 3, 1981, pp. 209–217.

Tom Nairn, *The Break-Up of Britain,* 2nd ed., Verso, London, 1981.

National Committee for the In-Service Training of Teachers, *Arrangements for the Staff Development of Teachers,* 1984.

National Committee for the In-Service Training of Teachers, *The Development of the Three Tier Structure of Award Bearing Courses,* 1984.

National Committee for the In-Service Training of Teachers, *The Future of In-Service Training in Scotland,* 1979.

J. Nisbet and P. Broadfoot, *The Impact of Research on Policy and Practice in Education,* Aberdeen University Press, Aberdeen, 1980.

P. Odor and N. Entwistle, *The Introduction of Microelectronics into Scottish Education,* Scottish Academic Press, Edinburgh, 1982.

G. S. Osborne, *Change in Scottish Education,* Longmans, London, 1968.

G. S. Osborne, 'Information Paper 3: The Committee of Principals of Scottish Colleges of Education', *Scottish Educational Review,* Vol. 11, No. 1, 1979, pp. 74–77.

J. T. Ozga and M. A. Lawn, *Teachers, Professionalism and Class: A Study of Organized Teachers,* Falmer Press, London, 1981.

Sir W. Pile, *The Department of Education and Science,* Allen and Unwin, London, 1979.

D. Raffe (ed.), *Fourteen to Eighteen: The Changing Patttern of Schooling in Scotland,* Aberdeen University Press, Aberdeen, 1984.

P. Rendle, *Scrutiny of HM Inspectors of Schools,* Report to Mr Alex Fletcher MP, Parliamentary Under Secretary of State for Industry and Education, Scottish Office, July 1981.

B. Salter and T. Tapper, *Education, Politics and the State,* Grant McIntyre, London, 1981.

J. Scotland, *The History of Scottish Education,* Vol. 2, University of London Press, London, 1969.

K. B. Scott, 'The Development of College Councils in Scottish Further Education Colleges', *Scottish Educational Review,* Vol. 15, No. 2, 1983, pp. 121–131.

Scottish Education Department, *Report of the Committee to Review Assessment in the Third and Fourth Years of Secondary Education in Scotland* (the Dunning Report), HMSO, Edinburgh, 1977.

Scottish Education Department, *School and Further Education in Scotland: A Single Examining Body?,* A Consultative Paper Issued by the Secretary of State for Scotland, September 1984.

Scottish Education Department, *The Structure of the Curriculum in the Third and Fourth Years of the Scottish Secondary School* (the Munn Report), HMSO, Edinburgh, 1977.

M. Shipman, *Education as a Public Service,* Harper and Row, London, 1984.

H. Silver, *Education as History,* Methuen, London, 1983.

J. V. Smith and D. Hamilton (eds.), *The Meritocratic Intellect: Studies in the History of Educational Research,* Aberdeen University Press, Aberdeen, 1980.

D. Warwick, *Bureaucracy,* Longmans, London, 1974.

Sir D. Wass, *1983 Reith Lectures,* reprinted in *The Listener,* November 24, 1983, pp. 18–25; December 8, 1983, pp. 21–27; December 15, 1983, pp. 12–17.

Sir T. Weaver, *Department of Education and Science: 'Central' Control of Education?,* Unit 2, Course E222, Open University, Milton Keynes, 1979.

R. Williams, *Keywords,* revised ed., Fontana, London, 1983.

T. Worthington, 'Lifelong learning: its battle against the enemy within', *TESS,* February 13, 1981, pp. 14–15.

T. Worthington, 'A profession can colonise the mind', *TESS,* February 20, 1981, pp. 16–17.

R. Young, *The Search for Democracy: A Guide to and Polemic About Scottish Local Government,* Heatherbank Press, Milngavie, 1977.

# Index